FREEDUMB'S CALLING

365 daily meditations on the art of living a great again American life

C.Z. RICHARDS

PALMETTO
PUBLISHING
Charleston, SC
www.PalmettoPublishing.com

Copyright © 2024 by C.Z. Richards

All rights reserved

No portion of this book may be reproduced, stored in a retrieval system, or transmitted in any form by any means–electronic, mechanical, photocopy, recording, or other–except for brief quotations in printed reviews, without prior permission of the author.

Paperback ISBN: 979-8-8229-5477-9

FREEDUMB'S CALLING

To my wife and partner, whose kindness and compassion inspire me everyday

Trigger Warning: the following contains graphic references to mind-numbing dumbness so extreme you could be shocked into the realization you may lack what it takes to reach full-fledged Freedumber status.

INTRODUCTION

Freedom or Freedumb?

That's the choice. For yourself. And for America.

This book is here to help. It's rooted in my own conversion from freedom-lover to Freedumb-fighter. Hopefully my journey can inform your own.

I once believed America was the place miracles happened. It was a place where love of country could make the hair on the back of your neck stand up in admiration, awe and pride. It was the first country to put a man on the moon. Unafraid to push boundaries, take risks and capture the imagination of all humankind. It was the country where good people fought for civil rights. Unafraid to right wrongs in service of liberty and justice for all. The land of the free and the home of the brave was a beacon of hope – the greatest country in the world. And freedom fuelled our greatness. Perhaps a bit wide-eyed, but that's what I believed.

Now I know better.

I believed America was the country that invited you to dream. It was a country that had chosen courage over cowardice. The courage to try harder, learn and get better. The courage to see diversity as an opportunity to build something exceptional. The courage to be the future, and define it by a vision of what could be. America was the country with the audacity to suggest that you ask yourself what you could do for it, rather than what it might do for you. Such was its confidence in what it had to offer. America was the good guy. And freedom fuelled our goodness.

Now I know better.

The truth is, freedom is long past its 'sell by' date. It has outlived its usefulness. It carries an outdated sense of responsibility, accountability and duty. Freedom has become a millstone around the neck of American greatness. It has lost its way and become something un-American. Freedom works to embrace tolerance and inclusion. It works to welcome all people and foster open-mindedness. Freedom works to encourage curiosity, understanding and compassion. It works to nurture learning and mutual respect. Freedom works for progress, toward justice, and with a deep commitment to democracy.

Freedumb's Calling | 1

Well, it's become pretty obvious that kind of shit has got to stop.

Enter what I have affectionately come to call the Freedumb movement.

It's a movement founded on the idea of liberty without the burden of responsibility. It is permission to do or say without conscience or shame. It's a movement committed to transforming America in a way that would have once been thought inconceivable. It's not paradigm-shifting, it's paradigm-shattering. And it aims to take us toward some combination of *Punishment Park*, *The Handmaid's Tale* and the 1936 Nazi propaganda film *Triumph of the Will*. Talk about making miracles happen. Maybe America really can be great again.

The idea that we, as Americans, are facing a fundamental choice as to who we are and where we are headed, has been on my mind a great deal over the last few years. My 'light switch' moment happened during the 2016 presidential election campaign, when the Freedumbest of all Freedumbers made fun of a disabled reporter: mocked him publicly, with a natural and impressive degree of cruelty, to the laughter and applause of all those around him. Was I converted to Freedumb right then and there? In honesty, almost, but not quite. Still, it opened my eyes to a movement that showed me an intriguing side of American greatness. After all, if you can't have a little laugh at someone's expense at the end of a hard day, what's the point – a gimp knows he's a gimp.

There was a 'great again' truth in that moment. And it introduced me to a whole different take on life, liberty and the pursuit of happiness. Clearly, this movement had a lot to offer.

Its rise forced me to reconsider everything I thought I knew about America, being American, and American greatness. Forget about the best and brightest. Dumbness wasn't something you ran from; it was something you ran toward. It was something you cultivated and even celebrated. Dumbness wasn't a problem; it was the solution. What better way to confront the forces not only pushing awareness of social and cultural inequities, but actually trying to do something about them? Besides, messing around with other people's lives looked kind of fun.

Who knew that getting back to greatness could feel so dumb and so right at the same time? It's pretty amazing when you don't think about it. And while it took me a number of years to fully commit to the cause, the important thing is, I'm there now. A full-fledged Freedumb Fighter. Proudly and patriotically so. When I finally understood that white nationalists are very fine people too, I knew I had found my tribe.

Now admittedly, I'm not a Freedumber of note. I'm just your normal dummy. But I do have some important credentials. I'm an old, white, straight man who grew up Christian. And those credentials come with a certain all-seeing, all-knowing, all-powerful capability.

So see me for what I am: an expert on pretty much anything you can name. Including being an oracle in the field of self-help.

And this book is primarily aimed at helping men like me. Sadly, I should note that not all such men are open to the fruits of Freedumb. I've had the honor, at least I used to think it an honor, to have met a lot of good American men – many of them white and Christian. They came in shades of both red and blue. Men of no particular fame or fortune, but men who, to me, were model American citizens.

These men are open-minded and big-hearted. They are builders, contributors and dreamers. They are smart, decent and civic-minded. They believe in mutual respect and are ready to show compassion. They believe in liberty and justice – for all. They are true competitors, unafraid of an equal playing field. They don't scare easy, and they love this country, warts and all. To me, they embodied what I once thought to be the quintessential American man. They were fellow Americans I liked and admired. Now, it goes without saying, I no longer associate with any of them. They just don't have Freedumbness in them. Sad, but true. Not one weirdo in the bunch. Losers and lost causes, all.

In truth, this book also offers help and guidance to any and all real Americans who have simply grown tired of the burdens of freedom, impatient with the expectations of civility that come with citizenship, and agitated by the demand that America progress into the future: Young men willing to follow the dumb example set by their elders and, even those special women capable of putting some real dumb into the heart of Freedumb – this book is for you too.

Over the course of 365 days the book will take you on a journey toward clarifying the kind of American you want to be – in the end, dumbness is a decision. Most of the daily meditations are structured around my own personal transformation from "Then" (freedom-loving) to "Now" (Freedumb-fighting). The quotes that open most of the days' entries are genuine; the quotes that follow from Freedumbers, while genuinely believable, are imagined in a way to make the movement most proud. The book can be read one day at a time or in chunks of your choosing. Just please be careful how much of the book you consume at any one time. There's only so much dumbness a reader should consume in one sitting.

Some terms you'll come across that warrant a bit of definition include:

Freedumb: freedom in its purest form, without responsibility or a moral compass.

Freedumb Fighters: these Freedumbers are the tip of the Freedumb spear. And bleed orange.

Wisdumb: a game-changing type of wisdom that makes common sense and reason unnecessary.

Christendumb: a beautifully twisted version of Christianity rooted in the teachings of Jesus of Orange here on earth.

Vicdumbhood: a state of mind in which white men blessed with the birthright of privilege feel that the world is out to get them.

Freedumbia: a mythical place where we have won the day, democracy is dead, and the grumpy old men of Freedumb have finally got everyone the fuck off our lawn.

My hope is that you heed the call, decide to embrace Freedumb, and help return America to greatness. In these pages, you have the opportunity to embody a Freedumbness that can take you, and America, to unseen depths. You, yes you, have the rare opportunity to hold the future of America in your hands and bury its brightness once and for all.

The fact is, there's never been a better time to close your mind, harden your heart, and darken your soul. Let's get this party started.

Let Freedumb reign!

JANUARY 1

What's your yardstick?

"I don't measure America by its achievement, but by its potential."
(Shirley Chisholm)

"I'll be the one measuring America."
(Freedumb Fighter)

Then ... I believed America's upside was limitless. A work in progress, characterized by moments of greatness embodying the promise of even greater possibilities. It's not that America hasn't achieved: our "imperfect union" has come a long way since the starter's musket went off in 1776. Our energy, our ambition and our determination have fueled the progress, as well as our sense of right and wrong. As the land of opportunity, America can perhaps claim, as no other country can, limitless potential as its birthright. We are imperfect but striving and hopeful. Imperfect but committed and capable. Imperfect but moving ahead. And while progress never happens fast enough, or in a straight enough line for the people who seek it, it does happen. The possibility of greatness always stands before us. What happens next has always been up to the American people.

Now ... We Freedumbers have created a whole new metric for measuring America.

We measure America on its capacity to limit the potential – of others. After all, their potential can challenge our advantage, our privilege, our entitlement. And that's not going to help anyone that counts. Well-intended change is unwelcome change. Well-intended change will push us further from greatness. Can't we all just light up some fireworks, have a picnic, hug the flag and call it a day? Let's forget about making progress. Remember when things were simpler, clearer and easier. Holding America to deliver on its upside is unfair, because it risks undercutting a bunch of guys who just want to keep the party going: sustaining racism, upholding injustice and fostering inequality.

Today ... Make a resolution to do more to limit America's potential. Helpful hint: Even small gestures can have a negative impact. Thought starter: Create 'unwelcome mats' and place them anywhere people are trying to do some good.

JANUARY 2

Could you care a little less?

"Wherever men and women are persecuted because of their race, religion, or political views, that place must – at that moment – become the center of the universe."
(Elie Wiesel)

"Unjust persecution is the best kind of persecution."
(Freedumb Fighter)

Then … Elie Wiesel was a Holocaust survivor and a fierce advocate on behalf of victims of hate and persecution around the world. At the risk of gross understatement, the man knew how hate and prejudice work to create immense pain and suffering – not to mention the eradication of minority rights. His 'center of the universe' thought inspired me: it's a clarion call to defend minorities and protect the most vulnerable. Fundamentally, it's about caring. Caring about liberty and justice for all. A genuine caring for each other as human beings, as fellow citizens. Wiesel spent more than half his life in the United States, and somehow this call to care felt very American, very appropriate in the land of the free and the home of the brave.

Now … I know us Freedumbers are the center of the universe.

It's dangerous to think or feel too deeply about other people. That kind of caring can breed a warped sense of fairness and can work to take your eye off the ball. There's nothing wrong with a little 'targeted' persecution. Those 'other' people need to understand the rights of Freedumbers are one thing, and that their own rights are another. Especially where liberty and justice are concerned. It's best to think of it as kind of a tiered system where some people have a lot of rights, others not so much. The top tier would be old white men. After that it doesn't really matter. If everyone could get their head around that truth, the stars would finally align.

Today … Take some time for self-reflection. Ask yourself, why on earth would you care about anybody other than yourself and your fellow Freedumbers. Minority rights? A women's right to choose? Migrant rights? Transgender rights? Enough already. The only right any of those 'others' deserve is the extreme right!

JANUARY 3

Have you closed your mind?

"The magic of America is that we are a free and open society with a mixed population. Part of our security is our freedom."
(Madeleine Albright)

"America would be a lot more magical if it didn't have a mixed population."
(Freedumb Fighter)

Then … I believed free, open and mixed were good things. American things. I thought diversity of belief, of behavior, of being, was foundational to America. And to its greatness. I thought our freedom provided a promise, if not a kind of certainty, that people of all races, sexual orientations, religious beliefs and socio-economic backgrounds had a genuine opportunity for life, liberty and the pursuit of happiness. And that promise, I believed, helped make America exceptional.

Now … Admittedly, I also once thought that Santa Claus was real.

Freedumbers have for a long time understood the downside of a free, open, and heaven forbid, mixed society. With dumbness as our guide, we see diversity for what it is – the devil at work. As followers of Christendumb, Freedumbers worship sameness – we are devout believers in godly intolerance. We see diversity as a threat, an abomination. You have to shut your mind to it. You're not going to get to being great again if you don't value purity. In fact, 'open' and 'mixed' are words that should probably be banned. It's for our own security.

Today … Make some magic. Work on your looks of disdain. Helpful hint: One look can say a lot. Thought starter: Identify a 'diverse other,' give them the side eye and, voila, you'll make them feel uncomfortable in your presence. That's a look that'll serve you, and the cause, well.

JANUARY 4

Today, reflect on the power and poignancy of:

The Freedumbness Questionnaire

1. *What is your idea of perfect happiness?*
I like long walks on the beach, feeling the sand between my toes and watching the sunset as I reflect on what I would have been like as a slave owner.

2. *What is your greatest fear?*
Hmm. Probably having a woman for a boss.

3. *What trait do you most deplore in yourself?*
There's not really anything to deplore. Although I did enjoy watching an episode of *Queer Eye* awhile back. And I was so disgusted with myself.

4. *What trait do you most deplore in others?*
Kindness.

5. *What do you consider the most overrated virtue?*
Remind me of what a virtue is again.

6. *What talent would you most like to have?*
I've always admired conspiracy theorists and the way they dig for the real truth.

7. *What do you consider your greatest achievement?*
Being white.

JANUARY 5

What is essential?

"I have never lost faith in America's essential goodness and greatness. I believe no challenge or threat is too dangerous or difficult for us to meet, if we work together, if we have sensible policies, if we cross the partisan divide that too often substitutes for reason, and come together around our shared values and a commitment to that future we want for our children and grandchildren."
(Hillary Clinton)

"Good has nothing to do with being great."
(Freedumb Fighter)

Then … I always thought the link between goodness and greatness was an essential one. For me, America's goodness has always been core to its greatness. It's a goodness that tirelessly works toward liberty and justice for all. It's a goodness that advocates for those who are unable to do so for themselves. It's a goodness that knows the difference between right and wrong, and endeavors to do right. It's a goodness that crosses the partisan divide, and is anchored in character and courage. The courage of conviction. The courage to stand up against wrong-headedness and wrongdoing. The courage to fight the good fight, and never give up. The courage to defend the common good. Not only because it's the right thing to do, but because our children and grandchildren depend on it.

Now … I see the sinister side of goodness.

We Freedumbers realize that goodness actually prevents American greatness. In fact, goodness may be the greatest of all threats to the future of America. After all, good might lead to inclusiveness, and that's a highway to hell. Good might lead to compassion – an off ramp to the apocalypse. Good might lead to mutual respect – that's just un-American. We must turn the tide against goodness. The future of our children and grandchildren depends on it.

Today … Don't let goodness get the better of you. Try a 30-day 'good-for-nothing' challenge: Do no good, and see great again things start to happen.

JANUARY 6

Is your cup full?

"I've always thought New Year's Day was an especially American tradition, full of the optimism and hope we're famous for in our daily lives – an energy and confidence we call the American spirit. Perhaps because we know we control our own destiny; we believe deep down inside that working together we can make each new year better than the old."
(Ronald Reagan)

"I've always thought Insurrection Day was part of a great American tradition, full of the fear and anger we're famous for in our daily lives – an aggression and recklessness we call the American spirit."
(Freedumb Fighter)

Then ... When people asked me what it is about America that makes it different, I always started by saying: the energy. The energy of its people. The collective energy of the whole. The energy of possibility, of 'can do'. I believed President Reagan's hopeful remark nails that sentiment. The combination of optimism and determination is high octane fuel able to generate amazing advances and achievements. And America has always had that kind of fuel – in abundance. How could you not be excited and confident about where that kind of energy might take us?

Now ... I realize hope and optimism is a waste of time.

Each new year can't be better than the next or we'll lose sight of the good old days. That's why the energy around hope, the energy around belief in better, is a bad thing. We have to stop trying to improve and focus on what's going to get us back to greatness. More intolerance. More overt prejudice. More targets for our intolerance and prejudice. We need to think less and let our fear run rampant. And perhaps most importantly, we need to respect less. That's why us Freedumbers hold on to the idea that the insurrection of January 6, 2021 was just the beginning for the biggest step backward this country, and its people, have ever taken.

Today ... Honor the insurrection. Helpful hint: Work to instill fear and anger in your kids. Thought starter: Resolve to turn them into little insurrectionists, and encourage them to storm the principal's office to protest the lack of the Ten Commandments in the classroom.

JANUARY 7

What should you be called?

"Sometimes people call me an idealist. Well, that is the way I know I am an American ... America is the only idealistic nation in the world."
(Woodrow Wilson)

"Nobody calls me an idealist. That's the way I know I'm an American. America is no country for idealists."
(Freedumb Fighter)

Then ... I bought into every single word of President Wilson's quote. Idealists and idealism are part of what makes America great. Maybe it's a function of America still being a relatively young country, maybe it's our Constitution or our immigrant roots, but I believe idealism works to differentiate us as a people. We're dreamers. Pursuing happiness. Embracing life and liberty. There's an optimism that underpins our idealism that I've always found appealing. It makes America a promise of what could be. Without idealism, what of the American dream? Without idealism, what of the land of opportunity? Of justice for all? Of freedom for all? Idealism is oxygen for better, for making America better, by being a better American.

Now ... I've discovered that there's always a dumber way to look at things.

Freedumbers see idealism as a threat. Idealism can put too many ideas in people's heads. Ideas for a better life, a better community, a better country. And how is that going to do anything other than damage? Goddamned do-gooders! Sure, we Freedumbers talk about an ideal such as the American Dream, but only as 'cloud cover' for our belief that we own the dream. It's ours and we are not letting go. It's a possession to be doled out at our discretion. So too the ideals of justice, equality and opportunity. And, for the record, Freedumbers will never be mistaken for big givers. Ideally, everybody would just accept that and get with the program.

Today ... Imagine Freedumb's America - Freedumbia. Helpful hint: feel free to take some inspiration from apartheid-era South Africa, Nazi Germany or present-day Russia. Now we're talking ideal!

JANUARY 8

Is better really beneficial?

"True patriotism springs from a belief in the dignity of the individual, freedom and equality not only for Americans but for all people on earth, universal brotherhood and good will, and a constant striving toward the principles and ideals on which this country was founded."
(Eleanor Roosevelt)

"Striving for better just gets us further from perfection."
(Freedumb Fighter)

Then ... Eleanor Roosevelt was one of my heroes. And I believed as she did. Fully and completely.

Now ... My first thought is "What could a woman possibly know about patriotism?"

More to the point, we Freedumbers believe America is perfect, or at least it used to be. Before women got the vote. Before the dismantling of Jim Crow. Before President Johnson and the Voting Rights Act. Before the decriminalization of homosexuality. Before people worried about gun control or the environment.

True patriotism is about going backward. Back to when things were great for old white guys – which was great for everyone. Back to when old white men were the answer and held all the power. Back to when men had the balls to be manly. Back to when prejudice and intolerance got the respect they deserved. It takes a special kind of courage and patriotism to run away from the possibility of something better. Fortunately, Freedumbers have what it takes.

Today ... Try a creative visualization exercise. Imagine you are the king of your castle. Uninformed but all-knowing. Narrow-minded but all-seeing. Limited in capability but all-powerful. Now go out there and make things happen!

JANUARY 9

Are you a winner?

"Freedom is never really won. You earn it and win it in every generation."
(Coretta Scott King)

"I'm a winner. Freedumb rocks."
(Freedumb Fighter)

Then ...The idea of not taking freedom for granted, of seeing it as something that must be forever earned, spoke to its importance, fragile nature and unrealized potential. And maybe I was reading between the lines a bit, but I also took away from Mrs. King's words the idea that winning freedom should be a victory for us all. For our country and our people. Every single one of us. Regardless of color, creed or sexual orientation. Freedom for all is a worthy challenge for every generation of Americans.

Now ... Freedumb has taught me that some people are meant to lose.

From where us Freedumbers sit, we are the winners. Others? The losers. And Freedumbers aim to keep it that way. We see our winning as birthright. If you're white, you win. A man? You win. Straight? You win. A man of Christendumb? Of course you win! We dedicate our lives to ensuring everyone is clear on who the winners are and who the losers are, and always will be. We live to help losers understand that they'll never win. Ever. That's the Freedumbers' burden. Somebody needs to protect unearned privilege and advantage.

Today ... Try this 'winning exercise'. Imagine losing at something – a game, a competition, an election for your local school board or, dare to dream, an election to be President of the United States – and then imagine declaring that you won a tremendous victory. You're not a real Freedumber unless you refuse to lose!

JANUARY 10

Do you measure up?

"There is no second tier citizenship. You are an American, period. With hard work, learning English and getting involved, there is no limit to what you can achieve."
(Arnold Schwarzenegger)

"Yes, there is second tier American citizenship. But don't forget the other tiers as well."
(Freedumb Fighter)

Then ... I was all-in with Governor Schwarzenegger. For me, that was America, period. Hustling, learning, contributing toward limitless opportunity. That's energizing. That's motivating. And it's certainly every immigrant's dream upon coming to America. Limitless hope is the magnet that draws those "yearning to breathe free." All an immigrant wants is a chance. A genuine chance. A chance to prove they're up to the promise America offers, the promise of opportunity. I believed America gave immigrants the right, along with every other American citizen, to take their best shot at fulfilling their potential. For this I said: God bless America.

Now ... What I didn't realize is that the God of Christendumb likes to play favorites.

We Freedumbers see ourselves as his chosen ones. So, of course there are second tier American citizens. The real question is how many tiers are there? Immigrants typically range from the second tier on down. It's basically a color-coded system, although gender, sexual orientation and religious belief can also push you further down the ladder. Not surprising that us Freedumbers, ever vigilant, see the lower tiers as a threat. A threat to our comfort, our advantage and our inherent superiority. We don't care about any immigrant's hopes or dreams. Or rights, for that matter. What we care about is outsiders knowing their place – that place being on the outside, looking in. And for this I say: God bless Freedumb.

Today ... Be a real American and tell a few immigrants to go back where they came from. Helpful hint: Extra points if they come from a Freedumb-designated "shithole" country.

JANUARY 11

'Woke say, We say': Let's dumb some stuff down:

Woke say … Privilege is the good fortune you enjoy without having to think about certain obstacles. Other people face these obstacles because of their skin color, gender, sexual orientation, religion or mother tongue. Sure, you may have worked hard and deserve everything you've achieved. But while you've been running life's 100-meter sprint, an awful lot of people out there are running the 110-meter hurdles.

We say … Privilege is other people being allowed to live in our country despite all their skin colors, sexual orientations and various godless religions, while we Freedumbers work tirelessly without help from anybody. Ever.

Woke say … Advantage is what you gain by running 10 meters less than other people and not having to jump over any hurdles.

We say … Advantage belongs to the fastest runner, and we're just faster than those other people.

Woke say … Entitlement is a refusal to believe that anyone is running the 110-meter hurdles, while acting like you own the track.

We say … Entitlement is other people refusing to believe that Freedumbers don't just own the track, but the country and all their sorry asses as well.

JANUARY 12

Have you made openness an enemy?

"Freedom is the open window through which pours the sunlight of the human spirit and human dignity."
(Herbert Hoover)

"I like my windows closed, with the drapes drawn."
(Freedumb Fighter)

Then … I always thought openness was a good thing. This quote from President Hoover struck me as a powerful bit of poetic language about what openness can bring. With openness come understanding and learning. With understanding and learning come empathy and compassion. And ultimately, a respect for people, places and things that are different. And that's the kind of growth that makes us better people. Better Americans. I mean, how could human dignity and the best of the human spirit be a bad thing? I've always seen America as both an advocate for and defender of that kind of sunlight.

Now … Sunlight gives me a rash.

The road to Freedumb is littered with epiphanies. One being that humanity, human dignity, has no part in being an American. In fact, for us Freedumbers, the very idea of humanity poses an existential threat to all things American. Our privilege. Our entitlement. Our advantage. All at risk. Dignity isn't something that is just given to anyone. All that would do is confuse everybody. And it could lead to uncertainty, and worse. Imagine, for example, if the superiority of Freedumb's mediocre men was ever called into question? That kind of insanity opens the window to the apocalypse. Equality? Justice? Opportunity for all? Screw "the sunlight." Life is great again in the dark.

Today … Show your indignation at the thought of human dignity. Helpful hint: Find reasons to fly the flag upside down. Thought starter: In addition to the 2020 election being stolen, do you realize poor people are still getting food stamps on your nickel? Do you realize do-gooders are still leaving food and water for migrants at our southern border? Do you realize there are still states where it's OK to say "gay"?

JANUARY 13

What would God do?

"Be kind and compassionate to one another, forgiving each other, just as in Christ God forgave you."
(Ephesians 4:32)

"God forgives if the end justify the means."
(Freedumb Fighter)

Then ... I believed in a kind and compassionate God. A forgiving God. She wasn't an advocate for the 'whatever it takes' approach. My God wanted you to be a good person. If you were trying to be a good person, and messed up once in a while, she'd cut you some slack. My God's hope was that we understand what being good means: being good to one another. Being good means respecting one another. Being good does not mean you can 'lord over' others. My God didn't need us to assert dominance over others in her name. She didn't need us to marginalize or demonize others just because they're different. She didn't need us to put liars on the Supreme Court or pussy grabbers in the White House. Really all my God asked for, when she gave America her blessing, was for all of us to try our best to be decent human beings.

Now ... I've been introduced to the badass God of Christendumb.

First, it should go without saying, but God is a 'he'. I mean, to think about God as anything other than a man is plain stupid. Second, a Freedumber's God sees kindness and compassion as unnecessary – which, among other things, is a bit of a stress reliever. The most important thing is to win. Freedumb's God loves winners. He's less concerned with how you get there. Freedumb's God knows that you may have to be cruel and callous to let his holiness (and your own) shine through. He realizes that being an asshole, a misogynist or a racist may be what it takes to get his job dumb. And as long as the job gets dumb, all is good. That's a pretty awesome God when you think about it.

Today ... Live in God's image. Do something dumb to win the day in his name and all that is holy.

JANUARY 14

What do you cherish?

"These are moments to be cherished in American life: The realization of a common dream, unique, really, to this land – a college education, a privilege not confined to the well-born or wealthy. Here the working class sits side-by-side with old and new fortunes; here new Americans from distant lands and cultures mingle with the sons and daughters of the Americans who came on the sailing ships, some to proclaim their freedom, others in the holds and chains of slave ships."
(Tom Brokaw)

"January 6, 2021, a moment to cherish."
(Freedumb Fighter)

Then ... I thought Tom Brokaw nailed it with his description of 'cherishable' American moments. Dreams. Diversity. Determination. These create moments that are woven into the fabric of what makes America. For me, these were elements that fueled our greatness. I believed they sat at the foundation of what makes us exceptional. They unlock possibility and hope. They open the door to the opportunity for better. They foster moments that provide oxygen for our progress. They foster moments that make us proud to be American. Very proud. What's not to cherish?

Now ... I see it's best to put your pride elsewhere.

A common dream? Not there. Equality of opportunity? Not there. New Americans from distant lands? Ah, not there. Mingling of cultures? Please, please, not there. Instead, we Freedumbers stand strong to proclaim a more perfectly pure union, and cherish moments that bring us closer to that goal. Such as the overturning of Roe v. Wade. Or legislation that bans the teaching of Black history. Or the passing of 'Don't say Gay' laws. And of course, the big moment: that day when the sunshine of Freedumb broke through the clouds of democracy. January 6, 2021. Keep the faith. A greater again America is on the horizon. Be proud of that.

Today ... Go to a new citizen naturalization ceremony – in protest. Helpful hint: be the 'unwelcoming committee'. Thought Starter: Begin booing as they begin the Pledge. Or boo as each new citizen stands when their country of origin is recognized. Or both. Or just boo throughout the entire ceremony.

JANUARY 15

When is enough enough?

"I say to you that our goal is freedom, and I believe we are going to get there because however much she strays from it, the goal of America is freedom."
(Martin Luther King Jr.)

"I say to you enough already."
(Freedumb Fighter)

Then … I believed Martin Luther King was among the greatest Americans to ever live.

The thought of freedom being a goal, an eternal goal, was a powerful one. Freedom must have a dynamic quality to it. The struggle on behalf of minorities and the marginalized must never end. It rang true as an essential American aspiration. I believed there was nobility in it. Nobility in the idea of it. In the struggle for it and in the striving toward it. Freedom means equal opportunity. Freedom means justice for all. Freedom depends on a shared responsibility to one another, an unwavering commitment, and an endurance that will last for generations, because the road is a long one. Yet it's a road I know my fellow Americans will always travel.

Now … I understand the importance of living your life as a roadblock.

We Freedumbers believe some Americans have too much freedom already. Minorities only warrant a minor amount of freedom. A minor amount of justice and opportunity. They've been given too much. And it's time to pull it back. Women began to believe they were equal; gays not only came out of the closet, they actually came out proud; and how did black people ever start to think their lives mattered? A course correction is needed.

Think suppression. Think repression. Think banning, muzzling and stifling. Think quashing, squashing and crushing. Think clampdown, crackdown and stamping out. Freedumb aims to stop freedom dead in its tracks.

Today … Turn back the clock. On women, for example. Take inspiration from the Supreme Court of Arizona reinstating a Civil War era (1864) law which for all intents and purposes banned abortion. We can't go back far enough in our quest to make America great again!

JANUARY 16

Today, a Freedumber makes a speech for the ages:

"I have a dream that one day on the rolling hills of America, the sons of former slaves will be slaves themselves, and the sons of former slave owners can sit down at a table together and celebrate their newly acquired possessions.

I have a dream that one day we can warm up our anger on the sweltering heat of injustice, the sweltering heat of oppression, and transform it into a raging fire that forces out the enemies of Freedumb.

I have a dream that my little children will one day live in a nation where they will be judged only on the color of their skin, not by the content of their character or their contribution to any common good. I have a dream today.

And when this happens, and when we allow Freedumb to ring, when we let it ring from every village and every hamlet, from every state and every city, we will be able to speed up that day when all of God's white male children will be able to join hands and sing, 'Victory at last. Victory at last.'"

JANUARY 17

Is gratitude really necessary?

"Out of profound gratitude for my adopted country, I can only say that I would like in this land to live and die, and while I live to help other people as much as possible, believing that only in service to other people can I possibly express my gratitude for all that America has done for me."
(Peter Marshall)

"You're an immigrant? Keep on thanking me."
(Freedumb Fighter)

Then ... Peter Marshall was a Presbyterian preacher who became a chaplain of the United States Senate. This quote really resonated with me. Whether immigrant or natural born American, a degree of gratitude should play a part in being a citizen. An immigrant's experience tends to be a very personal one, but they all come into America believing. They believe America is the land of opportunity. The land of dreams. They believe in hard work, determination, personal responsibility, and the pursuit of happiness. They believe in contributing to the country that is their new home. They believe in the land of the free and the home of the brave. And they are thankful for it. So should we all.

Now ... Freedumb has taught me that all I have to say is 'You're welcome'.

Freedumbers like to be thanked. Which just feels right, because gratitude is kind of a minority thing. An immigrant thing. It's not a thing real Americans have to bother with. Which is so cool. Basically, we Freedumbers should be thanked for pretty much everything. Thanked for our privilege and our advantage. Thanked for our whiteness and our straightness. Thanked for our conspiracy theories. Thanked for making sure other people know how lucky they are. Thanked for driving America back to greatness.

Today ... On National Nothing Day, commit to being a complete ingrate. You're probably almost there anyway. Thank your fellow citizens for nothing. Thank your community for nothing. And thank your country for nothing - except the Freedumb you've been given.

JANUARY 18

What is your responsibility?

"With freedom comes responsibility, a responsibility that can only be met by the individual."
(Ronald Reagan)

"Responsibility isn't the only option."
(Freedumb Fighter)

Then ... I believed that although responsibility isn't often sexy, exciting or fun, it was a mandatory. For our government, for our companies, for our communities, for all of us as individuals. Freedom doesn't function without responsibility. Greatness doesn't happen without responsibility. A better life for our children and grandchildren doesn't happen without responsibility. Our pursuit of happiness depended on it. Our rights and democracy depended on it. I have always believed that America at its core, Americans at their heart, were anchored to a sense of responsibility that put us on common ground and fostered our desire to stand united.

Now ... Freedumb has shown me that responsibility is a virus to be eradicated.

For Freedumbers, responsibility is an unnecessary and unfair burden. It gets in the way of our predestined greatness. In fact, Freedumbers believe it's our duty to be irresponsible. Irresponsibility is the right of each and every American and works to unlock the kind of inhumanity that will get us back to greatness. Think of it as Freedumbing down in order to rise up.

Today ... Work on your 'irresponse - ability'. Create a list of all the things you're not responsible for. Thought starter: What you say and what you do should lead the list. You can get more specific after that.

JANUARY 19

What's so remarkable?

"Our Constitution is a remarkable, beautiful gift. But it's really just a piece of parchment. It has no power on its own. We, the people, give it power. We, the people, give it meaning – with our participation, and with the choices that we make, and the alliances that we forge."
(Barack Obama)

"Our Constitution is a remarkable, beautiful thing that allows us to do whatever we want."
(Freedumb Fighter)

Then ... I read the Constitution. It's an inspiring document. It's a document full of possibility and ambition. Indeed, as President Obama suggested, it ultimately derives its power from the American people – from "we the people." That said, as a gift, it's one open to interpretation. I believed that it operated at its full potential when anchored in wisdom, even-handedness and conscience of the American people. And as such, I never had any doubt that the 'gift' of our Constitution was in good hands.

Now ... I know better who to listen to. And it's not some guy born in Kenya.

We Freedumbers, as always, can be depended on to set the record straight. First off, President Obama can't be trusted. Have you noticed he's black? Strike one. And you know, that funny name of his, how can he be American? Strike two. And he's a wise, even-handed man with a conscience. Enough already! Strike three and he's out. Yes, he's out.

On the Constitution bit, Freedumbers see it not as a gift but as a weapon. And we use it to knock the crap out of common sense, minority rights, and pleas for equal opportunity and justice for the most vulnerable. We use it to justify mass shootings, book bans and the killing of Mother Nature. In the hands of us Freedumbers, the Constitution is the most nuclear of nuclear weapons. Don't you just love explosions!

Today ... Take a break. No weaponizing needed. Helpful hint: Do something else to make yourself smile. Thought starter: Pleasure yourself between a couple of couch cushions.

JANUARY 20

What are you doing?

*"Ask not what your country can do for you,
ask what you can do for your country."
(John F. Kennedy)*

*"Go ahead and ask, I'm not doing it."
(Freedumb Fighter)*

Then ... These words, spoken on President Kennedy's Inauguration Day, was *the* American call to action. It was American patriotism in a nutshell, American citizenship at its most distilled. It was being American at its core. There are moments in time when citizens must step up and help their country. Military service is the obvious example, but I'm talking about civilians stepping up in everyday life. In big ways, yes, but in small ways too. How can we help our country progress? Be better? Build? Or heal? Kindness is one way. So are compassion and mutual respect. And civility too. Americans want to 'do' for our country. Our country needs us to 'do' for it. On good days, and bad. Every single day. That's how we've solved problems and overcame obstacles. That's how we reached for greatness. That's how we made a difference. Together.

Now ... We Freedumbers have a different take on difference-making.

It has nothing to do with solving problems, getting better or doing anything together. You can't ask us Freedumbers to *do* anything. Among the things that Freedumbers won't do is make progress possible, work for the greater good, or help create the possibility of better. We aren't big on governing either. We prefer petulance and chaos, and the entertainment it provides. That takes a lot of negative energy. Fortunately, we have that in limitless supply. And we'll use every ounce of it in service to a vision of greatness only we can see.

Today ... Identify a difference-maker. Helpful hint: Make it fun for the whole family by playing a game of 'I Spy'. Thought starter: Start with the greatest of them all – I spy with my little eye something that is orange.

JANUARY 21

Have you seen the ocean?

"We can't be afraid of change. You may feel very secure in the pond that you are in, but if you never venture out of it, you will never know that there is such a thing as an ocean, a sea."
(C Joybell C)

"It's my pond and I'm sticking to it."
(Freedumb Fighter)

Then ... C Joybell C is a writer and cultural critic. I thought her statement about change was both poetic and poignant. I didn't see Americans as "pond people," afraid to venture out into the unknown, because a sense of adventure and exploration is very much a part of the American spirit. We embrace the possibilities inherent in new frontiers. With new frontiers come the experiences that open our eyes, hearts and minds. And while venturing out of our comfort zone is no guarantee of change, change doesn't happen without some degree of discomfort. Too much comfort can shrink our minds, harden our hearts, and solidify our resistance to change. If that was something we needed to guard against, a trip to the ocean sounded like the perfect antidote.

Now ... We Freedumbers aren't big water people.

Venturing out isn't our thing. We love our little ponds. We love them so much! A pond is our comfort zone. The world as we know it, and like it. The ocean petrifies us. And with good reason. Why jump into an unknown and unpredictable vastness? Sure, the ocean may hold beauty and inspiration. It might expand our horizons and alter our worldview. It might unlock our humility, our humanity, and give us a sense of being part of something bigger. And that's the problem. Thankfully, we recognize it as such. Life on the pond never changes. Life is as life should be. Nothing different. Nothing challenging. Nothing to inspire awe, imagination or progress. Bliss.

Today ... Put on your swimsuit, jump into your pond, and soak your body to your heart's content. You can always throw in some salt and pretend you're an 'ocean person.'

JANUARY 22

Under what circumstances?

"In America, nobody says you have to keep the circumstances somebody else gives you."
(Amy Tan)

"Some circumstances are just meant to be. It's God's will."
(Freedumb Fighter)

Then … I believed the idea that your circumstances don't define you was a very powerful one. It encourages drive. It promises opportunity. It's an invitation to take your rip at a better life. It's the right to life, liberty and the pursuit. That's the fuel for the American dream. It's about overcoming obstacles, transcending expectations, and doing the seemingly impossible. And that dream is the most potent dream on the planet. We need to continue to work at giving every American their fair chance – that's got to be a priority – but the invitation to take your best shot will always be there.

Now … Freedumb has taught me not to give a shit about anybody else's circumstances.

Freedumbers don't care about the hardships and obstacles the others might confront. We have a 'Freedumber First' perspective. If we – the straight white men of Christendumb – don't take care of ourselves, who will? And a big part of that caring comes down to screwing everybody else around us. Some people are just meant to have less, to lead a more difficult life, and to feel the sharp edge of unfairness. It's simply God's will. And Freedumbers, with our limitless generosity, are willing to contribute in any way we can to maintain the unfair circumstances of others. The amount of energy 'the work' takes, the attention it demands, and the creativity it requires add up to a burden not everyone can carry. Still, we Freedumbers soldier on. Amen to us.

Today … Create 'Freedumber First' bumper stickers to help spread the word. Thought starters: "I'm more blessed than you" or "Stop hoping" or "Disadvantage looks good on you." Time to put on your dunce cap and have some fun!

JANUARY 23

Is hope really a good thing?

"America is hope. It is compassion. It is excellence. It is valor."
(Paul Tsongas)

"I'm hoping for the end of hope."
(Freedumb Fighter)

Then … If I believed that America was one thing, I believed it was hope. Genuine hope. Hope for better. Hope for equality of opportunity. Hope for even-handed justice. Hope for freedom for all. As Senator Tsongas realized, hope is energy-giving. Hope is idea-generating. Hope is a building block for progress. Hope brings compassion, encourages excellence, and puts a premium on valor and courage. The courage to fight complacency and make a difference. The courage to make things right. In America, hope should always spring eternal. Hope is the oxygen needed to be optimistic, to search for common ground, and to aspire toward the greater good.

Now … Hope is carbon monoxide to me.

On Freedumb's endless 'most wanted' list of enemies, hope may be Public Enemy #1. Hope attacks the core Freedumb. It invites the kind of improvement that can only hurt Freedumbers. Hope invites better opportunities for others. Hope invites more robust rights for others. Hope invites greater acceptance of others. America doesn't have to wrap its mouth around the exhaust pipe of hope. Time to hold your breath until all hope is gone!

Today … Find a cure for hope. Fast! Helpful hint: Don't even think about a vaccine. Thought starter: invermectin!

JANUARY 24

What does love look like?

"I love America more than any other country in this world, and, exactly for this reason, I insist on the right to criticize her perpetually."
(James Baldwin)

"Criticizing America is un-American. Except when I do it."
(Freedumb Fighter)

Then ... I respected James Baldwin's push to critique what you love. You can't get better as a country or a people if you're not willing to call out shortcomings and wrongdoings. Offering up that kind of criticism can be tough, but sometimes tough love is what's needed to maximize potential. The American love of country brings out an almost one-of-a-kind passion, energy and depth of feeling. America is a big promise and, objectively, has some ways to go before fulfilling its ultimate potential. That's the American struggle – the struggle to match its potential. And it's every citizen's obligation to do what they can to help in the struggle. That obligation demands the integrity and courage to identify flaws and address them on our way to achieving the best of what America could be.

Now ... Freedumb has shown me why America's flaws are what makes it great.

Freedumbers' love of America is an extra special kind of love. For example, we don't worry about racism. We love it because, after all, it works in our favor. Talk about a great flaw! Freedumbers understand that unequal opportunity is great when you're on the right side of the equation. Intolerance is great when you're not the target. So instead of trying to fight inequality and intolerance, find a flag and give it a big hug. Obligation fulfilled. Freedumbers are smart enough not to criticize things that work to our advantage. If you're going to criticize, take aim at some minority for being lazy, rail against some woman for being uppity, accuse some LGBTQ-type of being a predator, blame some woke nutcase for caring about the environment. Then, OK – but otherwise, mouth shut.

Today ... Organize a lovefest. Invite a racist, a couple of Incels and some homophobes to dinner, and discuss what you love about America. It's the type of discussion that can only make America greater again.

JANUARY 25

Are you divisive enough?

"The essence of America, that which really unites us, is not ethnicity or nationality or religion. It is an idea – and what an idea it is – that you can come from humble circumstances and do great things."
(Condoleezza Rice)

"When divided, we can do really great things."
(Freedumb Fighter)

Then ... I loved the power and simplicity of Secretary Rice's thought. The way I read it is that, in America, we are united by the most powerful idea there is: possibility. The possibility to take our best shot and make our dreams come true. The possibility to create something of value and give our children a better life. The possibility to leave our community and country in a better place. The color of our skin, our sexual preference, our religious beliefs should not impact what's possible. Our differences should feed our curiosity, accelerate our understanding, energize our creativity, and expand our horizons. America, at its best, is an incubator for what could be – for each and every one of us.

Now ... I think we need to celebrate all that divides us.

Common ground is quicksand. Common good is bad for privilege and entitlement. And common sense – well, that's just nonsense. So, for us Freedumbers, it's not enough to simply disagree, it's time to deepen the American divide. Stop trying to understand and empathize. Stop trying to include and embrace. Stop trying to improve. Man up and make our dreams come true. Just imagine an America that is authoritarian, intolerant, small-minded and backward-thinking. There really can be a heaven on earth! Time to divide and conquer – our fellow Americans.

Today ... Formalize the conquest. Stop calling us The United States of America. Freedumbia does have a nice ring to it, especially since "Russia" and "North Korea" are already taken.

JANUARY 26

Is that a lie?

"Freedom lies in being bold."
(Robert Frost)

"If you're going to lie, lie boldly."
(Freedumb Fighter)

Then ... I liked Robert Frost's simple, direct connection between freedom and boldness. It suggests freedom is a living, breathing thing. To expand and strengthen freedom, it needs to be used. This speaks to the courage to push boundaries, question conventional wisdom, and challenge the status quo. It speaks to the courage needed to experiment, to address tough problems with new initiatives, to harness our untapped potential, individually and as a nation. It's about being brave enough to attempt the yet to be done. All in service to something that breaks the mold, something impossibly inspiring, something that just might take your breath away. As the saying goes, let freedom reign.

Now ... Let it rain on freedom's parade.

So, let's talk lying. Freedumbers love lies, and love to lie. We love to listen to lies, build on them, and make them even bigger lies. Why? Because lies have the potential to create an alternative reality. Sure, this requires something more than simple embellishments or exaggerations. Greatness demands bold, mind-numbing, absolute untruths. For example, white men always know best. No discussion. All migrants are felons. Full stop. Blacks are lazy. End of story. All gays are groomers. Blindingly obvious. Women are weak. Naturally. Freedumb's reality is so clear and easy to understand. Big lies are a beautiful thing. Impossibly inspiring and breathtaking: it makes you well up with tears.

Today ... Take your lying to the next level. Helpful hint: Create a 1-10 scale to rate your lies. 1 = embarrassingly small. 10 = full-on Freedumb mode. Grade your lies daily. And when you're consistently hitting 8 out of 10, consider yourself genuine leadership material for the Freedumb movement.

JANUARY 27

Do you have a big idea?

"America is not just a country, it's an idea."
(Bono)

"You have no idea what America is."
(Freedumb Fighter)

Then … I saw Bono as a thinking man's musician. His vision of America as an idea is an interesting one. That America is something more than land mass and borders – that it stands for, symbolizes and has meaning beyond itself – speaks to its potential exceptionalism and greatness. America stood for something aspirational, elevated, noble even. Is it opportunity? Is it freedom and justice for all? Is it the pursuit of happiness? Ultimately, wherever you landed, the idea of America was a big one. It was an idea that could make a difference, an idea that aimed at better. It was an idea we needed. We were all a part of this idea. We were all invited to contribute to it.

Now … Well, we Freedumbers don't really like ideas.

Especially ones that burden us with the unhelpful expectation of doing and being better. Besides, Freedumbers spend too much time trying to save America than to waste time on ideas. White advantage isn't simply going to take care of itself. Lack of tolerance for the others under the rainbow doesn't just happen. Even systemic racism needs to be oiled and tightened every now and again. Coming up with new ways to fuck with migrants and frighten the undocumented isn't as easy as it looks. Book banning, pseudo-science, the spreading of conspiracy theories: all this demands time and effort. Not to mention the sheer energy it takes to ignore facts and evidence, and to reject the truth. We Freedumbers know no rest!

Today … Work on your Freedumb-fighting fitness. Helpful hint: Instead of daily push-ups, do some daily put-downs. Thought Starters: Put down democracy or education. Put down science or black history. Put down learning. Put down compassion. Better has got to be stopped. You get the idea.

JANUARY 28

What do you value?

"A people that values its privileges above its principles soon loses both."
(Dwight D. Eisenhower)

"I value the principle of privilege."
(Freedumb Fighter)

Then ... This seemed like a great 'watchout' from President Eisenhower. To me, the American man has always tried to be a man of principle. At its core, that means there were some things that you just wouldn't do. Lines that you wouldn't cross. A lot of principles come down to what you say 'no' to. Saying no helped you safeguard your integrity, your honor, and ultimately your self-worth. Saying no to racial injustice made you a better person. Saying no to intolerance for those searching for their gender identity made you a better person. Saying no to inequality made you a better person. A person of principle. And you can't have a principled country without a principled people.

Now ... Freedumb has taught me that privilege is a principle.

So, forget about racial injustice, intolerance and inequality. And focus on your privilege. Privilege trumps integrity, decency and fairness. And the cool thing is, for us Freedumbers, privilege isn't something you have to earn. If you're white, welcome to our privilege. If you're a straight white man: go ahead have an extra helping of privilege. And get ready to protect all the privilege you can get. It's a lot of fun. You don't just get to be selfish you get to be shamelessly and unapologetically selfish. On principle.

Today ... Regress. Helpful hint: Access your inner toddler. Thought starter: Brainstorm the different types of tantrums you could throw beyond the classic 'kick and scream.'

JANUARY 29

What's your one thing?

"The one thing in the world, of value, is the active soul."
(Ralph Waldo Emerson)

"The one thing in the world, of value, is my opinion."
(Freedumb Fighter)

Then … For me, the idea of soul spoke to the essence of a person, place or thing. Soul is cultivated through experience, through existence over time. It develops as you live life. It is a source of goodness and our best self. Emerson's quote gets to the heart of what we need from our soul. That is, it must manifest itself in action. There's not a lot of point in knowing in your soul what is good and right if you don't act like you do. There's not much use in knowing in your soul what is decent and respectful if you don't act like you do. Knowing better is worthless if you don't act on it. A person with a good soul, a community with a good soul and a country with a good soul can accomplish great things. I believed the American people knew this. And would always act on the knowledge.

Now … A soul isn't something we Freedumbers think a lot about.

We're too busy focussing on our opinions. A Freedumber's opinion is a sacred thing. A special thing. Often unfounded and incomprehensible, it's a point-of-view powered by the twin engines of fear and loathing. And there's a lot to fear and loathe out there. Competent women. Blacks who think they matter. Immigrants who yearn. Anybody out of the closet. And, of course, librarians. Threats to our greatness each and every one.

Today … Form an opinion based on absolutely nothing. And make it sacred. Helpful hint: List out all the things that scare you, and threaten America. Vaccines, masks, words that start with L or G or B or T or Q, science that isn't pseudo, losers who actually think about what they recycle … the list is a long one.

JANUARY 30

Do you harness the power of denial?

"The greatness of America lies not in being more enlightened than any other nation, but rather in her ability to repair her faults."
(Alexis de Tocqueville)

"The greatness of America lies in not being enlightened."
(Freedumb Fighter)

Then … De Tocqueville's observation may have been my favorite quote about America ever. It hit at America's super power. The power to be better. I never thought of America as being afraid to take on its problems and shortcomings. Americans have always known what they need to do.

Now … I know it's always better to deny than repair.

If acknowledging faults is one way to step onto the path of getting better, denial is a much easier step to get us on the yellow brick road to Freedumbia. Talk about a super power! Why acknowledge and address when you can merely deny? Racism? Not in America. Injustice? Nothing to see here. Inequality? Gone the way of the dinosaurs. Pandemics, climate change, mass shootings? Hoax, hoax, hoax. The power of denial knows no bounds.

Today … Make it a day of denial. Strive for implausible deniability. Do it with a straight face and no shame. Work on your finger-pointing (great for shifting blame), hone your 'whataboutism' skill (great for changing the subject) and, of course, refine your conspiracy theory skills (great for so many reasons). If we stay strong, we can deny our way to being great again.

JANUARY 31

Do you have a hero inside you?

"A hero is someone who understands the responsibility that comes with his freedom."
(Bob Dylan)

"If you're asking, I think I'm an American hero."
(Freedumb Fighter)

Then ... Acting responsibly isn't always easy. It can require stepping up, saying no, opening your eyes, and doing something outside of your comfort zone. It can require curiosity and learning. Not to mention sacrifice. And patience. As Bob Dylan points out, freedom is ultimately a test of character. It demands that you think about consequence. Consequences for yourself, sure, but more importantly, the impact of your actions on others. Acting responsibly is not for the faint of heart. Then again, what could be more appropriate in the land of the free and the home of the brave. I believed there was a hero inside every American. Ready and waiting.

Now ... I realize I had no clue of what heroism was.

Of course, it has nothing to do with responsibility. Responsibility is for the disadvantaged and marginalized – they better damn well take responsibility for the burden they are! Freedumbers are a different breed. We believe a hero is someone brave enough to be cowardly when it counts. Brave enough to run to Cancun when millions of your constituents lose their heating and lighting. Brave enough to take a vaccine while telling your followers not to. Brave enough to suggest that white supremacists are nice people too. Brave enough to bully people who, by the way they live and love, just bug you. Talk about superheroes. Some Freedumbers, might with all humility suggest they were simply born heroes, but that's not giving themselves enough credit. Having no conscience or moral compass requires putting in the work.

Today ... Put in the work.

FEBRUARY 1

What are you buying?

"The white man's happiness cannot be purchased by the black man's misery."
(Frederick Douglass)

"Sure it can, but it can be bought by the misery of other minorities as well."
(Freedumb Fighter)

Then ... I thought happiness at the expense of another is hollow and immoral. And un-American. Throughout our history, and still today, much in America comes down to race. Happiness is no exception. The quote from Frederick Douglass is truth. Black History Month was an opportunity to recognize the misery put upon black Americans as shameful – in the absolute. That said, I believed America, and the American people, stood squarely on the moral side of the struggle to right this wrong. There can be no genuine happiness without liberty and justice for all. There can be no true happiness without opportunity for all. And America will never fully achieve its destiny, and the possibility of a more perfect union, until it achieves a foundational happiness shared by each and every one of its citizens. Or so I thought.

Now ... I get that there's only so much happiness to go around.

We Freedumbers want more than our share, but that's only because we deserve more. And if we get more, they get less. And the less they have, the more miserable they are. And their misery fosters our happiness. And the white, straight men of Christendumb deserve all the happiness they can get. In the end, aren't black people really better off miserable? Isn't that how they are most comfortable? Or look at all those desperate people (sorry, desperados) coming to our southern border: misery is their destiny, yes? We Freedumbers can't help but smile. Unfair is fair, as long as you're on top.

Today ... Ponder others who might be made more miserable. Thought starter: People wearing masks? People getting vaccinated? People who care about the environment? People who believe in democracy? Healthcare workers? Scientists? There's more happiness out there for the taking.

FEBRUARY 2

How happy are you?

"Our greatest happiness does not depend on the condition of life in which chance has placed us, but is always the result of a good conscience, good health, occupation, and freedom in all just pursuits."
(Thomas Jefferson)

"I'm not happy with this idea of happiness as a thing for everybody."
(Freedumb Fighter)

Then ... I believed that in America, happiness should be a force for good. As President Jefferson suggested, the combination of a good conscience, hard work and just pursuits can orient happiness with a kind of moral sensibility. I'd never taken Americans to be selfish people, or America to be a selfish country. Ambitious, yes. Driven, yes. But also inherently generous and big-hearted. I believed there was a moral fiber to the American makeup that kept its relentless pursuit of happiness from going off the rails.

Now ... I understand that nothing of value results from a good conscience.

Thankfully, Freedumbers don't carry the burden of a conscience. And the thought of one makes us unhappy. Don't tell Freedumbers that pursuits have to be just. That would stop our pursuit in its tracks. Don't say that happiness doesn't depend on color. Happiness's favorite color is white. Happiness's favorite gender is male. Happiness's God is the God of Christendumb. In the name of that God, happiness's favorite pursuits are those that benefit the white men of Christendumb. The mere thought of not being happiness's favorite son makes a Freedumber very unhappy – and vicdumbized.

Today ... Reflect on what's holding you back from being happier. Helpful hint: It could be a remaining fragment of conscience. Take out what's left, lock it in your sights, and pull the trigger. Your smile will be immediate with 'that little voice inside' dead and gone.

FEBRUARY 3

Is kindness your weakness?

"Imagine what our real neighborhoods would be like if each of us offered, as a matter of course, just one kind word to another person."
(Fred Rogers)

"One kind word is a dangerous thing."
(Freedumb Fighter)

Then ... I never knew of Mr. Rogers growing up. As I became familiar with his neighborhood later in life, I thought he was a pretty cool guy. For me, he was a teacher. One who taught us to be good people. One who saw the good in people. One who taught that a little gesture could make a big difference. The thought above is a perfect example. What does a kind word cost anyone? A kind word can elicit a smile, create a happy moment, or even make someone's day. It seemed like that kind of impact would make any big-hearted American feel pretty cool himself. And who knows, maybe that one word of kindness could lead to more compassion, understanding and mutual respect. His neighborhood felt like a place I'd be happy to live in.

Now ... Mr. Rogers' neighborhood ain't in my zip code.

Every Freedumber knows that nothing opens a can of worms like kindness. A kind word represents the beginning of the end. It might bridge misunderstandings and bring us closer together. What is this, Kumbaya country? Freedumbers see the danger in heading that direction. Kindness could make us less scared and angry. Maybe even hate less. How the fuck is that going to help the cause? How is that going to help sustain prejudice and intolerance? How is that going to keep migrants out and minorities in a state of fear? How's that going to fuel our unearned sense of superiority? Bottom line, kindness is no friend of the Freedumber. That big American heart has got to get smaller and harden up if we're serious about recapturing our greatness. Imagine that!

Today ... Do some creative visualization. Contemplate your ideal neighborhood. Helpful hint: Ban any Mr. Rogers fans. Thought starter: You could name the street you live on 'Callous Crescent' or 'Ill Will Way' or 'Bitter Boulevard'.

FEBRUARY 4

Do you have a moral code?

"Human happiness and moral duty are inseparably connected."
(George Washington)

"Immorality is the new morality."
(Freedumb Fighter)

Then ... What makes an American happy is a big question. The answers are as varied as the people themselves. President Washington's idea of connecting happiness with a sense of duty gave me pause to think. No doubt it sets a high bar. And it grounds happiness in a kind of goodness. I liked that. If you talk about being a great country, if you take pride in its exceptionalism, a moral thread in pursuit of happiness feels almost mandatory. To me, it was a rich vein for introspection. And, ultimately, action.

Now ... We Freedumbers see the duty in immorality.

It's a necessary twist of a moral code. And the immoral fiber of a Freedumber is formidable. Lie, cheat, fabricate, harm, marginalize, demean, or look the other way – just do whatever it takes. No exceptions. Morality won't get you to the finish line, or to the promised land of Freedumbia where greatness comes again. And again.

Immoral behavior, on the other hand, makes shit happen. You can ban books (you don't even have to read them!), you can undermine healthcare workers during a global pandemic, and you can disparage people trying to protect Mother Nature. You can take away a woman's right to choose, you can dismiss black history, and you can demean every migrant you see for causing every problem you can think of. You can vote for leaders who redefine the religious high ground by giving misogyny, racism and narcissism a pass in service to God's will. When you don't think about it, immorality is a beautiful thing.

Today ... Formalize your immoral code. Helpful hint: Give the Ten Commandments a once over. Thought starter: Is loving thy neighbor as thyself really necessary?

FEBRUARY 5

Now, for a little spiritual inspiration, the Freedumber movement brings you:

The Ten Commandments of Christendumb

1. Thou shalt worship no other than Jesus of Orange.

2. Thou shalt not make idols except orange miniatures of you know who.

3. Thou shalt not take his name and put it anywhere except in big letters on the front of buildings.

4. Thou shalt keep holy the Sabbath day by reading posts from Truth Social.

5. Thou shalt honor thy father, tolerate thy mother, and dishonor everybody else.

6. Thou shalt not let a mass shooting go by without asking Santa for more ammo.

7. Thou shalt not commit adultery, but pussy grabbing is OK.

8. Thou shalt steal from others, especially their dignity and hope.

9. Thou shalt embrace lies of all kinds and bear false witness whenever possible.

10. Thou shalt covet only the stuff Jesus of Orange sells on-line.

FEBRUARY 6

Seize the opportunity?

"In periods where there is no leadership, society stands still. Progress occurs when courageous, skillful leaders seize the opportunity to change things for the better."
(Harry S. Truman)

"I can imagine a place where society stands still. And then heads backwards."
(Freedumb Fighter)

Then ... Standing on the shoulders of giants like Washington and Lincoln, Roosevelt and Kennedy, Reagan and Obama carried with it a high expectation. An expectation of leadership filled with vision and integrity. With courage and determination. With optimism and a desire to make America the best it could be. American leadership at its best carries a kind of audacity that makes you believe anything is possible. That makes you believe America is a resolute force for good. That makes you proud to join in and be part of a country that understands its obligation to its Founding Fathers, its fellow citizens and the world at large. In big moments, when the opportunity came to take a step forward and move closer to fulfilling America's destiny, ultimately the best of American leadership would seize the moment and take us to a better place.

Now ... I'm happy to imagine another kind of place. It's called Freedumbia.

Granted, Freedumbia is only a place that exists in the mind of Freedumbers. Still, it's a place to be proud of. It's not a place that puts a premium on integrity or decency. And it's certainly not a place from which goodness grows. Getting to that kind of dream state may not require courage per se, but it does demand we have the fortitude to shrink from obligation. And in a moment of opportunity, never hesitate to take America to a place that feels somehow less than what it should be. A place that feels smaller and less inspired. A place where racists can be nice people too. Or where intolerance is simply standing up for what's rightfully yours. Or where toxic masculinity is just a way to make it clear to other people that men are the answer. To everything.

Today ... Spend some quality time in Freedumbia. Would our national anthem be Russian? Would our police motto be "Protect and Kill"? Would it ban any color other than white? Would every white man wear a crown? Let your imagination run wild!

FEBRUARY 7

Is honesty really the best policy?

"The life of a nation is secure only while the nation is honest, truthful and virtuous."
(Frederick Douglass)

"Honest? Truthful? Virtuous?"
(Freedumb Fighter)

Then ... The more I've read about Frederick Douglass, the more I've come to appreciate his perspective. His wisdom. I found it refreshing to think about our nation's security in the context of character traits such as honesty, truthfulness and virtue. Americans are a people of character. America is a country of character. That character protects our democracy. That protects our pledge to liberty and justice for all. We could not be the land of the free and the home of the brave without being secure in the knowledge that we stand together in upholding those things that make America the country of our dreams.

Now ... Can you hear us Freedumbers laughing?

For Freedumbers, dishonesty is the best policy. If you're not lying, then chances are you're not helping. Nobody stole the 2020 election, but 'Stop the steal' is the big lie Freedumb loves to hear. Truthfulness is the enemy. Things like facts, evidence and proof are to be denied – immediately. Especially if they have anything to do with vaccines or climate change. Or black history. Or 'gayness' being something other than a bad choice. And virtue is something you weaponize to attack others. Pro-life really means pro-birth. Fooled you! After that, you and your baby are on your own. There's an undeniable audacity to our parallel universe. And we've got operating in it down to an artform. We should all dare to dream of being so unabashedly warped.

Today ... Find your truth. Helpful hint: You have to lie to yourself get there. Thought starters: 'Being uncivil is just being real' or 'Hating means you care more' or 'Willful ignorance is God's will.'

FEBRUARY 8

Does pessimism drive you?

"Life can only be understood backwards; but it must be lived forward."
(Soren Kierkegaard)

"If you're not moving backward, the future is apocalyptic."
(Freedumb Fighter)

Then ... Kierkegaard, the Danish philosopher, focused on the need to learn from the past so as to live a better future - a task both difficult and essential. America, the land of opportunity, the country that pursues happiness like none other, the place of dreams, has to me always represented a better future. We're a country and a people that look forward to what comes next. We learned from the past but never lived in it.

Now ... I see how tragic it would be to leave our idyllic past behind.

Forget about learning from the past, we've got to live in it. We Freedumbers wonder why things can't just be the way they used to be. A time when overt racism, intolerance and misogyny were appreciated, even celebrated. A time when men always knew best. A time when minorities knew their place. A time when you didn't have to think so hard about the gays, because they were more or less out of sight. A future focused on what could be is the doomsday scenario for us.

Be pessimistic about the future. Anchor yourself in fear, and everything begins to fall into place. Expecting the worst helps you lose faith in your fellow citizens, it helps shake your belief in our capability to solve problems for the common good, and it helps undermine the confidence necessary to find common ground. All of which works to encourage a big courageous step backwards.

Today ... Look backward to be backward. But it's not enough to simply yearn for the good old days. Helpful hint: Strive to be backward - in how you think, feel and live. Thought starter: Should women be forced to wear whalebone corsets?

FEBRUARY 9

Do you find it difficult?

"It's better to hang out with people better than you ... If you're picking associates, pick out those whose behavior is somewhat better than yours, and you'll drift in that direction."
(Warren Buffett)

"Real men need to circle the wagons."
(Freedumb Fighter)

Then ... When Warren Buffett says something, you'd be crazy not to listen. Nobody's better at dispensing common-sense wisdom. His comment seemed like a good one in general, but it really hit me as one that American men would do well to latch onto. Why wouldn't you choose men of integrity, generosity, intelligence, compassion and accountability to be around? There's been a lot of talk about men being lost and struggling. And it would seem that searching out men better than ourselves would be a good way to get found. Associating with men that you could take something positive from couldn't help but make you a better man. Maybe even a happier one. This search might take a bit of effort, but in the end, it's not that complicated. Kind of a no-brainer.

Now ... I know the Freedumb movement can't be outdone in the no-brainer department.

Freedumbness doesn't make room for qualities such as integrity or generosity, compassion or accountability. Let alone intelligence. It's more about gravitating toward men who are fearful, angry and bitter. Men who see themselves as vicdumbs. A vicdumb of women's independence. Not fair. A vicdumb of immigrant energy. Not fair. A vicdumb of gay rights. Not fair. A vicdumb of a woke mob calling you on the dumb shit you say and do. Not fair. It's hard not to long for the days when everyone was asleep, so you could get away with the dumb shit you did best. It's just so hard to be a straight white man. The odds are stacked against us every day.

Today ... Spend some quality time feeling sorry for yourself. Helpful hint: Be dumb about it. Thought starter: Hang with someone even Freedumber than you, and you'll be a world-class vicdumb before you know it.

FEBRUARY 10

Do you learn from mistakes?

"You build on failure. You use it as a stepping stone. Close the door on the past. You don't try to forget the mistakes, but you don't dwell on it. You don't let it have any of your energy, or any of your time, or any of your space."
(Johnny Cash)

"I don't make mistakes."
(Freedumb Fighter)

Then ... The man in black said it like it is. Achieving anything worthwhile requires a focused energy. Informed by the past but not dependent on it. Mistakes are learning opportunities and teachable moments. It's OK to take a hard look at failures and shortcomings as a way to get it right next time. Americans want to get things right, and we don't give up until we do. No matter how long it takes. That persistence, that determination and that never-say-die attitude is oxygen for those wanting to step up and be better, do better. For the difference-makers. For those needing and wanting a second chance. America is a country for the committed – for those committed to the best of what a life of liberty can bring.

Now ... Freedumb encouraged me to look at stepping stones and see objects to throw.

We Freedumbers don't make mistakes. Learning from mistakes is some woke self-help bullshit. Besides, there's no point in learning when you already know. And Freedumbers are all-knowing. So the thought of acknowledging any shortcomings, missteps or mistakes – past or present – doesn't really enter our mind. Nor should it. If accused of such things, we will deny, avoid, blame, finger-point and, of course, lie. It's never about building on failure, it's about reframing your mistakes, failures and even crimes to show why you're so hard done by. Undermining democracy is an act of patriotism, baby. Feel free to dwell on that.

Today ... Look in the mirror and practice saying stupid stuff. Just because. For example, 'mistaking' gazpacho with the Gestapo and using it in a sentence might help get you elected to Congress. That's what Freedumbers call thought leadership.

FEBRUARY 11

Can you close your eyes?

"Each of you, as an individual, must pick your own goals. Listen to others, but do not become a blind follower."
(Thurgood Marshall)

"If you're not a blind follower, you're not much of a follower."
(Freedumb Fighter)

Then ... There is an independent streak to being an American that I always admired. Even aspired to. Loyal and patriotic citizens of the US of A have a mind of their own. We think for ourselves. Ask questions. Use common sense to see things clearly. Americans, I believed, could always be counted on to take the measure of a circumstance, an event or a person with a clear and critical eye. We carry the courage of our convictions everywhere we go. Blind following has never been part of the equation.

Now ... The bald eagle has had its day. Freedumb's mascot is a sheep.

Freedumbers have the courage to not think for ourselves. Blindly following is a big part of how we find our bliss. The less thinking we do, the more Freedumb we feel. And Freedumb loves a groundless conspiracy theory, a harmful half-truth, and of course an outright lie, no matter how wacky. Freedumbers happily kiss common sense goodbye. So too our critical eye – blind followers are the best followers. It's true that Freedumb's leaders don't much respect us, but we love them for their blindness. We're willing to forgive bad behavior, hypocrisy, stupidity and cruelty, and even celebrate such behavior – without hesitation. The cynical leading the blind: it's the magic elixir that aims to show the world what real American greatness looks like. Can't you just see it?

Today ... Practice shutting your eyes to reality. And baa-baa-baaing like a sheep. Never let go of this old bit of wisdumb: "To think is to overthink."

FEBRUARY 12

Could you be more intolerant?

"Freedom of thought and the right of private judgment, in matters of conscience, driven from every other corner of the earth, direct their course to this happy country as their last asylum. Let us cherish the noble guests, and shelter them under the wings of a universal toleration."
(Samuel Adams)

"There are a lot of things I cherish. 'Noble guests' don't make the list."
(Freedumb Fighter)

Then ... America always stood tall as a safe haven. A haven of hope and opportunity. A place for dreamers and "noble guests." And those desperate for freedom. You know, "Give me your tired, your poor, your huddled masses yearning to breathe free ...". That's a big-hearted invitation from a big-hearted country with a big-hearted people. It's an invitation rooted in the American conviction about what's right and just. It's anchored in an openness that feeds our exceptionalism and is core to our greatness. Emma Lazarus's sonnet "The New Colossus" is etched into the Statue of Liberty for all eternity. So too, I believed, into the hearts and minds of every American.

Now ... I see the Statue of Liberty for what it is – a really cool tourist attraction.

It makes for a great photo op, but we Freedumbers don't read anything more into Lady Liberty. Can you imagine thinking of immigrants as "noble guests"? Get real. One of the things Freedumbers like to think about the least is the wider world – other countries and especially the people who live in them. We might tolerate them as tourists, but fellow citizens? NFW. Especially, anybody coming from a 'shithole' country as called out by the Freedumbest of us all. How about making a small-hearted invitation from a small-hearted country and a small-hearted people? That's Freedumbia!

Small can get America to greatness. Small can protect the status quo. Small can protect against different, against new, against change. And, maybe most importantly, small can protect purity. Beautiful things can happen when small-heartedness meets small-mindedness. Besides, being small is so much less a burden. So much less is expected of you. So much less to concern yourself with. Can't you just feel the cool breeze of liberation at your back?

Today ... See how small you can get. Do you have it in you to tolerate absolutely nothing that makes you feel the least bit uncomfortable? Come on, you can get smaller.

FEBRUARY 13

Today, some poetic inspiration from the Freedumb movement:

The New Catastrophe

Much like the brazen giant of Greek fame,
With conquering weapons showing off his brand;
Here at our Trump-towered, sunset gates shall stand
A mighty woman with a torch, whose flame
Is now extinguished, and her name
Mother of Wreckage. From her beacon-hand
No welcome gleams; her wild eyes command
The fortified harbor that twin cities frame.
"Keep, ancient lands, your freeloaders!" cries she
With twisted lips. "Take back your tired, your poor,
Your huddled masses yearning to breathe free.
You're wretched refuse on my pleasant shore.
Send none of your homeless, tempest-lost to me,
I break my lamp and lock the golden door!"

FEBRUARY 14

The power of love?

"Love recognizes no barriers. It jumps hurdles, leaps fences, penetrates walls to arrive at its destination full of hope."
(Maya Angelou)

"All this talk about love makes me want to puke."
(Freedumb Fighter)

Then … Maya Angelou's words gave me oxygen. I'm not sure love can really conquer all, but I know without it, something better doesn't have a chance. Without it, the likes of happiness, possibility and ultimately hope don't stand a chance. Without it, the pledge of liberty and justice for all will fall on deaf ears. All of which wouldn't say much for the future of American greatness.

Now … To this, we Freedumbers would say; "Take your love and shove it."

Love is one of those woke words, isn't it. A gateway to hell. To kindness. To compassion. To, heaven forbid, hope. Love will jump, huddle and leap us to the apocalypse. So, if Freedumbers are going to love anything, we're going to love to hate. Hate is the antidote for all that ails us. Hate works to fend off liberty, justice, opportunity for others. As an added bonus, hate doesn't require the effort love does. Doing harm, hurting another or being destructive isn't the heavy lift that love is. It does take the courage to give in to your worst fears, to aim your anger at the vulnerable. Throw in a mind-numbing lack of compassion, and the possibility of sustaining hope is a pipe dream. Next stop: hopelessness.

Today … On Valentine's Day, practice your hate stare. Helpful hint: Grab some pictures of others you don't like and work on the look that'll let 'em know what you think of them. When you've nailed the look, take to the streets and help bring America a step closer to greatness.

FEBRUARY 15

Are you vicious enough?

"Each year one vicious habit rooted out, in time might make the worst man good throughout."
(Benjamin Franklin)

"Viciousness takes practice and commitment."
(Freedumb Fighter)

Then ... Ben Franklin's thought hit hard. We can all be better people. To me, a vicious habit is one that does genuine harm. It's not a word that any of us want to be associated with, but viciousness can take many forms. That includes, for example, enabling those who do harm. Being an enabler is a vicious habit. Standing idly by and enabling intolerance is a vicious habit. Standing idly by and enabling racist taunts and vitriol is a vicious habit. Standing idly by as one's freedom is weaponized to suppress the freedom of others is a vicious habit. Rooting out any such habits can only make us better people. Better citizens. Americans are not idle or passive by nature. We rise and stand strong. Franklin's wisdom is practical, constructive, and challenging. Still, Americans have never shied away from the tough stuff.

Now ... I understand it's better to add a vicious habit than root one out.

Freedumbers, ever the provocateurs, feel that viciousness has gotten an unfairly bad rap. Whether a passive or active habit, the benefits of vicious habits are too often underappreciated. Take cruelty, for example. Such a sweet form of viciousness. Incuriosity and ignorance help, but a capacity for cruelty is key to being a great again man. And key to making America a great again country. Cruelty is terrific for keeping the others in their place. And making them feel worthless and somehow lacking. Cruelty is terrific for making the vulnerable feel even further marginalized and without hope. And obviously, cruelty in the name of God is a higher calling that can only help get you closer to heaven. All this with an unfeeling kind of Freedumber flair? That just can't be a bad thing.

Today ... Have the guts to challenge yourself. Do you have any remaining good habits you could root out? The time is now.

FEBRUARY 16

Knock knock, who's there?

"If we were to select the most intelligent, imaginative, energetic, and emotionally stable third of mankind, all races would be represented."
(Franz Boas)

"If we were to select the most intelligent, imaginative, energetic, and emotionally stable third of mankind, it'd be a sea of white."
(Freedumb Fighter)

Then ... Franz Boas has been called the "Father of American Anthropology." And he made a fundamental point. No single race has the market cornered on the best humanity has to offer. No single race has the market cornered on intelligence or creativity. No single race has the market cornered on determination or common sense. To me, that's part of what makes America special: the vast and varied resources of humanity we can draw upon; the depth of diverse capability we can access; the rich tapestry of experience and perspective we can bring to bear on our obstacles and opportunities. And that's no joke.

Now ... Freedumbers everywhere are pissing themselves laughing.

When Freedumbers open the door and step out into America, all we want to see is white. White intelligence. White creativity. White determination. White common sense. Obviously, we don't believe in equal capability across races – because it's not there. It doesn't exist. White men are the gold standard. Always have been, always will be. And we won't be convinced otherwise. Proof, data or evidence to the contrary, be damned. If a person of another race has something to offer, it's simply the result of a white man's generosity. As always, we Freedumbers like to keep things simple. And this perspective is about as simple-minded as we can make it.

Today ... Take credit. As a white man, you're responsible for all that is good in America. Helpful hint: Get beyond all the benefits of mass shootings. Thought starter: Could Beyoncé have come up with the genius of "Texas Hold 'em" without the vast creativity of white men? Duh, I think not.

FEBRUARY 17

What's your question?

"The important thing is not to stop questioning."
(Albert Einstein)

"Why ask when you know."
(Freedumb Fighter)

Then ... Questions challenge us. They can provoke new ideas and lead to different ways of doing things. Questions can make us pause and reflect. Progress comes from asking questions; so does accountability. Questions can lead to wisdom and greater understanding. They can work to inspire us. Questions help define who we are as a country, as a people, and as citizens of the United States. What makes America a great country? How can we be a more perfect union? What can we, as individual Americans, do to contribute to our country's greatness? What can we do to foster life, liberty and the pursuit of happiness? And how can we ensure liberty and justice – for all? I believed the greatest countries are never afraid to ask 'the question'. Whatever that question might be.

Now ... We Freedumbers see asking questions as a waste of time.

Our answer to everything is pretty simple, if somewhat lengthy. If we want to be great again, we need to be whiter. And straighter. And more patriarchal. And Christendumber. We need to be less of a democracy. And less tolerant. And less civil and decent. And less thoughtful. And we definitely need to be less curious. Less curious about how we might improve or get to a better future. Less curious about others' circumstances and feelings. Less curious about black history and police reform. Less curious about climate change and the discoveries of science – especially allegedly life-saving vaccines. Less curious about the world outside our borders. Why? The only thing questions ever lead to is problems.

Today ... Make up flash cards. You can't stop others from asking questions, but you can always have your answers ready-made. Helpful hint: Dumb is as dumb does. Thought starters: 'That's woke,' 'You're woke,' 'They're woke,' 'That's so woke,' and 'That's so fucking woke.'

FEBRUARY 18

Will you do the work?

"America is a great country, but we still have a lot of work to do to make it truly great for all of its citizens."
(attributed to Harry Belafonte)

"America needs to be better for us white people."
(Freedumb Fighter)

Then … I believed greatness could never fully be achieved until it is great for all. That seemed to me a pretty difficult one to argue with. America can't rest until every single one of us shares equally in its opportunity. Regardless of race, color or creed. Greatness doesn't leave people behind. Greatness doesn't marginalize or discriminate. It doesn't put systems in place to keep people down. It doesn't create victims. Americans know this. We are working to fix this. And we will continue working until our country is truly great for all our citizens. I believed that to be an American obligation.

Now … I understand Freedumbers are America's biggest vicdumbs.

The weight we carry is indescribable. The obstacles we face are unfathomable. The unfairness we're confronted with is beyond belief. No single group you can name is on the receiving end of more prejudice and intolerance. No other group you could think of feels the blunt force of systemic injustice more than we do. What we wouldn't give to be black, gay or a woman. To be a white straight man in America is to be deeply, sadly misunderstood and disadvantaged. All we want is what's best. For ourselves. All we want is for others to genuflect at the altar that is us. I mean, what the fuck is happening!

Today … Wallow. Wallow in how hard it is to be you. Helpful hint: Sometimes the best way to wallow is to share your misery. Thought starter: Pull aside the first migrant you see, and lecture them on how lucky they are and how difficult it is to be a white man in America. It may be hard for them to hear, but there's no sugar-coating the truth.

FEBRUARY 19

What makes you happy?

"The art of being happy lies in the power of extracting happiness from common things."
(Harriet Ward Beecher)

"The art of being happy lies in the power of extracting happiness from other people."
(Freedumb Fighter)

Maybe happiness, like beauty, is in the eye of the beholder.

Then: Start a Gratitude Journal and note one little act of kindness that filled your cup, but …

Now: Go out and find someone holding a Gratitude Journal. Take it off their hands and throw it in the trash.

FEBRUARY 20

Do you have any questions?

"It's good to be curious about many things."
(Fred Rogers)

"Curiosity killed the cat and it's going to kill America."
(Freedumb Fighter)

Then ... I believed that being curious is how we learn and grow. It's how we get smarter and understand more deeply. Being curious about different people, cultures, lifestyles and religions builds empathy and connection. Being curious is a trait of the open-minded. It's a trait of those who have the courage to challenge what they know and delve into what they don't. Could you imagine white people finally beginning to *truly* appreciate the experience of being black in America? Could you imagine straight people *truly* appreciating the experience of being queer in America? Could you imagine men *truly* understanding the experience of being a woman in America? I mean, could you imagine? Could you imagine what a little less 'us versus them' might feel like? Could you imagine the upside potential in a little more 'us and them'? The progress it might harness? I felt like it would have been great to find out.

Now ... We Freedumbers may be incurious, but we have a few choice questions of our own.

Questions such as: What's so great about being open-minded? What's the big deal about learning and growing? Why should you appreciate different people, cultures, lifestyles or religions? Doesn't curiosity make you vulnerable? What if you start to see things differently? What if you begin to empathize, and the strange or foreign becomes a little more familiar? What if you start to question some long-held assumptions and attitudes? How does curiosity help to foster prejudice and intolerance? How does it help encourage cruelty? And how the hell is any of all of this potential learning, understanding and appreciating going to help America embrace our greatness again? Huh? How? Huh?

Today ... Put your foot down. Helpful hint: Take inspiration from the great again Governor of South Dakota. Thought starter: You may not be able to kill curiosity, but you can take your dog out back and blow his brains out. Bad dog!

FEBRUARY 21

Are you holding on tight enough?

"Some people believe that holding on and hanging in there are signs of great strength. However, there are times when it takes much more strength to know when to let go - and then do it."
(Ann Landers)

"Never let go. Of anything. Ever."
(Freedumb Fighter)

Then ... This little nugget from Ann Landers offered good advice: that life can be better when you learn to let go. But it's no easy thing. I always thought great countries and great peoples ultimately have the strength to let go of the things that hold them back. Perhaps fear being first and foremost among them. If the past was unjust: acknowledge it, and try to make things more just. If the past was intolerant: acknowledge it, and try to be more tolerant. If the past was racist: acknowledge it, and try to be an anti-racist. Acknowledging and 'owning' our past, our current societal shortcomings, and our future challenges requires letting go of our fear. Letting go tends to happen over time, not overnight, but the struggle to let go of what holds us back is part of the American way. They don't call us the home of the brave for nothing.

Now ... Me and my Freedumber friends don't like letting go - especially of our fear.

And why would we ever take some fluffy-assed advice from some woman.

Today ... Scare your kids stupid. It's never too soon to put the fear of God, and country, in them. If we let go of our fear, we put America's greatness at risk. And if that happens, the white, straight, manly God of Christendumb will fuck us up big time in the afterlife.

FEBRUARY 22

Are you accountable?

"But more is required. Men want to be part of a common enterprise, a cause greater than themselves. And each of us must find a way to advance the purpose of the Nation, thus finding new purpose for ourselves. Without this, we will simply become a nation of strangers."
(Lyndon B. Johnson)

"Requirements are for other people."
(Freedumb Fighter)

Then ... I believed more was required of an American. Great countries need their people to step up. If America aspires to be the greatest nation on earth, a big step must be taken and sustained. You can't be the greatest country in the world without purposeful people, people concerned with something greater than themselves. You can't be the greatest country on earth with men who aren't their best selves, men who default to comfort over courage, men who think the old ways are the only ways, men who choose tribe over nation. Being an American man requires carrying your weight and a little bit more, but I never doubted our capacity to rise to meet the challenge of the day. The truth will always hold: the greater the country, the greater the requirement.

Now ... Slow down there, buddy boy. It's time to slam the brakes on all that requirement talk.

First off, Freedumbers don't believe that requirements apply to us. Requirements suggest burden, and worse yet, responsibility. So any talk of requirements is dead on arrival in Freedumbia. Secondly, Freedumbers believe men's lesser selves are key to American greatness. For example, can one mediocre man make America great again? No, but the cumulative impact of millions of men committed to something less than their best is a game-changer. Being not very good requires very little. We Freedumbers are relentless in our drive to underdeliver.

Today ... Commit to falling short of your potential. Way short. Be the man you shouldn't be, and help get America back to greatness.

FEBRUARY 23

Should you give a little less?

"I have no other view than to promote the public good, and am unambitious of honors not founded in the approbation of my country."
(George Washington)

"I have no other view than to promote what I see in the mirror."
(Freedumb Fighter)

Then ... I believed that love of country was inherently connected with a contribution to the public good. Not always in big ways, because little ways can matter a lot in the lives we lead and, in their way, can be just as significant a contribution. Sometimes the most effective way to promote the public good is to simply be a good person. To be a person who knows what's right – and acts like it. An actively good citizenry would work to make things better, would work to protect democracy, would work for the rights and freedom of all. A good citizenry would respect Mother Nature and would be determined to leave this world a habitable place for the children and grandchildren. Promoting the public good demands a conscience. And I always believed America's conscience was as big as its heart.

Now ... I realize that anything 'public' reeks of do-goodism.

Freedumbers are tired of giving. Give. Give. Give. That's all we do. The public good and its promotion are draining us dry. Physically, mentally, emotionally and spiritually dry. Now, self-promotion, that's another thing altogether. We Freedumbers never tire of that. Take. Take. Take. Take without conscience. Take advantage. Take what's mine and take what's theirs. Take more to leave less. Now you're talking! How does defending women's rights help the men of Freedumb? It doesn't. What does supporting the gays give the straight men of Freedumb? Nothing. How do equal voting rights protect the power of the Freedumb? They just don't. So let's put all this talk of the public good to bed.

Today ... Resolve to give nothing. Don't help. Don't support. Don't foster. Don't fight for the rights of others. Protect yourself against any promoting of the public good.

FEBRUARY 24

How's your math?

"There are no mathematical equations for good citizenship."
(Tom Rosenstiel)

"Reciting the pledge + hugging the flag + referencing the Constitution = the right kind of American."
(Freedumb Fighter)

Then ... Being a good citizen wasn't simply a box-checking exercise. No matter what it is, *how* you do it always makes a difference. I believed good citizenship came down to how you contributed. It came down to: How are you making things better for your family, your community and your country? Is reciting the pledge an act of patriotism if you don't contribute to liberty, or help cultivate justice for all? Is flying the flag an act of patriotism if you're not working for equal rights? And is referencing the Constitution an act of patriotism if all you do, in the face of mass shooting after mass shooting after mass shooting, is send your thoughts and prayers? That just doesn't add up.

Now ... Not to worry. Freedumbers are here to correct everything, including your math.

Give us Freedumbers credit, we are very mathy. And we know a good equation when we see one. For example,

   a. Hugging the flag = permission to do whatever you need in the name of getting America back to greatness again.

   b. Reciting the pledge = permission to say anything you want in the name of getting America back to greatness again.

   c. Referencing the Constitution = permission to undermine whatever you like in the name of getting America back to greatness again.

Today ... Take a selfie of yourself hugging the flag and post it on X or Truth Social. Treat Old Glory like you would a woman, and hug her just long enough to make it uncomfortable.

FEBRUARY 25

Have you forgotten something?

"I've learned that people will forget what you said, people will forget what you did, but people will never forget how you made them feel."
(Maya Angelou)

"I'm not interested in how other people feel."
(Freedumb Fighter)

Then ... Great countries are, in many ways, like great people. Their influence comes from their words and actions, but as Maya Angelou suggests, their lasting impact is connected to how they make people feel. A great country, like a great leader, makes you feel something positive and uplifting. And I always felt a tremendous sense of pride in what our country stands for. I felt a sense of hope and possibility in what we could accomplish together, to make our country a better place. To make the world a better place. I felt confident in our determination to do the right thing. To lead by doing the right thing. I felt, with everything I had, that above all else, we were and would always be the good guy. And all that made me feel pretty good.

Now ... Well, best forget all that woke woo woo.

To us, considering other people's feelings is a waste of time. With one exception. Making another person feel less valued as an American, as a human being, is somehow both life-affirming and gratifying to a Freedumber. Other people's feelings have no real role in making America great again, but making somebody feel lousy can be energizing and empowering. Almost intoxicating. Sometimes we Freedumb Fighters deserve a little 'feel good' too.

Today ... Do something for yourself. Helpful hint: Dish out some misery. Thought starter: Ask yourself WWJD, er, that is, WWJOOD – What Would Jesus Of Orange Do?

FEBRUARY 26

Are you blinded by the light?

"I refuse to accept the view that mankind is so tragically bound to the starless midnight of racism and war that the bright daybreak of peace and brotherhood can never become a reality."
(Martin Luther King Jr.)

"The light has always bothered my eyes."
(Freedumb Fighter)

Then ... I believed in Dr. King's hope for the future. Call it a naive view. Call it a romantic notion. Call it optimistic in the extreme. I called it an American perspective. If we, as a country, were all about possibility and what can be, then why couldn't we expect a brighter future? If we were the country of dreamers, then why couldn't we imagine a brotherhood anchored in peace? If we were the country that can-do, why would we remain "tragically bound"? We could strive for common ground. We could seek to understand and learn to mutually respect. We could see each other for who we are, beyond the color of our skin. I believed that. Nothing was impossible in America. For America. And America would never settle for "the starless midnight" as its destiny.

Now ... We Freedumbers aren't freaked out at the thought of an eternal dark night.

You can get away with a lot when the lights are off. And we love when we can get away with shit. Keeping the light out can only help make good things happen. In this day and age, you don't have to wear a white sheet to be a good racist – although you'd be passing up the chance to meet a lot of great people. In fact, you don't even have to be a white supremacist to get things done – even though it's always fun to sit at the cool kids' table. The reality is, you can just stand by and be an enabler. Not all of us Freedumbers have what it takes to get our hands dirty, but that doesn't mean we can't smile, laugh and backslap while others do the dirty work. A "starless midnight" is no tragedy. And rest assured, the bell is about to toll.

Today ... Play in the dark. Helpful hint: Doing nothing can be fun too. Thought starter: Never make a racist feel uncomfortable. That would be rude and counter-productive.

FEBRUARY 27

Have you fully embraced dishonesty?

"Neither the wisest constitution nor the wisest laws will secure the liberty and happiness of a people whose manners are universally corrupt."
(Samuel Adams)

"Corruption can be very constructive."
(Freedumb Fighter)

Then ... When all is said and done, you can't legislate destiny or greatness. Or moral behavior. Morality rests solely in the hearts and minds of people. Full stop. I always believed that Americans live by a kind of code. We work hard and play hard. We take our best shot and leave nothing on the field. We are the ultimate competitors. Relentless. Innovative. Resourceful. We're unafraid to push boundaries and challenge convention in our full-throated embrace of life, liberty and the pursuit of happiness. Still, there are lines we won't cross, things we won't do, and prices we won't pay. That integrity anchors our code, fuels our destiny, and fosters our greatness.

Now ... That kind of talk signals a Code Red for us Freedumbers.

One of the greatest things about Freedumbers is our absolute disdain for the rights of others. We've put democracy on notice. There isn't a line we won't cross. And if some see our behavior as corrupt, so be it. We see corrupt behavior as part of our privilege and patriotic duty. We recognize we'll have to do a lot of bad shit to get America to a state of real greatness. And fortunately, we have the Freedumbness to feel completely at home in 'whatever it takes' territory.

It's the code we live by.

Today ... Take a crack at amping up the Freedumber's code. Helpful hint: Give it a logo to help it get the attention it deserves. Thought starter: For creative inspiration consider the swastika. Russia's golden double eagle is also pretty cool.

FEBRUARY 28

What do you depend on?

"Remember, happiness doesn't depend upon who you are or what you have; it depends solely on what you think."
(Dale Carnegie)

"Happiness depends upon who you are or what you have, no matter what you think."
(Freedumb Fighter)

Then … I thought that America is nothing if not an attitude. A can-do attitude. A 'nothing's impossible' attitude. An unrelentingly determined attitude. That's quintessentially American. It's the attitude that drives our pursuit of happiness – and the beating heart of that attitude is self-belief. Hope is our oxygen. Opportunity, our life's blood. Count us out at your peril. Don't think we can do it? Just watch this space. Belief fuels our passion. None of this is dependent on your circumstance or situation. It's just dependent on you being American. And that makes us happy.

Now … Freedumbers depend on a different attitude.

We know that happiness is meant to be exclusively white property. People of color can see happiness, they just can't have any of it. Happiness is also a Christendumb thing. Non-believers might hear about it, but it can never be within their grasp. And, of course, happiness is the sovereignty of the straight. The gays can dream of it if that's how they want to waste their time. In the end, white men are the boss of happiness. If happiness knows what's good for it, it goes where we tell it. And if you don't like it, you can go fuck yourself. How's that for some attitude?

Today … It's time for an attitude adjustment. Don't worry, make them unhappy. Remember, if you're not happy enough, somebody undeserving is too happy. Regardless, the marginalized aren't miserable enough, it's time to get to work.

MARCH 1

Are you ignorant enough?

"There is nothing which can better deserve your patronage than the promotion of science and literature. Knowledge is in every country the surest basis of public happiness."
(George Washington)

"Knowledge is an enemy."
(Freedumb Fighter)

Then ... George Washington's words struck me as an important bit of wisdom. A commitment to education and knowledge as a service to our collective happiness. And while the observation is one any country would be wise to embrace, for an America with big dreams, a belief in its exceptionalism and aspirations of sustained greatness, it seems essential. I believe America is always hungry to learn, be smarter, and understand better. So too the American people. Know-how is an American thing. Know-how is leadership. Know-how is the future. Know-how is the key to better. Know-how, ultimately, is the answer. And America knows how. That should make us all very happy.

Now ... Freedumb has shown me that knowing doesn't really matter.

Knowledge and genuine understanding are no help to Freedumb's cause. In fact, knowledge is a menace; all it offers is insight. Science is a menace; all it does is offer possibility. Literature is a menace; all it does is encourage thinking and, God help us, mutual understanding. And don't get us Freedumbers even started on history – all it encourages is questioning of our great, white, patriarchal past. Genuine knowing gets in the way of the greatness we envision. We don't want people thinking, learning and growing. The solution? Willful ignorance.

Today ... Learn absolutely nothing. Helpful hint: Disavow knowledge. Deny fact. Dismiss proof. Thought starter: Being willfully ignorant takes hard work, so don't let yourself get into a rut by letting verbs beginning with the letter 'D' do all the heavy lifting for you.

MARCH 2

Are you in a good place?

"This country will not permanently be a good place for any of us to live in unless we make it a reasonably good place for all of us to live in."
(Theodore Roosevelt)

"We need to make this country a permanently good place for me."
(Freedumb Fighter)

Then ... I didn't believe America meant good for some and not for others. Good doesn't come easy, or with a guaranteed outcome, but it comes with opportunity. It comes with liberty. It comes with justice. For all. When we pledge allegiance to the flag, we're pledging that we're in it together. When we stand for the national anthem, we are committing to stand together. And if we kneel during the anthem, maybe, just maybe, it's a sign that America isn't yet a "good place for us all to live in." Achieving that goal takes strength, resolve and shared purpose. I never had any doubt we were up to the challenge, committed to the struggle. And that wasn't a bad place to start.

Now ... Well, for us Freedumbers that's a terrible place to start.

First off, American greatness has nothing to do with being good. Goodness is one of those soft, woke words that cause nothing but trouble. Second, the notion of 'for all' has been taken out of context for far too long; 'for all' was never meant to suggest for everybody. That would be inclusive, and that's ridiculous. Properly understood, "for all" is an exclusive, members' only club. Third, America needs to stop struggling and challenging itself. Why make things better for anybody who's not us? Let's just remember, father knows best.

Today ... Be the antidote to goodness. Helpful hint: Embrace the old saying "Keep a bad thought." Thought starter: family dinners are great for bonding, so work to keep the conversations toxic, and at the first sign of a good thought – pound your fist on the table and put an end to it. You could earn yourself a 'Dad of the Year' coffee mug!

MARCH 3

What do you remember?

"Let us at all times remember that all American citizens are brothers of a common country, and should dwell together in the bonds of fraternal feeling."
(Abraham Lincoln)

"Let us at all times forget that all American citizens are brothers of a common country."
(Freedumb Fighter)

Then … United we stand. No president understood this better than President Lincoln. His plea for "bonds of fraternal feeling" is as important today as when he spoke. Americans are an energetic, passionate, independent and rebellious bunch. As such, America needs common ground. It needs ties that bind and a genuine sense of togetherness. Of brotherhood and sisterhood. This is true at all times, but in particular when the things we hold dear are under threat, from forces foreign or domestic. I always believed our country carried the kind of sense of shared purpose that is necessary not only to survive, but to thrive. We are the answer. We are the solution. We are what makes us great. We, the people of the United States of America.

Now … Divided we stand.

I've learned that forgetting is actually fundamental to Freedumb. Forget about any kind of fraternal feeling. Brothers, my ass! Forget common ground. It's quicksand. Forget ties that bind. They're handcuffs. Forget liberty and justice for all. That's just nonsense. Forget any sense of shared obligation. It's too hard! Forgetting puts a whole different spin on what it means to be a citizen. Forget responsibility and duty. And while you're at it, forget about prejudice, injustice and inequality. Remembering only brings problems and guilt. If we're brave enough to forget enough, we can be great again sooner than you think.

Today … Just one thing. Forget you're an American. Pledge allegiance to a group where you can really make a difference. Helpful hint: the Incels and Proud Boys are currently welcoming new members.

MARCH 4

True or false?

"True patriotism hates injustice in its own land more than anywhere else."
(Clarence Darrow)

"True patriotism loves injustice."
(Freedumb Fighter)

Then ... Americans are always up for fighting the good fight – first and foremost, the fight against injustice. The struggle for justice is in the American DNA. Injustice has no place in the land of opportunity. Injustice has no place in the American dream. One of the things I bought into was that belief – the belief that America wanted people to get a fair shot, a fair deal. I believed that all things American, from the Constitution and the Bill of Rights to the Statue of Liberty, pointed to the commitment of every citizen, every true patriot, to making America the land of justice and respect for all. If you're going to hate anything, injustice was a great place to start.

Now ... We Freedumbers take a more sympathetic view of injustice.

When you don't really think about it, is injustice so bad? The truth is that justice must be served up judiciously, meaning it must be served up disproportionately to those who deserve it. Ourselves, that is: the white, straight men of Christendumb. After that, justice becomes less important. In fact, as you go through the list and get all the way down to people of color, women and gays, injustice actually becomes very nice. A helping hand, if you will. Injustice serves to maintain the natural order of things. It serves as a reminder of who's in charge and how things work. It helps the others open their eyes and see the limitations and obstacles placed in front of them -- for their own good. We Freedumbers believe it's time to give injustice more of the love it deserves.

Today ...Take your fight for injustice to the next level. Let injustice anchor your personal code of conduct. If it seems unfair, support it. If it seems discriminatory, embrace It. If it seems indefensible, defend it. And if it seems bigoted, welcome it.

MARCH 5

Are you a cheerleader?

"Two cheers for democracy: one because it admits variety and two because it permits criticism."
(E.M. Forster)

"Three cheers for the death of democracy."
(Freedumb Fighter)

Then ... This quote from the English novelist E.M. Forster used to make me smile. I get that democracy is messy. American democracy would definitely fit that description – precisely because it fosters a range of critical views, tough questions and innovative solutions. Messiness is part of democracy's power. Messiness isn't an excuse for obstructionism and irresponsibility – messiness is debate, listening to understand, and compromise. Messiness is two steps forward and one step back. Messiness pushes us ahead, slowly. Ultimately it should lead to wisdom. And that is worth all the frustration, anxiety and tumult embodied in the democratic process and the progress it pushes us toward. Maybe democracy deserves three cheers after all.

Now ... Freedumbers have schooled me on something even better to cheer for.

Freedumbers certainly aren't fans of the mess that is democracy. Any variety in voice or representation and any criticisms of country are non-starters for us. Our solution to the mess has the potential to surprise and delight. The Freedumb movement means to clean up democracy through imposing a dictatorship of minority rule. We are white. We are men. We are straight. We believe in the God of Christendumb. And we want to rule!

Instead of trying to work together to build a better America, we need to tell people what America is, and isn't, and get everyone to march in the right direction – the far right direction. We Freedumbers are willing to step up and stamp down on our fellow Americans. Think suppression. Think oppression. Think repression. Hip hip hooray!

Today ... Download Duolingo and start learning Russian. We can learn a lot from that country about the many benefits of authoritarianism. And what greatness looks like.

MARCH 6

What is your state of mind?

"The kingdom of heaven is not a place, but a state of mind."
(John Burroughs)

"The kingdumb of heaven is not a place that welcomes everyone. And the United States should follow heaven's lead."
(Freedumb Fighter)

Then ... To me, the idea of a heavenly mindset was anchored in the belief that we are all God's children. That kind of belief could create some seriously positive energy. An energy that would fuel respect for all. Kindness toward all. Curiosity about all. Being one of God's children would anchor your state of mind in gratitude. Imagine being grateful for the diversity offered by our fellow Americans. Imagine being excited by the inclusion of all. Imagine seeing people for who they are, as individuals, rather than simply as part of the group we identify them with. Imagine if we could take one small step forward toward that kind of acceptance and understanding. In the country where dreams drive reality maybe, just maybe, imagining a little heaven on earth isn't as far-fetched as it sounds.

Now ... We Freedumbers have no need for imagination.

This is especially true of all things religion-related. As devout followers of Christendumb, we know that any thought of heaven on earth is heresy. We also know that the proper state of mind needed to get to heaven is fear. And, we are, in fact, not all God's children. Remember, the God of Christendumb is one big badass. Think of him as kind of like a gang leader. Only much more vindictive and grudge-bearing. And taking his lead, we Freedumbers know that if you're not one of us, you're the enemy.

Today ... Get your mind right. Make life hell on earth for other people.

MARCH 7

(All written by Freedumb Fighter Pat Riarchy)

1. *Why Men Are Never Wrong*
An in-depth, faith-based analysis proving the superiority of men's decision-making. The chapter on how women can get the most out of their lives is transformative. An instant classic.

2. *One Thing Men Don't Know*
This book's title foreshadows the entertaining nature of the pages that follow. Obviously, suggesting any gap in men's knowledge is a tongue-in-cheek proposition. Still, the author manages to inject real wisdumb into a discussion around such women-related topics as 'Why right now is a great time to have a baby,' 'Why you should never ask for more money,' and 'Why it's fun to do what you're told.'

3. *We Can't Be More Supportive*
This heartbreaking work is comprised of a series of interviews with men who have put women on a pedestal and yet received little or no recognition for their efforts. The interviews are organized around four themes:
    1. I know what you should wear – why won't you just listen?
    2. Dinner was late, but did I make a fuss?
    3. If the house was cleaner, maybe you and I would both be happier.
    4. Why would you need any help? My guidance should be more than enough.

4. *The Manliest of Manly Men*
This ode to what a man should be is an essential for any nightstand. At a time when many men have sadly lost their way, this book pays homage to the North Star of masculinity. Chapters include 'Because I have a penis, that's why,' 'There's more to my penis than meets the eye,' 'Is thinking with your penis really wrong?' and the provocative and often misunderstood 'The world would be simpler and more fun if every man had two penises.'

5. *How Are You Helping?*
This book is a must read for any man, woman or child. It argues that the push for women's rights is fundamentally misguided. The author argues (very persuasively) that instead of fighting for their rights, women need to focus on their obligations. Not to God or country, but to the men in their life. The chapters ask questions on definitive topics such as "Why isn't the laundry done?", 'Why is what little I do never enough?' and of course the seminal 'If men are from Mars, why should anyone care about Venus?'

MARCH 8

What of the future?

"The women of my generation and my daughter's generation, they were very active in moving along the social change that would result in equal citizenship stature for men and women."
(Ruth Bader Ginsburg)

"If we put women on a pedestal, we get them out of our way."
(Freedumb Fighter)

Then ... RBG was a hero of mine. I'm fortunate to have been surrounded by strong, smart and independent women my entire life. Both in my personal and professional life. I always believed men and women are equal, and should be treated as such. In every way, in both rights and opportunities. Equal, as American citizens. It seems silly to have to say that out loud. The truth is, father doesn't always know best, he never did. We need everything that women can create and contribute in order to maximize America's potential greatness. In order to become a better people and nation. A nation of liberty and justice for all. Besides, a future that's female sounds kind of exciting to me. After all, their turn has been a long time coming.

Now ... Cue us Freedumbers shaking our heads in outraged disbelief.

Freedumbers see women as very special. So special that they need to be placed on a pedestal to protect them from their own inferiority. They are the weaker sex in every way. Not as smart, not as capable, although they're better changing diapers, of course. All of which makes them very attractive. Freedumbers love women so much that we endeavor to make their decisions for them – especially as it relates to their bodies. Freedumbers respect women so much that we endeavor to keep them in their place. And pay them accordingly. It's what's best for them. We should know.

Women can't take the pressure out there in the real world. Things are too complicated for them. Difficult choices have to be made. And women are simply too sensitive. The men of Freedumb won't allow women to experience the hard truth of a world outside the kitchen or bedroom or kid's playroom. They're too special for that.

Today ... On International Women's Day, reflect on manliness. Helpful hint: Reassert your authority in ways both big and small. Thought starter: Maybe a women's right to vote causes them too much pain and anguish and maybe the dinner the wife prepared just wasn't up to standard.

MARCH 9

What's reasonable?

"Women have another option. They can aspire to be wise, not merely nice; to be competent, not merely helpful; to be strong, not merely graceful; to be ambitious for themselves, not merely for themselves in relation to men and children. They can let themselves age naturally and without embarrassment, actively protesting and disobeying the conventions that stem from this society's double standard about aging. Instead of being girls, girls as long as possible, who then age humiliatingly into middle-aged women, they can become women much earlier – and remain active adults, enjoying the long, erotic career of which women are capable, far longer. Women should allow their faces to show the lives they have lived. Women should tell the truth."
(Susan Sontag)

"Wrong."
(Freedumb Fighter)

You are your choices.

Then: Reject the double standard, but ...

Now: Throw a fit. Without a double standard we have no standards at all.

MARCH 10

What nourishes you?

"The land flourished because it was fed from so many sources – because it was nourished by so many cultures and traditions and peoples."
(Lyndon B. Johnson)

"The land deteriorated because it was fed from so many sources – because it was corrupted by so many cultures and traditions and peoples."
(Freedumb Fighter)

Then ... I believed America was America because of its diverse tapestry. Different cultures, beliefs and traditions came together to strengthen the promise of America. The dream that is America. The diversity of cultures and traditions amplifies the energy behind the American dream. America has never been about a certain look, color or creed – America is freedom. It is an invitation to all. An invitation to bring your best. To achieve, contribute and build. The diverse fabric of America makes us more interesting, more energetic and more innovative. it also serves to capture the imagination of the world as a beacon of hope and dreams. That's a well-nourished land.

Now ... Whoa. Whoa. Whoa already.

Freedumbers see diversity as America's downfall. And for us, being American is actually about a very particular look, color and creed. Don't look into someone's heart, look at the color of their skin. Don't peer into someone's soul, find out where they worship. Don't see someone's desire to achieve, ask where they come from. Don't look on in awe and admiration at the dreams of others, question their lifestyle. Freedumbers see diversity as confusing, complicating and, ultimately, a threat. Real Americans are under siege. Where are all the white people? A Freedumber would rather starve than be fed by diversity.

Today ... Work at unlocking your real Americanness. Helpful hint: Purity is patriotic. Thought starter: Perfect your straight-arm salute and spend some time in the basement, goose-stepping your way to glory.

MARCH 11

What do you believe?

"For to be free is not merely to cast off one's chains, but to live in a way that respects and enhances the freedom of others."
(Nelson Mandela)

"The freedom of others is a slippery slope."
(Freedumb Fighter)

Then ... I thought Nelson Mandela was a great man. He was a hero of mine. I believed his words carried meaning for each and every one of us here in America. I believed his assertion served as a fundamental reminder of the obligation that we, as Americans, carry. America is freedom for all. None of us is free unless all of us are free. We must all work for the genuine freedom of others. Freedom to live and love as we choose. An essential thought. A noble thought. And a responsibility that I believed brought out the best in my fellow Americans.

Now ... I don't believe in the enhancement of freedom.

Chains can keep other people down. Where's the downside? Literal chains may, unfortunately, not be possible in our woke wonderland, but what of a foot on the throat? Some ideas simply don't warrant the oxygen to become living, breathing things – gay rights, women's rights, black lives mattering. Stop the madness. What's next, liberty and justice for all?

Today ... Buy some chains, keep them at your bedside, and let them be a tangible reminder of the dream that could be.

MARCH 12

What will you sacrifice?

"Men must be ready, they must pride themselves and be happy to sacrifice their private pleasures, passions and interests, nay, their private friendships and dearest connections, when they stand in competition with the rights of society."
(John Adams)

"Sacrificing for the rights of society is the beginning of the end."
(Freedumb Fighter)

Then ... For all the appetite and ambition in the American DNA, I have never doubted our capacity for sacrifice. Our love of country makes sacrifice, however difficult, something American citizens would willingly embrace for the greater good of our communities and country. Of course, the ultimate sacrifice is that made by our men and women in uniform, but there are other opportunities to sacrifice and show your love of country. Prejudice can be sacrificed. Intolerance can be sacrificed. Fear and anger can be sacrificed. Sacrifice can bring us to kindness, compassion, and a greater respect for our fellow Americans. Sacrifice can make us more curious. More generous. Sacrifice can solve problems and create opportunities. It can make us a stronger America. A greater America. That would all seem well worth the sacrifice.

Now ... Freedumb taught me to pump the brakes on the sacrifice thing.

We have the wisdumb to see sacrifice for what it really is: a weakness. Sacrifice means giving, letting go or relinquishing. And that's a non-starter for a Freedumber. Why give when you can take? It doesn't make sense. And Freedumbers have the strength and courage to resist sacrificing anything for anyone. Sacrificing for others doesn't do you any good. Acts of kindness and compassion don't get you any further ahead. Sacrifice doesn't foster your advantage. Besides, caring for others sends the wrong message about who you are and what you believe in. Let's call it what it is: encouraging everyday Americans to sacrifice is a woke plot. Screw society. That's not my concern.

Today ... Play a game of 'Would You Rather'. Helpful hint: Anything requiring sacrifice is out of bounds. Thought starter: Would you rather have been the guy proudly screaming at old Chinese women in the grocery store for causing Covid or the guy who proudly held a kick-ass Covid super spreader event?

MARCH 13

What happens tomorrow?

"What makes America exceptional are the bonds that hold together the most diverse nation on earth. The belief that our destiny is shared; that this country only works when we accept certain obligations to one another and to future generations."
(Barack Obama)

"This country only works when we refuse certain obligations to one another and to future generations."
(Freedumb Fighter)

Then ... President Obama knew that obligation to each other and the search for common ground are essential to the future of America. The obligations we acknowledge and fulfill have always been critical to the lives of our children and grandchildren. Every generation must consider itself a caretaker of all that makes America a great country. Democracy. Freedom. Justice. And opportunity. For all. The American Dream and the pursuit of happiness. For all. And at the heart of each generation's obligation is the ambition to leave our country better than how we found it. A stronger democracy, greater opportunity, a more equitable justice system, a fairer shot at the American dream. And, perhaps as urgent and important as any of the above: a habitable planet. The list is long and the struggle for better is both real and difficult. Still, here and now, the burden is ours to carry.

Now ... We're not picking up what 'Obamascare' threw down.

Freedumb works to lighten the load and unburden Freedumbers of any responsibility. For anything, including to future generations. Why struggle to leave something better off than you found it? Take more for yourself while the taking is good. What is sustainability anyway? Take from democracy until it devolves into authoritarianism: a white straight man making all decisions for us would be a heaven-sent blessing. Take from liberty until all you have left is the Freedumb of white Christendumb nationalists. Take from the justice system until fairness has no part in the weighing of its scales. And take from the earth and Mother Nature until our environment becomes a living hellscape. Liberate yourself from any obligation to the future, and let the good times roll.

Today ... Initiate 'Fuck Up the Future' monthly meetings for you and your pals. Thought starter: watch *The Stepford Wives* for ideas, laughs, and inspiration.

MARCH 14

Are you carrying?

"You are a citizen, and citizenship carries responsibilities."
(Paul Collier)

"I am an American, and an American always carries."
(Freedumb Fighter)

Then ... Citizenship isn't a free pass. Citizens must obey the law. They must respect democracy; they must pay taxes; they must serve on a jury if asked. That's pretty straightforward stuff. Then there's voting, which is a right and a privilege, and in my mind, a patriotic duty. There's a responsibility to stay informed, think through issues and make decisions, and take action in the best interests of your community and country. There's also the need to practice tolerance and to respect the freedom of our fellow citizens. It all adds up to a civic obligation. Clearly that's no freebie, but as Americans, it's the thing we carry.

Now ... We Freedumbers love nothing more than to carry!

Smith and Wesson 642. Sig Sauer P320. Glock G19 GEN4. Beretta 92FS. Ruger-57. Smith and Wesson M&P Sport II. Springfield Saint. Colt Python. Heritage Arms Rough Rider Revolver Rifle. Colt King Cobra. Baretta M9A3. Springfield Hellcat. KEL-TEC PMR-30. Diamondback Firearms DB15. Bushmaster XM-15. Remington 700. Glock G-17. CZ-USA CZ 75. Mossberg 500. Taurus Judge. KEL-TEC SUB-2000. Mossberg 590 Shockwave. IWI TS12 Shotgun. Benelli M4. Marlin 1895. Henry .410 Axe. Springfield XD-S. Smooth and Wesson M&P Shield. DPMS Oracle. Ruger AR-556. Smith and Wesson M&P15. AK-47. AR-15. Remington Model 870. Marlin Model 60. IMI Uzi. Carry on!

Today ... Be a good citizen, and buy yourself another semi-automatic assault rifle. Bonus points for buying your kid's teacher an Uzi!

MARCH 15

Do you practice mindlessness?

"Knee-jerk disobedience and anti-conformity are no more praiseworthy than the most mindless loyalty to a group."
(Christopher Peterson)

"Knee-jerk disobedience and anti-conformity go together with mindless loyalty to a group."
(Freedumb Fighter)

Then … I always admired what I interpreted as this 'rebel with a cause' mentality woven into the fabric of America. At its best, there was something noble about it. Something heroic. It wasn't about rebelling just for the sake of rebelling or simply acting the contrarian. It wasn't about being disagreeable, selfish or self-interested. It was about the dream of progress. A commitment to progress. It was about being innovative and creative. There's a tough problem to solve? Don't default to the conventional. There's an opportunity to be embraced? Do it, with open arms.

This rebellious streak carried a social conscience. A willingness to fight for the underdog. It was purposeful. It aimed to confront injustice, overcome unfairness, and right wrongs. And there was nothing mindless about it. It was about loyalty to the vision of a better country.

Now … We Freedumbers aren't so much rebels as rabble rousers. And we're world class at it.

Think dumb shit. Say dumb shit. Do dumb shit. We Freedumbers are in an unending tantrum. We violate. We undermine. We obstruct. We have no suggestions, no solutions, no ideas as to how to govern effectively. It's about loyalty to a greater greatness.

Today … Declare 'Dress Up for Freedumb Day'. Helpful hint: Cue video of the insurrection at the Capitol for some world class fashion tips! Beaver pelts and face paint, anyone?

MARCH 16

What do you respect?

"If we tolerate vulgarity, our future will sway and fall under a burden of ignorance. It need not be so. We have the brains and the heart to face our futures bravely. Taking responsibility for the time we take up and the space we occupy. To respect our ancestors and out of concern for our descendants, we must show ourselves as courteous and courageous well-meaning Americans."
(Maya Angelou)

"Oh for fuck's sake."
(Freedumb Fighter)

Then … The thought of being both courageous and courteous felt powerful, on a very human level. The home of the brave has room in it for civility. Showing regard for each other by being polite can't do anything but help. Being vulgar and coarse isn't being real and authentic, it's being vulgar and coarse. And vulgarity and coarseness often come in the form of cruelty and mean-spiritedness. I always believed that we Americans mean well. Positive intent is core to whatever greatness we've achieved. It's just plain ignorant to think that by revelling in rudeness and crudeness, we somehow respect those who have gone before us or do right by those who will follow in our footsteps. That's not an American thing.

Now … I must say, we Freedumbers, disrespectfully, disagree.

We think being crude and coarse is telling it like it is. No bullshit. Besides, nothing puts a fine point on intolerance and prejudice like a lack of civility. The less respect you show to the others, the more effective your fight for Freedumb. Fuck this, fuck that, and fuck them. That not only serves as a great again example, it should make you feel proud to be an American.

Today … Admit it, your profanity has grown stale and unimaginative. Especially as it relates to denigrating other people. Just saying 'fuck or fucking' before some different race, color or religion isn't good enough. Pick up a 'Profanisaurus,' do some homework and let some fresh expletives fill the air.

MARCH 17

How does the spirit move you?

"Citizenship is ... a sense of belonging to a community for which one bears some responsibility. In a word, citizenship implies public-spiritedness, and it is in this sense that it cannot be taken for granted; like patriotism, it has to be cultivated."
(Walter Berns)

"Citizenship is a sense of ownership."
(Freedumb Fighter)

Then ... I believed embracing citizenship should come with a heightened sense of obligation to your community and country. It is both a weight, and opportunity. American citizenship comes with a sense that you are part of something important. Something bigger than yourself. Something special. I felt a part of a country that made a difference. A country that the world looked up to. A country that led. A country where dreams come true. And I wanted to be the best of what an American citizen should be - civic-minded, public-spirited, a good neighbor. A good person. That's something we all needed to cultivate.

Now ... We Freedumbers cultivate only one thing: Freedumb.

Being American, for us Freedumbers, has nothing to do with obligation. Heightened or otherwise. It's about permission. And in that way, we feel exceptional, superior and specially chosen. Being a real American gives us a free pass to do as we see fit. Not surprisingly, this can lead to some extraordinarily dumbass behavior. Ultimately, it's all about permission to act in service to the dream that Freedumb will one day reign. Which has a kind of charm all its own.

It's time for the dumber and dumbest to take the lead.

Today ... Do something genius. Helpful hint: Become a name-caller. Thought starter: Making up derogatory nicknames like "Lyin' Kamala," "Laffin' Kamala" and "Kamabla" not only shows maturity and great again leadership, it just makes us all so proud to be an American.

MARCH 18

What should you dispense?

"Try to make at least one person happy every day. If you cannot do a kind deed, speak a kind word. If you cannot speak a kind word, think a kind thought. Count up, if you can, the treasure of happiness that you would dispense in a week, in a year, in a lifetime."
(Lawrence G. Lovasik)

"Being unkind is a real difference-maker. Dispense that, asshole."
(Freedumb Fighter)

Then … In America, we tend to go big or go home. Our pursuit of happiness is a case in point. Sometimes we forget how important small, everyday acts of kindness can be in defining happiness. How they can impact the happiness of others as well as our own. And how bringing a smile to someone's face can ultimately bring a smile to our own. Small acts of kindness can make a big difference. Sometimes all it takes is a kind word. Especially to people who might not be expecting it. And in my experience, Americans not only understand this, we act on it. Sometimes we just need a little reminder.

Now … We Freedumbers are here to remind you that kindness is the worst kind of weakness.

If you really want to make a difference and help America back to greatness, being unkind is the only way to go. Being unkind protects our interests. And protecting entitlement takes more than its fair share of cruelty. If you're doing a kind deed, saying a kind word, or thinking kind thoughts every day, that doesn't leave enough room for the mean and heartless thoughts and deeds you need to keep people in their rightful place. Besides, do you really want other people to be happy – because of you? That's not going to make a true Freedumber smile. What type of message does that send? One of hope? Togetherness? Understanding? Respect? Let's dispense with that bullshit once and for all.

Today … Go to war against pronouns. Forget China, Iran, or any terrorist organization you can name, we've got people here in America, yes right here, who want to use the pronouns they/them. Talk about an existential threat. The horror! Danger! Code Red! Battle stations!

MARCH 19

Are you capable of astounding yourself?

"If we did all the things we are capable of, we would literally astound ourselves."
(Thomas Edison)

"I'm dumbfounded by how astounding I am."
(Freedumb Fighter)

Then ... I don't know if Thomas Edison's remark represented a light bulb moment, but I definitely saw wisdom in his words. It's inspiring to think of America as an opportunity to astound ourselves. America offers us that chance. Some chances are closer to sure bets, others are more like moonshots, but in America you are invited to take your rip. To harness your capability, to maximize your potential. To astound ourselves with what we can accomplish, how we can contribute, and the good we can do. In this country, impossible isn't an obstacle, it's an invitation to show the world what we're capable of. An invitation for each of us to do our part in fulfilling the limitless potential of the American experiment.

Now... We Freedumbers already astound ourselves every day.

We astound in a lot of ways, but our wisdumb never fails to surprise and delight. For example, others may see AR-15s as unwanted killing machines, but we see them as a great Christmas gift for a loved one. Astounding. Others see queer folk as, simply, people. We know LGBTQ+ spells DANGER. Astounding. Others see racism as something we must confront and overcome. We know racism is something to take comfort in, but never take for granted. Astounding. Others think science is real, vaccines stimulate immunity, and healthcare workers are here to help. We know it's all part of a government conspiracy aimed at turning us into mindless zombies. That's some astounding wisdumb at work!

Today ... Do some astounding mansplaining. Helpful hint: Explain how women of color get to positions of power. Thought starter: DEI hiring. Nuff said.

MARCH 20

Have you unlocked the hero inside?

"I think of a hero as someone who understands the degree of responsibility that comes with his freedom."
(Bob Dylan)

"I know I'm a superhero."
(Freedumb Fighter)

Then ... I loved Bob Dylan's definition of a hero. The more freedom you have, the more responsibility you carry. Seemed fair enough when you think about it. Think of responsibility in terms of our ability to respond. We can fight prejudice, even if we're not the target. We have the ability to respond in that way. We can stand up to intolerance, even if we're not on the receiving end of it. We have the ability to respond in that way. We can support people searching to identify their gender and yearning to be comfortable in their own skin, even if that's not our reality. We have the ability to respond in that way. We can act to protect our environment from climate change, even if we haven't been impacted by a prolonged heat dome, hurricane, wildfire or drought – yet. We have the ability to respond in that way. That all sounds pretty heroic to me.

Now ... We Freedumbers push past heroic all the way to super-heroic.

Freedumbers see ourselves as superheroes who have thrown off the shackles of freedom, to access awe-inspiring super powers. For example, who knew shamelessness could be a super power? We Freedumbers have no shame. None at all. We cannot be embarrassed. No matter what we say, no matter what we do. No matter who we associate with or admire. No matter how low we go. Responsibility is for suckers. Disparage and demean others? No shame. Now that's super-heroic. Rape Mother Nature? No shame. That's super-heroic. Do nothing to stop mass shootings other than offer our thoughts and prayers? No shame. The Marvel universe has nothing on the superheroes of Freedumb.

Today ... Reimagine the Fantastic Four. Instead of 'Mr. Fantastic," think "Mr. Pussy Grabber." Rather than "Human Torch," how about "Human Chaos?" And instead of "The Thing," what about "The Dummy." In place of "Invisible Woman," try...actually Invisible Woman is pretty good as is.

MARCH 21

What's at stake?

"The rights of every man are diminished when the rights of one man are threatened."
(John F. Kennedy)

"I'd like to consider myself a threat."
(Freedumb Fighter)

Then ... I believed that we, as Americans, are in it together. It's a powerful thought, both inspiring and motivating. I know, it's an aspiration, but in the end that's what I believed America to be. An aspiration for better. For more decent, more fair-minded, and wise. Maybe even smarter. Rich or poor, black, white, Asian or indigenous, immigrant or native born, straight or otherwise – it didn't matter. We were all working with and toward the hope of a more perfect union with liberty, justice and equal rights for all. There was no downside to aiming high.

Now ... I see the upside in aiming low.

We Freedumbers see togetherness for what it is: an obstacle to overcome. There is no room in 'us' for the likes of 'them'. When you don't think about it, it becomes so crystal clear. The rights of us Freedumbers can only be fully realized if the rights of 'them' suffer as a consequence. So it's not enough to simply be a white man. You've got to use your sense of entitlement to sow division and discord. You've got to actively undermine the rights of others. And ideally, take them away. Be the kind of menace that would make a mother proud.

Today ... Threaten yourself. Helpful hint: Being a threat doesn't come naturally, it's something even the best of us have to work at. Thought starter: Get in front of a mirror, and bully yourself – practice makes perfect.

MARCH 22

What's your biggest lesson learned?

"We ought not to look back unless it is to derive useful lessons from past errors, and for the purpose of profiting by dearly bought experience."
(George Washington)

"When you know what's right, learning is a waste of time."
(Freedumb Fighter)

Then ... I held that learning from the past was a fundamental characteristic of a great nation. As an American citizen, I believed that understanding our history, taking lessons from it, helped our communities and country be smarter going forward. Learning from the past takes courage and conviction. In looking back we might experience discomfort, even shame, but that's the price of learning and growing. That's the price of progress. That's the price of greatness.

Now ... I realize the past isn't painful, but a future with promise and possibility could hurt.

We Freedumbers look into the past and see a solid gold success story. No warts. No blemishes. No need for any soul-searching. Why learn from prejudice and intolerance when you can celebrate them? We have to lighten up a little bit and give ourselves a break. Maybe slavery should be just a 'fun fact' to laugh about instead of an atrocity to, sigh, learn from. After all, white people flourished during slavery. Maybe 'Don't say gay' could be a new party game. After all, closeted gays would give straight people less to think about. Which sounds great to any true Freedumber. Bottom line, trying to learn from the past takes the fun out of everything, and creates an unwanted speed bump on the way to being great again.

Today ... Teach your kids some real history. Helpful hint: They want blemishes, then show them blemishes. Thought starters: When Lincoln freed the slaves or when Roosevelt brokered the New Deal or when LBJ pushed for the Great Society or when we elected a guy who wasn't born here as President of these United States.

MARCH 23

Are you well-protected?

"Against logic there is no armor like ignorance."
(Laurence J. Peter)

"Against logic, science, history, facts, the common good and compassion, there is no armor like ignorance."
(Freedumb Fighter)

Then … I thought logic was essential. It anchored reason, sound judgment and common sense. American greatness was similarly anchored. We Americans may be dreamers, but we dream with our eyes open. We don't depend on wishful thinking or look the other way. We see things clearly and keep things simple when looking at problems and perspectives. Injustice? We have to balance the scales. Inequality? We need to level the playing field. Prejudice? We have to foster mutual respect. Clear and simple, though none of it easy. Still, Americans know how to work our way through the struggles that hold us back – even if the progress is too slow for our liking. I saw logic as our armor against ignorance, and a key element in the progress we needed to make.

Now … When I meet logic, I say hello, and fuck off.

That's right, screw logic. And reason, sound judgment and common sense for that matter. Ignorance is not just a Freedumber's armor, it's our weapon of choice. Ignorance protects the Freedumber from confronting issues such as injustice, inequality and prejudice in any meaningful way. What's more, it allows us to hate without hesitation, demean on demand, and challenge reality without regard. In the mind of a Freedumber, a good offense is always offensive.

Today … Put your ignorance to work. Helpful hint: Call everything you disagree with a hoax or conspiracy. Thought starter: Climate change, a joke. Gun control, a conspiracy. COVID, a progressive prank. Affirmative action, a scam. Mass shootings, a hoax and a conspiracy. You get the idea.

MARCH 24

Can you hit a home run?

"The right of every American to first class citizenship is the most important issue of our time."
(Jackie Robinson)

"Black people are allowed to speak up on their issues, so are your Muslims, your Gays, your Asians and anybody else – just as long as we white people don't have to do anything about them."
(Freedumb Fighter)

Being a citizen means facing some issues that impact us all.

Then: I believed Jackie Robinson pointed to the most important issue in American history, but ...

Now: Jackie Robinson got a chance he didn't earn because of the limitless generosity of white people.

MARCH 25

Are you a man of character?

"It is part of the American character to consider nothing as desperate."
(Thomas Jefferson)

"It is part of the American character to consider nothing as out of bounds."
(Freedumb Fighter)

Then ... It was hard to argue with President Jefferson on this one. I'd never seen desperation as part of the American character. Resilience, yes. Optimism, absolutely. Courage, check. Problem-solving, yup. Common sense, for sure. Ambition, of course. The list would get very long, and never would it include desperation as an American thing. In fact, I always held onto the belief that Americans would respond to a desperate event or situation with anything but desperation. We would respond instead, with a collective strength, determination and fortitude. An 'in it together' kind of spirit. People of character never let desperation get the better of them. That's ingrained into the home of the brave.

Now ... I've learned that desperation is the new patriotism.

We Freedumbers are desperately hanging on to a past that was great – for us. We desperately want to have our place at the head of the table unquestioned and revered. We desperately need our lives and livelihoods to matter more than anyone else's. We desperately hope the complexities of diversity and inclusion will go away. We desperately want history to teach us nothing more than how to be proud. We desperately need women to acknowledge us as all-knowing, all-seeing and sexy. We are desperate for Mother Nature to just shut up, fall into line and do as she's told. All this, because it's what's best for America. Freedumb offers us a new kind of American hero: the desperate man.

Today ... Put your desperation to the test. Helpful hint: Get creative. Thought starter: Instead of the Olympic Games, what about the 'Desperation Games'. Events could include "Synchronized race-baiting," "Artistic name-calling," and the very challenging, "3X3 narcissism."

MARCH 26

Are you looking for signs?

"Without continual growth and progress, such words as improvement, achievement and success have no meaning."
(Benjamin Franklin)

"Continual growth isn't going to get us the improvement, achievement and success we're looking for."
(Freedumb Fighter)

Then ... I believed progress was as American as fireworks on the Fourth of July. The hope of America was that we were improving, achieving and succeeding – that is, growing as a nation and a people. In other words, getting better. For example, progress would include less systemic racism and more effective gun control. It would mean no draconian abortion laws and a genuine tolerance of those with a different sexual orientation. It would include more reading of books and less talk of banning books. It would include a recommitment to the obligations of citizenship, and maybe a little less focus on flag hugging. That would all mean a lot in terms of growth, achievement and success. I thought that opportunity continued to knock.

Now ... Freedumb sees 'growth' for what it is – another woke virus.

What's the big deal about growth anyway? Do you really want America to grow to be more fair? More Just? More wise? More caring, and decent? Of fucking course not.

Today ... Stop growth in its tracks. Helpful hint: Take inspiration from the brilliant 'Don't say gay' initiative. There are so many things WE SHOULDN'T SAY. Thought starters: A sign reading 'DON'T say science' would send a powerful message. So too 'DON'T say inclusion'. Or 'DON'T say Taylor Swift'. Or 'DON'T say equal pay'. Or 'DON'T say menstruation.' Eww, why would you?

MARCH 27

What do you revere?

"Duty, honor, country. Those three hallowed words reverently dictate what you ought to be, what you can be, what you will be."
(Douglas MacArthur)

"Nothing or nobody dictates to me."
(Freedumb Fighter)

Then ... I always had the utmost respect and gratitude for the American military. I realize they have their challenges – as does every other large organization on the planet – but they put their lives on the line for their country, their fellow citizens and the world. And, at the risk of understatement, that ain't nothing. We civilians could also learn a thing or two from the military 'mindset'. General MacArthur's quote is a great place to start. Duty. Honor. Country. Those are words that carry integrity, responsibility and sacrifice. You may not have the courage or capability to serve, but as an American citizen, you do have the courage and capacity to contribute something positive to your country. Good citizens don't stand idle – good citizens help, however they can. Bottom line, duty and honor never applied just to the military. I thought they were part of the deal. Period.

Now ... Freedumbers have a better deal on offer.

Fair warning, our deal requires a special kind of courage. Do you have what it takes to shrink from responsibility and call it duty? Do you have what it takes to blame people for their empty bellies and their tent homes? Do you have what it takes to attack people for loving differently? Believing differently? Granted, this kind of courage puts a whole different spin on the act of stepping up. You have to be willing to sacrifice common sense, let go of common decency, and reject the idea of common interest. That's Freedumb's deal. We Freedumbers can teach you a thing or two about what does and doesn't need to be revered.

Today ... Be brave. Brave enough to give the poor, hungry and homeless a piece of your mind. Helpful hint: A good opener is "Get your shit together or get out of sight." Not everyone will appreciate your heroics, but that's just another chance to play the vicdumb.

MARCH 28

Today, some words of wisdumb from Freedumbers:

About our planet …
"The best thing about earth is, if you poke holes in it, oil and gas come out."

On the FDA phasing out trans fats …
"They're coming for your donuts!"

On education …
"It is not the role of Congress to make college affordable and accessible."

On climate change …
"The biblical Great Flood is an example of climate change. And that certainly wasn't because mankind overdeveloped hydrocarbon energy."

On treatments for COVID-19 …
"I see disinfectant, where it knocks it out in a minute – one minute – and is there a way we can do something like that by injection inside, or almost a cleaning!"

On racism …
"My opinion of a white nationalist, if somebody wants to call them a white nationalist, to me, is an American."

On mass shootings …
"The United States Supreme Court sanctioned abortion on demand. And we wonder why our culture sees school shootings so often."

On immigration at the southern border …
"For every one who's a valedictorian, there's another 100 out there who weigh 130 pounds and they've got calves the size of cantaloupes because they are hauling 75 pounds of marijuana across the desert."

MARCH 29

How best to be?

"Be completely humble and gentle; be patient, bearing with one another in love. Make every effort to keep the unity of the Spirit through the bond of peace."
(Ephesians 4:2-3)

"God would never want me to be humble, gentle, patient and loving. Ever!"
(Freedumb Fighter)

Then ... I believed being humble and gentle took a certain kind of strength. The search for common ground was not for the faint of heart. Generosity of spirit required a degree of courage, and I never doubted that the home of the brave could access that kind of character if needed. Americans were confident enough in who they were and what they believed to not succumb to fear and anger. Strength and courage didn't have to be toxic. The notion of "bearing with one another in love" may come across as a bit of flowery language, but whether you read the bible or not, getting along with our fellow Americans seems core to being a good citizen. And a good person. Debate, sure. Demean, no. Disagree, sure. Get disagreeable, why? It's easier said than done, especially when tensions and emotions run high, but that's why patience is a virtue.

Now ... We Freedumbers see toxicity as the most virtuous of virtues.

Asking a Freedumber to be patient or gentle, let alone loving of "one another," makes us feel put upon. And disadvantaged. No disrespect meant to the holy book, but apparently it doesn't know what's required to get America back to greatness. Greatness demands the toxic fumes of Freedumb. Fortunately, the God of Christendumb, through his son on earth, Jesus of Orange, is there to guide us. And the greatness envisioned by Christendumbness demands embracing all that is toxic. Instead of humility, embrace resentment. Instead of love and patience, fear and anger. Instead of gentleness, cruelty. There will be no "unity of the Spirit" or "bond of peace" on the road to establishing the United States of Freedumbia. There will be winners and there are losers. A lot of losers. Lots and lots of losers. Let us pray.

Today ... Put the bible away and read "Field Ethos". It's a Freedumber magazine for manly men, and it will teach you lessons you didn't even know you needed. Spoiler alert: The bigger and badder the gun, the bigger and better the man. Words to live by.

MARCH 30

Can you hold your ground?

"What we need are critical lovers of America - patriots who express their faith in their country by working to improve it."
(Hubert Humphrey)

"Improvement sucks."
(Freedumb Fighter)

Then ... Enough said. I stood with Hubert Humphery.

Now ... I know that 'improvement' is an enemy within.

From where we Freedumbers sit, improving America will only make things worse. Can't we just be grateful that racism is more subtle now? And leave it alone. Can't we just be relieved that women no longer control their bodies - and don't need to get paid what men do for equal work? And leave it alone. Can't we be gratified that 'Don't say gay' is a real thing? And just leave it alone. Can't we be happy that climate change is not a real thing, that AR-15s are available to all, and that COVID was a hoax? And just leave it all alone. The way to make America great again is to stop trying to improve it. Just stop it. That's love of country.

Today ... Take the gloves off in our fight against improvement. Help America decline into greatness! Helpful hint: Your home is your castle. Thought starter: After every mass shooting put up a lawn sign that reads "It's a good day for Freedumb."

MARCH 31

We're all human, right?

"Human rights is the soul of our foreign policy. And I say this with assurance, because human rights is the soul of our sense of nationhood."
(Jimmy Carter)

"Human rights have nothing to do with our nation."
(Freedumb Fighter)

Then ... I thought President Carter's words pointed to the core of American greatness: our steadfast belief in human rights. No exceptions or caveats. It's the simple and transformational belief in equality of opportunity uninfluenced by race, gender, sexual orientation or religious belief. That means liberty, opportunity and justice for each and every person on the planet. And last time I checked, the planet still includes America. Americans advocate for the human race, because that's who we are. We are advocates for the underprivileged. We are advocates for the marginalized. We are advocates for those in need, and the forgotten. Not just for some. Not just in certain situations. Not just when it suits our purposes. It's a 'no caveat' kind of belief. One that makes the audacity of the goal seem almost possible.

Now ... We Freedumbers offer a lesson in goal-setting. Free of charge.

Freedumbers don't really see Americans as part of the human race. What concerns humanity is of little consequence to us. We have our hands full with more important stuff. Besides, this 'humanity' thing smells of wokism. It certainly doesn't have anything to do with our sense of being American. Human rights don't have a favorite color. Human rights don't blame the poor for their poverty. And human rights don't even like assault weapons. To make things worse, human rights actually respect the environment and embrace democracy. Bottom line, human rights are just plain wrong.

Today ... Put your inhumanity to work. Helpful hint: Write up a Charter of Inhuman Rights. Thought starter: see Project 2025. And say hello to a degree of authoritarianism that would make our pal Putin green with envy.

APRIL 1

What say you?

"Unless democracy is to commit suicide by consenting to its own destruction, it will have to find some formidable answer to those who come to it saying: I demand from you in the name of your principles the rights which I shall deny to you later in the name of my principles."
(Walter Lippmann)

"I wish democracy would commit suicide."
(Freedumb Fighter)

Then ... I thought Walter Lippmann had hit on a couple of timeless and timely points. First, democracy needs us all to be in it together. Sure, we can disagree and argue, but the give and take of getting things done takes a real commitment from all sides. Those we choose to represent us must have the integrity, resolve and strength to do what is right – in any given moment. They must govern and legislate in the best interests of the American people. In the best interests of the country. Second, representing your constituents isn't permission to be a 'bomb thrower' or 'chaos creator'. Governing is for grown-ups. It's not for narcissists looking for attention and social media fame. And it's not for people looking to weaponize government against their opponents – or against democracy itself.

Now ... I understand the problem with democracy is that it's too democratic.

To us democracy, and the rights and freedoms of other people, are at best a nuisance and at worst a threat. As a consequence, we stand ready and willing to weaponize ourselves against all things pro-democracy. We love causing chaos, creating obstruction and doing absolutely nothing constructive in service to the greater great. Democracy doesn't do enough to protect what we hold dear – our rights, our privilege, our entitlement. Time for an assisted suicide.

Today ... Weaponize a bullhorn. Get loud and proud as you walk around the block shouting "Death to Democracy." If things get out of hand with one of your neighbors, you can always say "April Fools!"

APRIL 2

What do you have to lose?

"At what point then is the approach of danger to be expected? I answer, if it ever reach us, it must spring up amongst us. It cannot come from abroad. If destruction be our lot, we must ourselves be its author and finisher."
(Abraham Lincoln)

"America will never be destroyed from abroad. We'll have to do it ourselves."
(Freedumb Fighter)

Then ... President Lincoln understood both the immense potential and fragile nature of the promise of America. For me, his thought was a reminder of the responsibility each and every American citizen carries with respect to fulfilling that promise. And defending the democratic principles on which the country is founded. That responsibility includes everything from being a responsible voter to being a responsible human being. We need to respect our fellow Americans and the institutions of government that hold us together. Improve our institutions? Sure. Evolve our institutions? As needed, of course. But respect them. As much as Americans love our country, respecting its basic principles and institutions didn't seem like much of an ask. We had been given much and had a lot to lose.

Now ... Freedumb has revealed that the only way to win is through destruction.

Hollowing out the promise of America is the only way to fulfill America's potential. That kind of logic underscores the genius of Freedumb. So let's burn it all down. That's real love of country. Set a match to democracy and the idea of governing. Set a match to common sense and common good. Set a match to liberty, justice and opportunity for all. No negotiation. No compromise. No collaboration. Don't lead. Don't contribute. Don't legislate. Don't solve problems. Don't build. That's real patriotism.

Today ... Undermine something. Helpful hint: Raise your hand and get into position in the electoral college. Thought starter: Volunteer to be a 'fake elector' and work to overturn the will of the people in the next presidential election in the direction of Jesus of Orange (or one of his disciples).

APRIL 3

What makes you comfortable?

"Too often we hold fast to the clichés of our forebears. We subject all facts to a prefabricated set of interpretations. We enjoy the comfort of opinion without the discomfort of thought."
(John F. Kennedy)

"We have the right to comfort of opinion without the discomfort of thought."
(Freedumb Fighter)

Then ... We can all get a little too comfortable with our opinions, perspectives and attitudes. President Kennedy's words came as a good reminder to stop. And think. Thinking means a willingness to reconsider what we believe: about the issues we face as individuals, about the problems we find in our communities, about the potential we see in our country. Thinking means coming up with different approaches and solutions to our challenges. Getting too comfortable isn't the way to make things better. And comfortable opinions aren't the fuel needed for progress. Some discomfort is part and parcel of creating constructive change.

Now ... We Freedumbers are uncomfortable with "the discomfort of thought."

Especially discomfort brought on by being forced to think about new or different. Or heaven forbid 'alternative'. The only thing we care to think about is how to confirm what we already believe. We're always on the lookout to get more comfortable with our prejudices. And why should we Freedumbers search for information that might add to our knowledge, or look at new approaches that might challenge what we know? We know what we know and we know what's best. We have all the answers. And we're very comfortable with that.

Today ... Comfort yourself. Helpful hint: If you can't stop thinking altogether, at least stop thinking responsibly. Thought starter: Help spread the fact that the measles vaccine causes kids to go gay.

APRIL 4

Are you prepared?

"Democracy cannot succeed unless those who express their choice are prepared to choose wisely. The real safeguard of democracy, therefore, is education."
(Franklin D. Roosevelt)

"The real safeguard of America is willful ignorance."
(Freedumb Fighter)

Then … If Democracy was the username, then education was the password. Still, education wasn't simply about 'book smarts' – I thought it could be any type of learning and growth that opens the eyes, the heart and mind. Any learning that forces a reckoning with past shortcomings. Any learning that fuels our curiosity and desire to more fully understand. Any learning that gives us the confidence to challenge preconceived notions and long-held assumptions that might hold us back from realizing our full potential. For our democracy, our country and the idea of America to work, we must, as Americans, commit to becoming lifelong learners.

Now … Freedumb has taught me that education isn't an answer. It's an enemy.

Education means learning. Learning means growth. Growth leads to a desire for better. A desire to understand more deeply. Appreciate more fully. Engage more constructively. None of that is going to help us get back to greatness. Forget about education, learning and growth. If you're looking for a silver bullet, try ignorance. The more willful the better.

Embrace the beauty of a closed mind. A closed mind only sees what it wants to. It kills curiosity. It isn't interested in better and it blocks out understanding. A closed mind has all the answers, improves nothing and is key to making America great again. Lesson learned.

Today … Tap your potential. Helpful hint: Every Freedumber has the capacity to be Freedumb-er. Thought starter: Go to your local school board meeting and try to get history, science and math off the curriculum. (Isn't algebra one of those Arab words? It must be dangerous for our kids to study).

APRIL 5

Do you ever blush?

"Man is the only animal that blushes. Or needs to."
(Mark Twain)

"I don't blush."
(Freedumb Fighter)

Then … I thought Mark Twain was a brilliant man. A very keen observer of the human condition. This observation always made me smile. It was a great reminder that we need not take ourselves too seriously. We all make mistakes. We get things wrong. We overstep and overstate. We misjudge. We swing and miss. We are an imperfect nation of imperfect beings, each of us with a wide range of faults and foibles – no matter your race, color or creed. We are all capable of embarrassing ourselves. And of making amends. We're human, after all. We only need to feel shame if we never fix our mistakes.

Now … We Freedumbers don't feel shame, confusion or embarrassment.

When you're both right and righteous, how can you go wrong? You can't. So it's unnecessary for us ever to blush. We can say the Freedumbest things, no matter how false or outlandish, without a hint of embarrassment. We're oblivious to shame. And unfamiliar with confusion. It's very empowering. And liberating. We never have second thoughts. Never feel a twinge of remorse or an urge to apologize. The idea of saying "I'm sorry" is only for the weak and wokey. Freedumb's man can't be humiliated, and never makes a mistake. (That said, in all humility, we find it easy to be embarrassed for other people).

Today … Say something really, really stupid. Put your 'no blush' capacity to the test. Helpful hint: Having fun with racism is always fertile ground to challenge yourself in. Thought starter: Try to beat "Shut up and dribble."

APRIL 6

Do you listen to the voice inside?

"Americans don't settle. We build, we aspire, we listen to that voice inside that says, 'We can do better'. A better job; a better life for our children; a bigger, better country."
(Mitt Romney)

"No can do."
(Freedumb Fighter)

Then ... I believed with everything I had that Americans were inspired by the thought of something better. Life, liberty and the pursuit was all about improvement. An improved life. And ultimately, an improved country. And to me, that little "can-do" voice was a big part of being American. I believed the can-do voice was what pushed us forward. It grounded us in common sense. It pushed us to solve problems. It enabled us to see opportunities where others didn't. It focused the extraordinary energy that is America. And it propelled us to moments of greatness. That little voice inside is one we need to listen to. It has always spoken to the best that America can be. And it always will.

Now ... We Freedumbers refuse to settle for better.

Freedumb has unleashed something new: the little 'can't-do' voice. Improving won't help us get back to greatness. Why? Because improving will disadvantage us. Improving will involve less entitlement and privilege. How are we going to get back to greatness if the playing field is levelled? How will our country be great again if the others are allowed equal opportunity and justice? Let's get real. Constructive ideas - no can do. Constructive dialogue - no can do. Constructive action - oh for fuck's sake, no can do.

Today ... Find your quiet place. Meditate on your 'can't-do' voice. Be patient, have faith, and you'll get strong enough to keep constructiveness at bay each and every day.

APRIL 7

Today, in Mathematics and Statistics Awareness Month, become a mathlete for Freedumb:

One suspected felon crossing our southern border = all immigrants are felons;
One white felon is a martyr with Presidential potential.

One lazy Hispanic man = all Hispanic men are lazy;
One lazy white man is just a guy taking a well-deserved break.

One trans person = the end of the world as we know it;
One white misogynist is just a man sticking up for himself.

One black man who does something idiotic = all black men are stupid;
One white man who does something idiotic is just a guy who was pushed too far.

One rich Jewish man = proof of a worldwide Jewish financial conspiracy;
One rich Christian man is proof the American Dream is alive and well.

One Indian gas station cashier = America is the land of opportunity;
One white man working at a gas station means the Dream is dead.

APRIL 8

What's your creed?

"The creed of our democracy is that liberty is acquired, liberty is kept by men and women who are strong, self-reliant, and possessed of such wisdom as God gives to mankind – men and women who are just, and men and women who are understanding, and generous to others – men and women who are capable of disciplining themselves. For they are the rulers, and they must rule themselves."
(Franklin D. Roosevelt)

"Liberty is acquired and kept by men immune to self-discipline."
(Freedumb Fighter)

Then ... The "creed" articulated by President Roosevelt was an inspirational one. Self-reliance, balanced with a desire to be just and generous with others, felt quintessentially American to me. It was a creed anchored in an admirable strength of character. A constructive character. A character that steps up and stands tall. One that builds and creates. One that helps and solves. As creeds go, we could do worse. Much worse.

Now ... I see that doing worse is the way to becoming great again.

Freedumb's creed has nothing to do with the shackles of democracy. It doesn't demand wisdom, understanding, generosity, or any sense of justice. It doesn't make room for a meaningful role for women. Or any other second, third or fourth tier type citizens. Our creed is the 'dicktatorship' of white men. Straight white men who are so strong they can't be disciplined by themselves or anyone else. All-knowing men with the wisdumb to dismiss common sense, learning and truth. Courageous men who will not be held back by integrity, thoughtfulness or conscience. Men who serve Christendumb by their lack of generosity, their aversion to justice, and willingness to leave others hopelessly behind.

Today ... One-up yourself. Helpful hint: Do something bad, then do something worse. Thought starter: Walk through a Native American sacred site. And then walk through the sacred site again leaving some garbage and calling any man you meet "Chief."

APRIL 9

What are you afraid of?

"We are not afraid to entrust the American people with unpleasant facts, foreign ideas, alien philosophies, and competitive values. For a nation that is afraid to let its people judge the truth and falsehood in an open market is a nation that is afraid of its people."
(John F. Kennedy)

"Foreign. Alien. Open. It's all scary."
(Freedumb Fighter)

Then ... I always held diversity, and the capacity to embrace it, as a core strength of America. I believed it to be an integral part of America's greatness. The American mind is open and inviting. So too our hearts. Fear is not our default setting. Americans do not fear something because it is different – be it a fact, idea or belief. The American mind judges fairly, questions respectfully and always, always, always values truth over falsehood. We know what's right and wrong. We know the difference between good and evil. And we Americans have the courage to act accordingly. I put my trust in that courage.

Now ... We Freedumbers know better than to trust anything other than fear.

It might be more than you need to know, but anything foreign, alien or open causes us to shit our pants. That's what you call a one-of-a-kind early warning system. By nature, Freedumbers are not a curious bunch. With 'foreign' comes discomfort. And we love our comfort zone. We love our comfort so, so, so much. And who can blame us? Foreign doesn't help us sleep at night. 'Foreign' doesn't let us breathe easy. Foreign invades our sense of serenity and disrupts the natural order of things. If it's not from here, it doesn't belong here, and we don't want it.

Today ... Diagnose yourself. Are you xenophobic enough? If an American band with the name 'Foreigner' doesn't bother you, you're not where the Freedumb movement needs you to be.

APRIL 10

What flowers in you?

"Did you, too, O friend, suppose democracy was only for elections, for politics, and for a party name? I say democracy is only of use there that it may pass on and come to its flower and fruits in manners, in the highest forms of interaction between [people], and their beliefs – in religion, literature, colleges and schools – democracy in all public and private life …"
(Walt Whitman)

"So, I suppose we best fuck flowers and fruits."
(Freedumb Fighter)

Then … I believed Walt Whitman's idea was a great expression of the power of democracy. It articulated the "flower and fruits" of democracy in its most human terms. Not simply as a form of government, but as a way of life. A way to live. In all its aspects. Democracy at its most potent should cultivate openness, mutual respect, learning and tolerance among its citizenry. It should foster competition in which the best ideas win – including ideas which cultivate common ground and common good. I believed American citizens have the lifeblood of democracy running through their veins. I also believed this made us stronger, more courageous and more genuinely freedom-loving than any other place on the planet.

Now … My fellow Freedumbers reminded me only gays and women like flowers and fruits.

Conversely, we men of Freedumb love our dicks so much, we aspire to be one. We like to think of our dick as the needle in our moral compass. A dick doesn't respect. Doesn't contribute. Doesn't tolerate. Doesn't learn. A dick isn't interested in governing or being governed. All a dick wants is more. More Freedumb, dignity and opportunity than others. More justice and respect than others. A dick just wants more of everything. Democracy is too open, too inviting and too giving. Freedumb is where the fruits and flowers of democracy go to die. The merciful cause of death being over-urination.

Today … Surprise yourself. Helpful hint: Try making a list of your favorite plants. Thought starter: Poison ivy, stinging nettle and finger rot all have their admirable qualities, but don't overlook the underappreciated water hemlock – "the most violently toxic plant in North America."

APRIL 11

How will you be remembered?

"I always remember an epitaph which is in the cemetery at Tombstone, Arizona. It says 'Here lies Jack Williams. He done his damnedest.' I think that is the greatest epitaph a man can have – when he gives everything that is in him to do the job he has before him."
(Harry S. Truman)

"Jack Williams was a loser."
(Freedumb Fighter)

Then … I couldn't have agreed more with this quote from President Truman. Doing your "damnedest" is the American way. It's inspiring. Doing our best, taking our best shot. Never quitting, never letting up. That's us. That's Americans. We're relentless; we're resourceful; we're risk-takers. We're rebels with a cause. So when our best shot is taken, it's one you'll remember. You can etch that in stone.

Now … Freedumb says trying your best is a waste of time when you can be doing your worst.

Why is doing your worst so underappreciated? Trying your best could mean working to help your fellow Americans – you know, the others. And that isn't going to help the cause. Trying your best could mean working to help our most vulnerable and marginalized. That just feels too helpful. Trying your best could involve opening your heart to be more compassionate and empathetic. I mean, please. Trying your best could mean attempting to be civil and respectful. Fuck that. The key to America becoming great again is people putting their best aside and putting their worst foot forward. And if that's not the way you're willing to goose-step, then damn you to hell. Etch that one in stone.

Today … Reflect on your worst self. Have you maximized your potential? If the answer is no, redouble your efforts and earn an epitaph that will inspire future generations of Freedumbers. Thought starter: 'He done his dumbest.'

APRIL 12

Is your heart hard enough?

"I keep my ideals, because in spite of everything I still believe that people are really good at heart."
(Anne Frank)

"You keep your ideals. I won't."
(Freedumb Fighter)

Then ... Anne Frank was born in Germany and lived in the Netherlands, but to me, she was definitely American in spirit. Strong, courageous, determined and good-hearted. I grew up believing that America's greatness was inextricably linked to its goodness. And that goodness included everything from an innate, fun friendliness to an instinctive generosity to an intrinsic desire to advocate for the underdog. That good-heartedness was something I was excited to be a part of. The thought of doing good in the context of life, liberty and the pursuit of happiness made me smile. With pride. With possibility. With a sense of patriotism.

Now ... I see goodness as any true Freedumber would – it's a crack in the armor.

Freedumbers are petrified at the thought of vulnerability. We equate goodness with weakness, because goodness opens you up. It softens the heart. It breaks open the possibility of inclusion and acceptance. It believes in true justice and equality of opportunity. It can open you up to greater understanding of and respect for others – in other words, goodness invites all kinds of unknown threats and dangers. It can even work to limit your anger and, as a consequence, the effectiveness of your uncaring cruelty. Goodness won't help the cause.

Today ... Fortify your armor. If you have to have thoughts, commit to making them bad ones.

APRIL 13

Where do you stand?

"The greatest nations are defined by how they treat their weakest inhabitants."
(Jorge Ramos)

"You mean mistreat."
(Freedumb Fighter)

Then ... He's been called "'the Walter Cronkite of Latin America," and from where I stand he spoke the truth on this one. Great nations don't leave people behind. And they don't make things more difficult for those who need help, understanding or acceptance because they are different in some way. America, as the greatest country in the world, must live by these words. Its greatness must have a big heart to let people in. Its greatness must have strong arms to lift people up and embrace them. Its greatness must keep its promises. The promise of opportunity, of a fair chance at a better life. The promise of a good education and good healthcare. The promise to not be limited or marginalized by the color of your skin, your religion, your gender, or who you love. The promise to live free.

Now ...I understand the weak have it coming to them.

We Freedumbers demand that the weak understand just how weak they are. That the vulnerable understand just how fragile their circumstances are. That the marginalized see the edge of the cliff every single day of their existence. Yes, conveying that kind of understanding takes vigilance and endurance, but we aren't afraid to hold ourselves to the standard necessary to get America back to greatness. The weak, vulnerable and marginalized have been given too much. Too much respect, too much dignity, too much understanding. Well, the time has come for a whole lot less respect, dignity, and understanding.

Today ... Build your strength. Helpful hint: Muscle-up. Thought starter: Purchase the Jesus of Orange Patriotic Pull-Up Bar on-line for the introductory low price of $19.99!

APRIL 14

Where do you put your trust?

"Whenever the people are well informed, they can be trusted with their own government."
(Thomas Jefferson)

"Whenever the people are misinformed, you can trust great again things are going to happen."
(Freedumb Fighter)

Then ... I always gave the American citizen a lot of credit. Among the things, I gave us credit for was our smarts. I believed we had the capacity to make smart decisions for our communities and country. Smart decisions to protect liberty and promote justice. Smart decisions that broadened and sustained the American dream. I believed Americans embodied a powerful combination of passion and common sense. All underpinned by the importance of staying informed. I believed that, at our core, Americans were problem-solvers. That's what we wanted in our leaders and from our government. That's what we expected of ourselves. Americans aren't ones to jump down rabbit holes. America was a country and a people you could trust.

Now ... Once again, Freedumbers stand tall as an exception to the rule.

It's misinformation that makes magic happen. We love rabbit holes. We jump into each and every one we come across. That's how we make sense of the world. Paranoia trumps passion. Conspiracies trump common sense. When lies become truth, the great again times roll. Democracy becomes the enemy. People die in a pandemic. Children get shot at school. Blacks get arrested for crossing the street. Women lose control of their own bodies. Muslims get bullied. Asians get taunted. And Native Americans get completely ignored. Turning the unthinkable into reality is the power of Freedumb. Trust me, just grab a bowl of popcorn and watch as a government of the Freedumbers, by the Freedumbers and for the Freedumbers takes your breath away.

Today ... Help make magic happen. Helpful hint: Celebrate Freedumb. Thought starter: Start a petition to make January 6th a national holiday. If America can't honor and revere some great Americans visiting 'The People's House' where does that leave us?

APRIL 15

Today, some more exercises in Freedumb math.

One black woman gets an abortion = abortion is a hobby for black women.

One black woman on welfare = all black woman are "welfare queens."

One black male CEO = the unfair treatment of all white men.

One black drug addict = a criminal; One white drug addict = a victim.

One black man with a gun = a threat; One white man with a gun = a constitutionalist.

One black man with binoculars = a menace; One white man with binoculars = an ornithologist.

APRIL 16

What do you believe?

"We are too great a nation to limit ourselves to small dreams. We're not, as some would have us believe, doomed to an inevitable decline."
(Ronald Reagan)

"We are doomed."
(Freedumb Fighter)

Then ... I thought President Reagan might have given us the best expression of American optimism ever articulated. Americans have the courage to dream big. Always have had, always will have. We don't bury our head in the sand. We are undaunted by obstacles and difficulties – all they do is stiffen our resolve. Problems aren't 'stop signs', they are invitations. Problems are the gateway to progress. They are an opportunity to think and do differently. I believed no problem could match American ambition, determination and creativity. And I believed there was no country or people in the world with a bigger appetite for a brighter future.

Now ... We Freedumbers have an appetite for something different.

It's important to understand that progress is a cause for pessimism. If black, brown or red lives are really going to matter, America as we know it will disappear. If women really do make the same money as men for the same job, America as we know it might as well be put on life support. If gay marriage continues to be legal, the America we know will dead and gone before you know it. If we have to actually respect our environment, America might as well call it a day.

Freedumbers embrace our pessimism as a permission slip to do what's necessary. If you're facing the apocalypse, you've got to let Freedumb get to work. Just look at the positive impact of taking away a woman's right to choose: more misery for poor, more vulnerable women and more hardship for women in general. That permission slip just might be a ticket to paradise.

Today ... Create some doom and gloom swag. Helpful hint: Do it to make yourself smile. Thought starter: A beer koozie that reads 'The best way to create the future is to kill it.'

APRIL 17

What's the big idea?

"What do I believe in? Belief means faith, and there's only one damned thing in the world I have faith in. That's the idea of American democracy, because it seems to me so obvious that that's the only sensible way to run human affairs."
(Rex Stout)

"What do I believe in? It's not democracy."
(Freedumb Fighter)

Then ... I always had faith in American democracy. It's anchored in the Constitution we revere – a living, breathing document giving us the freedom to create a more perfect union. And it demands a government of the people and for the people. So, faith in American democracy demands faith in the American people. And I believe that to be a pretty good foundation to work from, because the American people are good people. People with courage and common sense. While history teaches us that getting to better is no straight line, I have faith that America has the great good sense to slowly, if at times unsteadily, continue to get to a better place.

Now ... We Freedumbers are always wary of anything that's living and breathing.

For us, the Constitution should be considered a dead document – to facilitate guns for all and liberty for some. And look, we *own* the Constitution. So we'll be the ones who decide how much liberty and how many rights others are allowed. Trigger warning: If you're not a straight white male don't get your hopes up. Besides, not to state the blindingly obvious, but it's not really 'we the people'. The word 'people' is way too diverse and inclusive-sounding. A typo on the part of the Founding Führers.

Today ... Reimagine a tiered voter system. Helpful hint: Straight white men should get two votes. Women, non-whites and gays should get half a vote each – but in the end – those votes shouldn't get counted. That all adds up to Freedumb.

APRIL 18

Do you stand on convention?

"The conventional view serves to protect us from the painful job of thinking."
(John Kenneth Galbraith)

"Thank God it does!"
(Freedumb Fighter)

Then ... I held to the idea that Americans weren't big on convention. As dreamers, innovators, adventurers and rebels with a cause, the conventional didn't define what could be. Americans were built to challenge the status quo. It's the only way to make things better. You have to challenge what is, question the way things have always been done, and ask how they could be better. Not that everything is bad, but progress is built on possibility. And that's rarely unlocked by conventional. Granted, unconventional thinking is hard. It takes energy, courage and sustained effort – but that's the kind of thinking genuine greatness demanded.

Now ... We Freedumbers are pain averse.

Thinking? Ouch! Ouch! Ouch!

Today ... Spend some time with "The Oucher." You remember, the thing designed to help kids self-report the intensity of their pain. Helpful hint: Explore a wide range of pain points. Thought starter: The US women's national soccer team. Too independent for their own good. And they speak their minds on issues such as equal pay, when they're lucky to be getting paid anything at all for women's 'work'. That's got to be a 99 out of 100 on The Oucher.

APRIL 19

What's the real deal?

"Real liberty is neither found in despotism or the extremes of democracy, but in moderate governments."
(Alexander Hamilton)

"Real liberty can only be found in extremism."
(Freedumb Fighter)

Then ... I wasn't sure moderation was always the best policy, but for the functioning of a government, I thought it represented the sweet spot. Moderation is a healthy, beneficial result of differing views coming to a compromise. It doesn't give any one faction everything they want, but it works to give the country what it needs. Moderation tends to be practical. And prudent. It requires both common sense and a shared sense of common good. As Alexander Hamilton realized, extremism always undermines the one thing we all desire, the thing America is founded on: freedom. Moderation may not be sexy, but I thought America always respected what worked.

Now ... We Freedumbers yearn for a kind of sexy that moderation just can't deliver.

We're extremists. We want to strip America bare. Not because it accomplishes anything constructive, but because it accomplishes the exact opposite. Freedumbers don't see governing as debating and legislating; we see it as baiting, undermining and obstructing. Which is both fun and necessary! In truth, governing is bad for the nation.

Doing damage is sexy. It gets you lots of attention, and Freedumbers love attention. The attention you can get from undermining democracy, taking away the rights of others, and not giving a rip. Freedumb flourishes in the extreme. Common sense is un-American. Common good is wokism. Common ground is unpatriotic. The righter the future, the brighter the future. And, let's be real, there's no such thing as too far right.

Today ... Celebrate sexy. Helpful hint: Think great again swimsuit calendar. Thought starter: Put on a Speedo, spray paint yourself orange, and start posing for pics. No doubt that'll do some damage!

APRIL 20

What do you comprehend?

"On the dogmas of religions, as distinguished from moral principles, all mankind, from the beginning of the world to this day, have been quarreling, fighting, burning and torturing one another, for abstractions unintelligible to themselves and to all others, and absolutely beyond the comprehension of the human mind."
(Thomas Jefferson)

"I love religion because it gives you permission."
(Freedumb Fighter)

Then … I was born and raised a Catholic. And I believe in God. But when I grew up, I was no fan of organized religion. Any organized religion. President Jefferson's words explain why. Morality can and does operate separately from organized religion, its dogmas and its 'my way or the highway' approach. Being good is a choice we all have. Acting with empathy and compassion is a decision. Kindness, too. Those are moral principles in no need of 'organizational extremism.'

Now … I stand with Freedumbers who, ever on the lookout for justification, have found religion.

Thank God for Christendumb. What a religion! What a God! He blesses his flock in every way imaginable or unimaginable. There's no better God to have on your side. It's amazing what you can do when you feel like you've got a free pass from on high. The first thing Freedumbers do is throw morality out the window – Christendumb is in it to win it. And being great demands doing bad. Getting things right means doing things wrong. Racism, prejudice and intolerance aren't sins, they're sacraments. It's impossible not to feel blessed at the opportunity we've been given.

Today … Play word association. Use it as a game to strengthen your faith. I say 'bible', you say 'weapon'. I say 'Ten Commandments', you say 'weapon'. I say 'belief', you say 'weapon'. Just keep associating until you become a true believer.

APRIL 21

Do you give too much?

"Individuals entering into society must give up a share of liberty to preserve the rest."
(George Washington)

"If you're looking for a giver, you're looking in the wrong direction."
(Freedumb Fighter)

Then ... I saw freedom as a gift. It gives you possibility. It gives you a chance. Needless to say, it's a big gift. Still, it needs to be said, freedom doesn't mean doing whatever you want, whenever you want, to whoever you want. True freedom requires accepting some boundaries, embracing a measure of order, to allow liberty for all to flourish. In a way, properly understood, freedom is more about giving than taking. You can't use your freedom to take freedom away from other people. To take their opportunity. To take their justice. President Washington believed that respect for our fellow Americans helped define and frame what our freedom looks and feels like. That sounded to me like something worth preserving.

Now ... We Freedumbers don't give a tinker's damn about others.

We Freedumbers know who we are. And we should never be mistaken for givers. Taking, on the other hand, is something we are very interested in. Taking makes us feel that things are as they should be. Taking is control. Taking is advantage. Taking is power. To give away anything, would just make taking harder. Bottom line, you can't force a Freedumber to "enter into society" if the cost is giving something up. That kind of giving makes you vulnerable, and carries the stench of fairness. Although it should be said we're happy to give up on the hopes and dreams of other people. You're welcome.

Today ... Give up one thing. Just to prove you could if you wanted to. Helpful hint: Do it to help the cause. Thought starter: Donate your brain to pseudo-science – any true Freedumber is better off without one anyway.

APRIL 22

Do you respect nature?

"All nature is a vast symbolism: Every material fact has sheathed within it a spiritual truth."
(E.H. Chapin)

"Nature is trees, water and rock. And some animals."
(Freedumb Fighter)

Then ... I saw nature as a gift. Something to be cherished and respected. The words of the poet and minister E.H. Chapin hint at the magnitude of that gift. Nature, to me, provided three spiritual truths. First, humanity must know its place. Nature is bigger and stronger than we are – trying to beat Mother Nature is wrong, and it's also a losing battle. Second, interconnectedness. Failure to recognize the impact of our behavior on the natural world is already having dire consequences. And third, nature is immune to misinformation. Nature doesn't listen to what we say, it watches what we do. And responds accordingly. So let's practice some humility, act responsibly, and stop trying to bullshit our way through the climate crisis.

Now ... We Freedumbers see Mother Nature as our bitch.

We disrespect her. We inflict pain on her. We wreak havoc on her. We pollute, poison and deface her. It all comes from a place of superiority. We're man. We're the man. Symbolism and spiritual truth have nothing to do with it. Trees, water and rocks don't mean a lot to us – they're just trees, water and rocks. And animals are more fun to see in zoos anyway. Humility is weakness, and interconnectedness is wokeness. So, nature best bend to our will or suffer the consequences. Mother Nature is just another woman who needs to be put in her place. Wildfires, floods, heat domes and hurricanes are God's will – probably all because trans people want to go into the wrong bathroom.

Today ... On Earth Day, set off some fireworks to celebrate the prospect of America becoming great again in the driest forested area you can find.

APRIL 23

Today, some additional equations from Freedumb math classes.

One white man who shows empathy for others + wisdumb = the end of masculinity.

One white man who says only deranged people don't have kids + wisdumb = Vice Presidential potential..

One intolerant white man + wisdumb = a patriot.

One white man found guilty of sexual abuse + wisdumb = a boy being a boy.

One pussy grabbing white man hugging an American flag + wisdumb = President for Life.

APRIL 24

What do you call yourself?

"Democracy is a way of life. Democracy is sincerity, friendliness, courage and tolerance. If your life and mine do not exemplify these characteristics, we do not have the right to call ourselves full-fledged citizens of the world's greatest democracy."
(Melvin J. Evans)

"I'd like to sincerely ask you to kiss my ass."
(Freedumb Fighter)

Then ... I loved the quote above from Melvin J. Evans. A Virgin Islander, and a proud American citizen. As Americans, we must aspire, each and every day, to live up to the standard set for being a "full-fledged citizen of the world's greatest democracy." It's easy to take shots at America, for its shortcomings and problems, but I believed our greatness is, in part, a result of our commitment to the struggle for progress. The American citizen was ready, willing and able to fight the good fight – on behalf of our fellow citizens, our country and, yes, the world. Being an American citizen meant you are in the arena. The arena where justice for all is won. Or lost. Where opportunity for all is won. Or lost. Where freedom for all is won. Or lost.

Now ... Freedumbers prefer full-fledged fanaticism to full-fledged citizenship.

We Freedumbers dismiss the obligations of being a citizen. Sincerity? Not interested. Friendliness? Um, no. Courage? Only enough to do the dumb that Freedumb demands. Tolerance? Don't think so, no. We are loud and proud about being American, but citizenship doesn't really interest us. We aren't interested in building a country on tolerance. We aren't interested in being courageous enough to do what's right. We aren't interested in solving problems or pushing for progress. And yet we seek no praise or appreciation for our lack of effort or contribution. We just get on with the business of not helping.

Today ... Brag. Stop being humble about your lack of contribution to a greater America. Helpful hint: Keep it personal. Thought starter: Talk up how good you are at keeping your woman on the pedestal of submissiveness.

APRIL 25

How will you be judged?

"A man is judged by the company he keeps, and a company is judged by the men it keeps, and the people of democratic nations are judged by the type and caliber of officers they elect."
(William J. H. Boetcker)

"Nobody better judge me."
(Freedumb Fighter)

Men of good character and good company have nothing to fear.

Then: Do right and rest easy, but …

Now: Hit the panic button. Code Red!

APRIL 26

Are you ready for a rendezvous?

"There is a mysterious cycle in human events. To some generations much is given. Of other generations much is expected. This generation of Americans has a rendezvous with destiny."
(Franklin D. Roosevelt)

"This generation of Americans has a rendezvous with great againess."
(Freedumb Fighter)

Then ... I liked lofty language. And a "rendezvous with destiny" carried a lot of loft. It felt big. It felt essential. It felt noble. It felt like just the kind of thing America, and the American people, would step up to. We have done so in the past. We come together and rise. There is no challenge too big, difficult or complex for the American people. We will meet it and beat it - even if it takes a little longer than we'd like. Every generation faces some crucial choices. We are called to defend what is good, right and just. We are called to push the progress. It's what true greatness demands. So bring it on, whatever 'it' is: the home of the brave will be there, waiting.

Now ... Freedumbers aren't willing to take that meeting. We have other things to do.

That is, keeping America on the path to being great again. Being so great as to be almost incomprehensibly great. Vindictively great. Dishonestly great. Callously great. Dishonorably great. Freedumbly great. Now, that is big, essential and noble. And a rendezvous worth putting on the calendar.

Today ... Rendezvous with yourself. You're on a road less traveled, but don't even think about turning off at any 'signposts' for thinking, feeling or caring. Take a minute to pat yourself on the back for never rising to the occasion. It's the least you deserve.

APRIL 27

What's your dream?

"We shall nobly save, or meanly lose, the last best hope of earth."
(Abraham Lincoln)

"We shall nobly save America by abolishing the dream of hope."
(Freedumb Fighter)

Then ... The idea of America as 'the last best hope' captures what America means to minorities, the vulnerable, the marginalized, and all those who dream of better. It touches the heart of every single American citizen. In the struggle for freedom versus oppression, equality versus prejudice, justice versus inequity, hope is fuel for the fight. America must remain strong, determined, and always ready to strive through the struggle. Always. America must always be the eternal home of hope.

Now ... Freedumbers dream of an America without hope.

Hope for others, that is. We dream of a time when hate replaces hope as the American promise. Imagine, feeling great hate, immigrants might just stay where they belong. Minorities, feeling great hate, might just accept being disadvantaged. Feeling great hate, the vulnerable might just give up. Feeling great hate, those on the margins might simply disappear. All of which would be great for us Freedumbers. We'd get more privilege. We'd get more advantage. We'd get the full entitlement to opportunity we deserve. That's a next level kind of greatness ... America the eternal home of hate.

Today ... Be an advocate for hopelessness. Helpful hint: Frame your opinions by prefacing them with "I don't want to be an asshole, but...". Thought starter: "I don't want to be an asshole, but if black women didn't get themselves pregnant, we wouldn't have worry about all their baby issues." Or "I don't want to be an asshole, but do the homeless really have to be so fucking needy?"

APRIL 28

Have you heard the news?

"We must challenge this statement and this sentiment that the news media is the enemy of the American people. This sentiment may be the greatest threat to democracy in my lifetime."
(William H. McRaven)

"The truth can kiss my ass."
(Freedumb Fighter)

Then ... I agreed with Admiral McRaven. A healthy democracy needs a healthy, high-functioning news media: objective, focused on the truth, and willing to speak that truth to power. The American media play a critical role both as watchdog and information source for the American people. Social media, pundits, pretenders and conspiracy theorists have challenged the media landscape and made it more difficult to discern fact from fiction, but categorizing the news media as the enemy is both dangerous and lazy. We have to read and listen to people who disagree with us, and entertain the possibility that our opinions might need rethinking. And most importantly, we have to call out the nut jobs, chaos creators, and those who gain from using media to wreak havoc in our democracy.

Now ... Give us some credit, Freedumbers only dismiss or deform the news when it's factual.

We know an enemy when we see one. Fact, an enemy. Proof, an enemy. Evidence, an enemy. And any news outlet that dares report that kind of crap needs to be put on notice. Fact, proof and evidence are obstacles to America achieving greatness again. That's why we Freedumbers, rightly, balk at the truth. And I'll only say this once, but deep down we are fragile flowers – and the truth really upsets us. Most unfair of all, the truth vicdumbizes us. Just because we are bigoted and lacking in conscience doesn't make us bad people.

Today ... Become a fabricator. Fabricate truth, proof, evidence and fact. It's the blueprint to greatness. After all, it's working in Russia, China, North Korea and did right by the Nazis.

APRIL 29

What feels natural?

"It is now no more that toleration is spoken of, as if it was the indulgence of one class of people that another enjoyed the exercise of their inherent natural rights. For happily the government of the United States, which gives to bigotry no sanction, to persecution no assistance, requires only that they who live under its protection should demean themselves as good citizens."
(George Washington)

"I like to indulge myself."
(Freedumb Fighter)

Then … Equality isn't a gift. Freedom isn't an indulgence. These are not things given to one group of people by another. They are rights. Fundamental. Inalienable. I thought bigotry and persecution were unacceptable in these United States. Good citizens must be vigilant. We must protect against and confront any violation of people's "inherent natural rights." Democracy is meant to protect our citizens. And we, as citizens, are meant to protect democracy by living by its principles and ideals. The American citizen and our representatives in government must be all in on the American experiment of liberty and justice for all. Without that commitment, America begins to look like something very, very different.

Now … I appreciate the soft spot Freedumbers have for intolerance and bigotry.

Honestly, the only right we view as fundamental is our right to tolerate only what we want to, and persecute others as we see fit. We see ourselves in a class by ourselves. The rights of others should be served up at our discretion. Imagine it like kids lining up for their 'goody bags' at a birthday party – some may get a meager gift. Others may get nothing at all. The only ones happy are us gift-givers – who keep most of the goodies for ourselves. What a party! So, it stands to reason, the more intolerant, bigoted and narrow-minded we become, the better patriots we are. Freedumb is meant to protect and indulge *us* and *our* rights. So much for George Washington.

Today … Be the gift that never gives anything. Thought starter: Imagine yourself as an empty bag. With a bow on it.

APRIL 30

How blessed are you?

"How little my countrymen know what precious blessings they are in possession of, and which no other people on earth enjoy."
(Thomas Jefferson)

"I'm blessed in all I do."
(Freedumb Fighter)

Then ... I don't use the word 'blessing' very often. That said, I'd rather take my shot in America than any other country in the world. America invites and rewards unlike any place else. If you're ambitious, have at it. If you're innovative, let's see what you've got. If you've got an idea, feel free to make it happen. Freedom. That's an extraordinary blessing America offers its citizens. It's all wrapped up in life, liberty and the pursuit. That little phrase packs a big punch, and a precious one indeed. In America, you've got yourself a chance. A chance to dream and go for it. While the playing field isn't yet as level as it should be, the America I knew, aspired to make it so. And that's something of a blessing in itself. Let freedom reign.

Now ... Me and my fellow Freedumbers are differently blessed.

We answer only to the great God of Christendumb. And, of course his son here on earth, Jesus of Orange. We imagine them watching while we kick the crap out of others' chances for some life, liberty and happiness. 'Shit-kicking' is a blessedly important thing to do. The more vulnerable our fellow Americans, the harder we kick, and the more blessed we become. Those on the margins are there by their own choosing, or for their sins. And we're there to put a target on their back. Trans people, just for example. It's not that they are really hurting anybody, or actually doing anything any harm, but they need to understand that because they make us uncomfortable, there's a price to be paid.

Today ... Thought starter: Join America's 'Battle for the Bathroom'. Volunteer to be bathroom monitor at your kid's elementary school. And stand vigilant to ensure that any kid not wearing an American flag T-shirt, has to hold it until they get home.

MAY 1

Have you found your way?

"Find your own way, open your treasure house, invent your own answer to the chaos."
(Gertrude Stein)

"Find your own way, open your treasure house, invent your own chaos."
(Freedumb Fighter)

Then ... I saw Gertrude Stein's words as a poetic way to describe self-reliance. Americans pride themselves on their self-reliance. It's our answer to the chaos: control what we can. You've got to own your life and your liberty. Dream big. Whatever that might look like. America was an invitation to step up and take your best shot. It was an energizing and exciting invite. Imagine if every American citizen was given the genuine opportunity to take their best shot. Granted, we've got some distance to go before we make that a reality, but that's the reality we aspire to. So dream, and go for it – for yourself, your community and your country. There can be no better way to answer "the chaos."

Now ... I wonder why people say "chaos" like it's a bad thing.

We Freedumbers love chaos. And why not? We love the attention and drama that comes from creating absolutely nothing. We like that our chaos can mess with the lives of other people. If it hurts and harms, well, that's bonus points. It's time to eat, sleep and dream up some chaos.

Today ... Stop dreaming it and start doing it. Helpful hint: Invent a parade and declare yourself Grand Marshall. Thought starter: Call it the "Proud Parade" (not to be confused with a Pride parade). And have different floats showcasing the highlights of the January 6, 2021 Capitol attack. Chaos rocks!

MAY 2

Do you know better?

"It's better to be alone than in bad company."
(George Washington)

"Bad company is the best company."
(Freedumb Fighter)

Then ... I felt that President Washington got this one right. In the end, you are the company you keep. And who wouldn't want to keep the company of Americans? We are ambitious, fun, smart and generous. We are creative, energetic and compassionate. We are kind, resourceful and determined. We are adventurous and independent. We worked and played hard. I never considered the choice "to be alone" would ever be necessary here in America. Those are my people.

Now ... My people are different than those people.

Being in "bad company" can help you maximize your own potential for Freedumbness. And that can make the difference between being, say, just another grumpy old white guy and a real Freedumber. It can make the difference between being indifferent and actively cruel. It can make the difference between being happily uninformed and being aggressively ignorant. It can make the difference between topping out at being an enabler and ascending to leadership. If that doesn't get you excited, if that kind of upside isn't something you find motivating and inspiring, you need to take a hard look in the mirror.

Today ... 'Friend' Alex Jones on the 'socials'. Surround yourself with some great new friends and find a lot help in our shared quest, to keep on moving dumbward. If you really want to exercise your Freedumb, become a shareholder!

MAY 3

Today, the Freedumbers' all-time list of best-selling books:

1. Toxic Soup for the Soul
2. To Kill an Optimist
3. The Color Orange
4. 12 Years a Slave Owner
5. The Year of Magical Unthinking
6. The Incredible Lightness of Ignorance
7. The Great Again Gatsby
8. A Farewell to Gun Control
9. Crime and Impunity
10. Eat, Pray, Hate: One White Man's Search for Meaning

MAY 4

What are you scared of?

"Freedom makes a huge requirement of every human being. With freedom comes responsibility. For the person who is unwilling to grow up, the person who does not want to carry his own weight, this is a frightening prospect."
(Eleanor Roosevelt)

"Requirements? I'll take a rain check."
(Freedumb Fighter)

Then … I thought Eleanor Roosevelt spoke truth, but we in the home of the brave didn't scare easily. And of all the things we might be fearful of, having to grow up wouldn't make the list. Neither would carrying our own weight. Responsibility is something we can handle. Nobody said freedom was for the faint of heart. Freedom requires responsible adults in order to work the way it's supposed to. Adults willing to do their part, willing to step up. Freedom is meant to open doors, open hearts and minds, foster dreams. The dreams of each and every one of us. And it's best built on mutual respect. That seems a reasonable requirement for those of us who live in the land of the free.

Now … Responsibility gives Freedumbers a rash.

We get pissed off at requirements. We ignore requirements. We fear requirements. We avoid requirements. We object to requirements. We belittle requirements. We abhor requirements. We make fun of requirements. We abandon requirements. We explain away requirements. We neglect, overlook and pooh pooh requirements.

Why? Because Freedumb means not being fenced in. Freedom, as described by Eleanor Roosevelt, is the height of wokeness. Do you have any idea of the slippery slope that responsibility can set you down? Why don't you just ask us to be compassionate and considerate? Why don't you push us toward being understanding, tolerant and - heaven forbid - inclusive? Responsibility does nothing but turn Freedumbers into vicdumbs. How is that fair? How is that right? How is that just?

Today … Require nothing of yourself. At least, nothing that could be mistaken for something positive.

MAY 5

Are you a good example?

"No democratic world will work as it should work until we recognize that we can only enjoy any right so long as we are prepared to discharge its equivalent duty. This applies just as much to states in their dealing with one another as to individuals within the states."
(Anthony Eden)

"Your rights have nothing to do with my duty."
(Freedumb Fighter)

Then ... I believed that with freedom and opportunity comes obligation. Anthony Eden was a British prime minister, but what he said spoke to the foundation of American citizenship. American democracy. American greatness. We carry the weight of being an example. That 'shining city on the hill' kind of example. An example of good in contribution to great. An example of ambition, generosity and tolerance. An example of commitment to something bigger than oneself. An example of how democracy works, what it offers, and how it fosters progress. And I never doubted that we had both the courage and the strength to deliver on that obligation. Never.

Now ... Freedumb releases us from the duty to be a good example.

We Freedumbers enjoy every right and privilege we can get our hands on. Our duty? To enjoy every right and privilege we can grab – and keep them to ourselves. This frees up a lot of time and works effectively to focus our energy. For example, when you don't care about the rights of others, one thing that floats to the top of the priority list is protecting your privilege. You could take some time developing conspiracy theories to chip away at the faith in our institutions. You could work to suppress the vote. You could use social media to promote fear and hate of others. The hard truth is, messing with democracy and the rights of others is the burden Freedumbers must carry.

Today ...   Dare to dream. Helpful hint: Not all things are for all people. Thought starter: Why should immigrants be allowed into national parks? Why should trans people be allowed into any parks at all?

MAY 6

What's in your soul?

"I have found that among its other benefits, giving liberates the soul of the giver."
(Maya Angelou)

"My soul doesn't need to be liberated."
(Freedumb Fighter)

Then ... In a country that holds so dearly to freedom, the poetic notion of liberating the soul through giving really made me stop and think. Perhaps a liberated soul helps us more effectively tap into our humanity. Perhaps a liberated soul helps us push harder for progress, justice and equality of opportunity. Perhaps a liberated soul allows us to give other people a chance, other colors and creeds a chance, other lifestyles and attitudes a chance. Perhaps a liberated soul helps us give to those we haven't yet given to. I always believed America to be a giving country, and Americans, a giving people.

Now ... I prefer a soul that's locked and loaded.

When you hold Freedumb dear, when you want America to get back to being great, you need to be careful what you liberate. Still, we Freedumbers do believe in liberating. Most of all, we want to liberate white penis power. Meaning white dicks dominate. White dicks decide who gets what rights and what justice looks like. So forget about your soul, liberate your dick, and feel the cool breeze of Freedumb come your way.

Today ... Commit to being a real dick. Helpful hint: Give your penis the pep talk it needs. Thought starter: No matter how small the penis, just know the potential to be a big Freedumb-loving dick is within your grasp.

MAY 7

A life well lived?

"Each person must live their life as a model for others."
(Rosa Parks)

"Each person must live their life as a threat to others."
(Freedumb Fighter)

Then … I held up Rosa Parks as a role model. Talk about an invitation to greatness. Imagine if we all behaved as role models. Rosa Parks stood up against racism and injustice by refusing to sit at the back of the bus. That was a very American act. An act of protest to be modeled and built upon. I believed Americans wanted to be role models. We wanted to right wrongs and build a better country. We wanted to be living examples of what is good and right. We wanted to be people that others can look up to. People that others can get inspired and energized by. This would take integrity, compassion, fortitude and, perhaps more than anything else, courage. That's no small ask, but not to worry. The home of the brave was up to the task.

Now … I look elsewhere for inspiration.

What about the congresswoman who blamed wildfires on a secret Jewish space laser? Or the congressman who accused the FBI of planning the insurrection? Or the governor who made his toddler daughter chant "Build the Wall"? Or the senator who introduced the "Love America Act" aimed at denying funds to schools trying to teach black history? Or the former big city mayor who was found guilty of defaming two black female election workers in Georgia? Or the congressman who said the insurrection looked like a normal tourist visit? With this kind of inspiration, we Freedumbers rightly ask, "Was Rosa Parks really that big a deal?"

Today … Take some time to brainstorm names for us Freedumb-fighting superheroes. Helpful hint: Unfortunately, Superman is already taken. Thought starters: The White Lantern, the Incredible Sulk, Dumbdevil, and the Great Again Hornet.

MAY 8

What's your question?

"The noblest question in the world is what good may I do in it?"
(Benjamin Franklin)

"What's so great about a noble question?"
(Freedumb Fighter)

Then ... I believed a good question was a powerful thing. And a noble question could change everything. It felt like Benjamin Franklin spoke to our morals and ideals, and the goodness to which we aspire. The goodness of a country or a people must never be separated from greatness. There are infinite ways to do good, big and small, but you must first ask yourself the question. You must have the desire. You need to state the goal. We Americans must challenge ourselves to ask how we can do good. How we can contribute to the greater good, the common good. I always believed America to be a country of noble intent.

Now ... We Freedumbers hate noble questions.

Who can blame us? Noble questions take us outside our comfort zone. Words synonymous with noble include honest, virtuous, decent, upright, heroic, valiant, uplifting, principled, just, moral, ethical, respected. Why would any righteous Freedumber want anything to do with noble – in a question or any other form. Instead, how about wallowing in the ignoble? Wallow in what's disreputable, mean, shabby, shameful, contemptible, despicable, dishonest, unprincipled, wrong, improper, uncharitable, reprehensible. And disgraceful. Now that's hitting our sweet spot.

Today ... Dive into the ignoble. Helpful hint: Come up with a useful battery of questions to keep you living in your sweet spot. Thought starters: Are you vulgar enough? When's the last time you did something disrespectful? What's the last truly Freedumb thing you've done?

MAY 9

What in the name of God?

"Those who deny freedom to others deserve it not for themselves and, under a just God, cannot long retain it."
(Abraham Lincoln)

"God knows denying freedom to others won't solve all our issues, but it's a place to start."
(Freedumb Fighter)

A just God will have the final say.

Then: I believed we supported the freedom of others so that God might bless America, but ...

Now: We Freedumbers follow the lead of Jesus of Orange, his son here on earth.

MAY 10

Can you be counted on?

"When angry, count ten before you speak; if very angry, a hundred."
(Thomas Jefferson)

"When angry, yell. If very angry, yell louder."
(Freedumb Fighter)

Then ... I saw anger as the lazy man's favorite emotion. We're all capable of anger. And in the times we live in, there seems to be an abundance of things to get angry about. Counting to ten or one hundred may seem a bit trite, but the point President Jefferson was making is a crucial one. Angry words seldom help. Angry words don't build or solve or seek to understand. Anger clouds our judgment, puts a lid on our compassion, and blinds us to the truth. Anger doesn't help us be better. It doesn't solve problems or yield constructive solutions. Anger wasn't something great countries or great people would build on. Restraint is a tough thing. Moderation seems out of fashion. Prudence doesn't get us attention or 'likes' on social media. Still, we needed them. Our country needed them. 1-2-3-4-5 ...

Now ... I realize asking Freedumbers to count to ten is asking way too much.

Anger doesn't get the best of a Freedumber, it *is* the best of a Freedumber. Anger is a Freedumber's happy place. We love being angry. We look to be angry. And we are pretty much angry about everything. Being angry is fun and as easy as 1-2-3.

Today ... Challenge yourself to count to ten at your first angry moment. You won't get there, but at least you can bitch, moan, complain, lash out and label yourself a vicdumb for having been forced to give it a try.

MAY 11

What are you a part of?

"All great qualities are never found in any one man or in any one race. The whole of humanity, like the whole of everything else, is ever greater than a part. Men only know themselves by knowing others, and contact is essential to this knowledge."
(Frederick Douglass)

"All great qualities are found in the white man."
(Freedumb Fighter)

Then ... I thought the point made by Frederick Douglass was a fundamental one. Every race, color and religion have good and bad. No race, color or creed has the market cornered on good character, or on the qualities required for greatness. Americans know we are better together. We are stronger, smarter, more innovative together. Diversity opens our eyes. It stimulates our minds. It expands our hearts. I thought diversity made everything more interesting, including we, the people. Besides, being exposed to the whole of humanity made life more fun.

Now ... That's not the kind of fun we Freedumbers like being exposed to.

We prefer making fun of the rest of humanity. For Freedumbers, there is no 'in it together' spirit. Diversity serves only to weaken our tribe. It weakens the white tribe. The male tribe. The straight tribe. The Christendumb tribe. Knowing others doesn't help us know ourselves, it only encourages us to forget who we are. How does it help maintain our advantage or hold on to the upper hand? It doesn't. So best keep our eyes closed, our minds shut, our hearts hard. And our lines drawn. Freedumbers know exactly who we are.

Today ... Go tribal. Remove any hint of diversity from your life. Different people are out. Different ideas are out. Even different foods should be out, except for all-American foods like tacos, pizza and beef chow mein.

MAY 12

What do you recognize?

"A feminist is anyone who recognizes the equality and full humanity of women and men."
(Gloria Steinem)

"A feminist is the enemy."
(Freedumb Fighter)

Then ... My view was that by Gloria Steinem's definition, shouldn't we all be feminists at this point? It seemed a bit strange to have to say, but recognizing the full humanity of women is something that benefits us all. It can make us smarter, more innovative and thoughtful. It can encourage us to have different conversations about the issues and problems we face, and help us develop better ways to address those issues and problems. It can bring us closer together, foster understanding and help us grow, individually and collectively, as Americans. And as human beings. That all seemed rather obvious.

Now ... I have too much wisdumb to recognize the obvious.

We Freedumbers see independent women as a problem. Always have. Always will. Freedumbers understand that recognizing the "full humanity" of women is an attack on men. It attacks our power and privilege. It attacks our superiority and self-esteem. It attacks our all-knowingness. It basically makes it more difficult and less fun to be a man. The full humanity of women does nothing but bring a lack of proper reverence for the manliness of our manhood. That all spells the beginning of the end of civilization. And more importantly, the end of America as we know it.

Today ... Know thy enemy. Helpful hint: To know a woman's mind you might try asking her what she's thinking. Thought starter: Time for another round of 'Would You Rather'. First question: "Would you rather meet a man or bear when alone in the woods?"

MAY 13

What do you pray for?

"Let us close the springs of racial poison. Let us pray for wise and understanding hearts. Let us lay aside irrelevant differences and make our nation whole. Let us hasten the day when our unmeasured strength and our unbounded spirit will be free to do the great works ordained for this nation by the just and wise God who is the father of us all."
(Lyndon B. Johnson)

"Oh Jesus of Orange, help us."
(Freedumb Fighter)

Then ... I saw Lyndon Johnson as a President who accomplished a great deal. Good things. He pledged to build a 'Great Society', more prosperous and more just. And he took his best shot at pushing the country in that direction. He also called things as he saw them. The speech he gave after signing the Civil Rights Act carries as powerful a punch today as it did back in 1964. The end of "racial poison"? That was prayer-worthy. "Wise and understanding hearts?" That was prayer-worthy. The laying down of "irrelevant differences?" That was prayer-worthy. The strength, spirit and freedom, as a nation, to do the great works America is destined for? That seemed like it's worth a prayer or two as well.

Now ... Freedumb demands if you're going to pray, you pray for the right shit.

Pray for privilege. Pray for advantage. Pray for entitlement. Pray that we keep our minds open to the upside of racism. Pray that we hold onto irrelevant differences of all kinds – especially as they relate to our superiority. Pray for the strength and spirit necessary to confuse, denigrate, and destabilize. And please pray that nobody else's prayers get answered. Amen to that.

Today ... Strengthen your spirit. Pray to his almighty Jesus of Orange for guidance in how to make this day great again.

MAY 14

Is your glass half full?

"I'm an optimist in the sense that I believe humans are noble and honorable, and some of them are really smart. I have a very optimistic view of individuals."
(Steve Jobs)

"I can see the apocalypse."
(Freedumb Fighter)

Then ... I admired Steve Jobs. Talk about a difference-maker. To me, he was a quintessential American. A man who put his heart and mind, all of his formidable energy and talent, into what could be. He changed the world. He changed people's lives. He changed how we live. He dreamed the impossible – and then made it happen. I find his belief in human beings both inspiring and reassuring. Optimism is *the* essential ingredient. It encourages you to see the good in people. To assume positive intent. To expect decency. And it fosters the belief that people want to do what's right. Optimism is the belief we can be better. Without optimism, what are we to believe about our fellow Americans, about our country and the world? Without optimism, what are we left with?

Now ... I'm with my fellow Freedumbers in focusing on what can't be.

Other people want progress. That can't be. Other people want inclusiveness. That can't be. Other people want equality of opportunity. That can't be. Other people want fairness. No. Other people want justice. No. Other people want compassion and understanding. No! Other people want, want, want. How can we ever expect to be great again with all these other people wanting better? Thankfully, we're here to save the day.

Today ... On National Decency Day, go the opposite direction. Helpful hint: Send a bad thought. Thought starter: Imagine a line of disrespectful greeting cards targeting minorities. Send them your worst wishes and hope they get ill soon.

MAY 15

What's the problem?

"Our problems are manmade; therefore, they can be solved by man. And man can be as big as he wants. No problem of human destiny is beyond human beings."
(John F. Kennedy)

"No problem caused by do-gooders is beyond men like us to solve."
(Freedumb Fighter)

Then … I thought President Kennedy's statement felt like a very American thing to say. Have a problem? OK, let's figure out how to solve it. There was no American problem that ultimately couldn't be solved by the American people. Nothing was beyond our brainpower. Nothing was beyond our willpower. Whatever our issues, I thought, we the people are the solution. We want liberty and justice for all. We want an end to racism, intolerance and prejudice. We want an American dream within reach of all who yearn for it. We are fair-minded and big-hearted. There is no problem too big, no issue too complicated, no obstacle too daunting. Put it in front of the American people and, as the saying goes, watch this space. Americans are world class problem-solvers.

Now … I know it's best that others leave well enough alone.

Well enough for others feels great to us Freedumbers. Women? Fun to have around, but the future will never be female. Just leave well enough alone and be happy posing on the weaker sex pedestal. Blacks and browns? Entertaining to watch on the field or court, but we don't want to watch them walk through our neighborhood. Just leave well enough alone and stay on your own side of town. Immigrants? Good on the golf course landscaping crew, or working at jobs I wouldn't touch, but the American dream is mine and mine alone. So please just cut the grass and leave well enough alone. The Orientals? Haven't they done enough causing COVID? Just stay out of my sight and leave well enough alone. There now, all good.

Today … Petition to get movies like *Crazy Rich Asians* and *The Joy Luck Club* banned. Words like 'rich', 'joy', and 'luck' have no business being associated with the Orientals. Problem solved.

MAY 16

Are you conscientious?

"Nothing in the world is more dangerous than sincere ignorance and conscientious stupidity."
(Martin Luther King, Jr.)

"Nothing in the world is more inspiring than sincere ignorance and conscientious stupidity."
(Freedumb Fighter)

Then ... In my experience, Americans were a lot of things, but stupid wasn't one of them. Americans were grounded in common sense. Our passion was balanced by pragmatism. We wanted to know the implications and consequences of our words and actions. We wanted information, not misinformation or disinformation. Americans genuinely wanted to know because we cared. We cared about our families, our fellow Americans and our country. Americans wanted to know because we understood the inherent risks of ignorance and stupidity. We knew they didn't help. We knew they did harm. Thankfully, the dangers of ignorance and stupidity were no match for American level-headedness and reason.

Now ... I respect what we Freedumbers might call uncommon sense.

More specifically, we have the sense to embrace ignorance. We possess a unique kind of all-knowingness rooted in not knowing, and in not caring enough to want to know. We don't care to know the facts, proof or evidence. We don't care enough to want to know about consequences. That's why we can be passionately pro-life right up until the time a baby is born – then, sweetie, you are on your own. That's why we can say guns don't kill people. That's why we can say climate change is just a bit of bad weather. And that's why we can say "Stop the steal" – as loudly and as often as possible. That's the kind of uncommon sense that can push us to greatness again, and transform America into Freedumbia.

Today ... Put your uncommon sense to work. Helpful hint: Give a lecture at your local library. Thought starter: Topics might include "The functionality and fashion of bulletproof backpacks," "Why women are to blame for the baby you don't want," or "Why Freedumbers never lose elections."

MAY 17

What pleases you?

"May we think of freedom not as the right to do as we please, but as the opportunity to do what is right."
(Peter Marshall)

"May we think of freedom as the right to do as we please."
(Freedumb Fighter)

Then ... I believed freedom was the greatest gift one could receive, and it came with the most essential of opportunities: to do what is right. As Rev. Marshall notes, freedom can never be seen as simply permission. Rising to the opportunity of doing what's right takes integrity, courage, and a willingness to contribute. And empathy. Freedom asks as much of those in its possession as it gives. Americans get that. For freedom to flourish, it must rest in the hands of people of character – good people. People with integrity. Thoughtful people. People less anchored in doing what they could, and more committed to doing what they should. People unafraid to do something that actually helps.

Now ... The land of the Freedumb rests in different hands.

Embrace Freedumb and there is no obligation to act with anything resembling integrity. Contribution is dismissed out of hand. There's no need to be encumbered by empathetic thoughts or concern ourselves with the common good. There's no desire or intent to build. Freedumb makes it cool to go full-on narcissist. And once you go full-on, the fun will never stop. So please, please, please, do as you please.

Today ... Please yourself. Helpful hint: The second best way to please yourself, is by taking potshots at other people. Thought starter: No condom necessary.

MAY 18

Are you rising?

"We must prepare to live in a new world ... The first thing is this, that we must rise above the narrow confines of our individualistic concerns, with a broader concern for all humanity."
(Martin Luther King Jr.)

"We must prepare to live in a new world in which we rise above humanity."
(Freedumb Fighter)

Then ... I'd always been inspired by the words of MLK. His words and actions had made America a better country, and Americans a better people. Living in the land of the free didn't mean every man for himself. Being American meant having a big heart and big shoulders. It meant being willing to help out as needed. That meant caring about equality of opportunity, caring about injustice and prejudice, caring about living wages and affordable healthcare. I never saw America becoming a 'nanny state', but we must continually strive to make the American dream something within the grasp of all Americans. Our pursuit of happiness can't mean survival of the fittest. The bar for America and for every American was always set higher than that. And we had always been a people ready to rise.

Now ... Freedumb has convinced me not to take this rising business too far.

Again, we Freedumbers adhere to a 'Freedumber First' agenda. Our desires will always trump any broader concerns of all humanity – after all, 'humanity' includes other people. We Freedumbers refuse to lumped in with the human race. So we'll rise to separate ourselves from humanity and all things humane. We'll rise to hate. We'll rise to discriminate. We'll rise to defend injustice. We'll rise to restrict the rights and liberties of others. All in the spirit of helping America taste the fruits of its great againess.

Today ... Rise by going low. Helpful hint: Take the lead of the greatest of all Freedumbers. Thought starter: Make fun of a disabled person, or call a war hero a loser, or purposely mispronounce someone's name. Remember, we Freedumbers are nothing if not a class act.

MAY 19

What do you think?

"Modern life means democracy, democracy means freeing intelligence for independent effectiveness – the emancipation of mind as an individual organ to do its own work. We naturally associate democracy, to be sure, with freedom of action, but freedom of action without freed capacity of thought behind it is only chaos."
(John Dewey)

"I don't think thinking is all that helpful."
(Freedumb Fighter)

Then … I believed we needed to heed the words of John Dewey. The opportunity to harness democracy and unlock the full power of freedom is dependent on our capacity to think for ourselves. To think through challenges and opportunities. Objectively, based on facts, with common sense and a reasoning mind. Thinking leads us to ask questions. It encourages us to seek truth, and pause when confronted by misinformation or wild-eyed conspiracy theories. It enables us to challenge our assumptions and biases. Thinking encourages us to consider others. Think hard enough, and you arrive at thoughtfulness. Thoughtfulness in the positions we advocate for, in how we vote and who we send to Congress, in how we contribute to American democracy and the future of our country. That all felt like it was well worth thinking about.

Now … Freedumbers see any thinking as overthinking.

Why do you need to think if you're free to act? Thinking slows you down. Thinking forces you to consider alternatives. Thinking gets you to look deeper into issues. Thinking just makes you engage with other people's point-of-view. And that could lead to thoughtfulness. Why would you think, if it might make you more understanding and considerate? Why would you think, if it might make you more compassionate? Why would you think, if it might make you more open and curious? The truth is, thinking is a headache waiting to happen.

Today … Consider a lobotomy. It'll set you up as a future leader of the Freedumb movement, and get you one step closer to being the man of action America needs.

MAY 20

Do you like to laugh?

"I sometimes think that the saving grace of America lies in the fact that the overwhelming majority of Americans are possessed of two great qualities – a sense of humor and a sense of proportion."
(Franklin D. Roosevelt)

"We are the saving grace of America. And that's no laughing matter."
(Freedumb Fighter)

Then ... One of things I always loved about Americans is that as much as we love our country, when push comes to shove, we can keep things in perspective and not take ourselves too seriously. As President Roosevelt noted, those qualities come in more than a little handy every now and again. Keeping things in perspective can be really beneficial. Not every issue is life or death. Not every crisis signals the end of the world. Not every misstep is a mortal wound. Perspective demands calmness and clear-headedness. It requires a degree of thoughtfulness and humility. It calls for presence of mind – and a fundamental confidence in who you are and what you stand for. In my experience, Americans understood this.

Now ... We Freedumbers are very serious people.

And we take ourselves very, very seriously. Heroes that we are – preventing common sense from capturing the airwaves, rescuing Americans from civility and decency – there's not a lot of time to take our eyes off the prize. No one is better equipped than us Freedumbers to save this country from itself. From do-gooders. From tree huggers. From those who advocate for immigrants. From the pussy hat wearers and independent women everywhere. From all the people who think it's OK to say 'gay' and watch re-runs of *Will and Grace*. From all the teachers and parents who think black history and science are real things. From the defenders of democracy and civil rights. The list goes on and on. The burden is heavy. And definitely no laughing matter.

Today ... With all that you're doing, don't forget about taking care of YOU. Commit to the Freedumber diet. Helpful hint: Make sure the colors of your food match the color of your skin. Thought starter: Why should we be forced to eat yellow corn or black beans or brown rice? The whitest foods are the purest and most palatable.

MAY 21

Today, the first of several Freedumber Public Service Announcements:

PSA #1:

Have you ever been promoted at work when you were less qualified, less talented, and less experienced than your colleagues? If the answer is no, you may be one of the few straight white men who haven't benefited from the most powerful gender-color combination America has ever known. This anomaly, this oversight, is a travesty of justice. Call 1-800-FREEDUM to talk to a representative with a sympathetic ear. He'll understand the shock and betrayal you must be feeling. And he will not only listen, but work with you to get your undeserved rewards.

PSA #2:

Have you ever heard police sirens behind you and never once thought something such as "Damn, I hope I don't get a ticket" or "Is that Mikey Johnson from Glenwood High?" or "I pay their salaries, we can work something out"? Well, you may be black. Call 1-800-FREEDUM to speak with a self-important, unsympathetic representative. He will explain to you why your race was better off when your ancestors worked on plantations and burning crosses were the order of the day.

MAY 22

Where are you on principle?

"Democracy is not so much a form of government as a set of principles."
(Woodrow Wilson)

"Democracy is for losers. So are principles."
(Freedumb Fighter)

Then ... I always believed that, as a form of government, democracy was intended to bring out the best in its citizens and institutions. In order for it to work, what's required is our very best. Our best effort. Our best judgment. Our best minds and hearts. Our democracy was founded on principles: liberty, justice, and a government of the people, by the people, for the people. These principles both underpin and transcend government. These are principles that guide us as American citizens. They guide us in what we say and do – as neighbors, voters and volunteers. They feed our dreams and fuel our ambition. For ourselves and for our country. They provide common ground and hold out the possibility of common good. They anchor our future, our potential, and our shot at greatness.

Now ... Freedumbers have anchored ourselves in the principle of being unprincipled.

If you're courageous enough to be genuinely irresponsible, letting a lack of principle be your guiding light can be a really cool and fun thing. It allows you to mess with everyone and everything. Democracy included. Truth be told, we Freedumbers have, for a long time, felt that democracy was an obstacle to the ultimate greatness of America. Paying lip service to liberty and justice, opportunity and happiness, are all well and good for cloud cover, but they must never be taken as a serious invitation to all. Make the promise, fine, but break the promise as and when necessary. Ultimately, civil rights must crumble and go the way of the dinosaur.

Today ... Don't be a loser. Helpful hint: Reflect on your integrity and rid yourself of any last remnants. Thought starter: Come up with reasons why there don't need to be any polling stations in the inner city. Or why public schools should be left unfunded. Or why we should ban the word "abortion."

MAY 23

Are you meeting your obligation?

"It is every man's obligation to put back into the world at least the equivalent of what he takes out of it."
(Albert Einstein)

"It is every man's obligation to take out of this world as much as he can."
(Freedumb Fighter)

Then … I thought Albert Einstein's call to action gave us words to live by. In the land of the free, the obligation to put back at least as much as you take was essential to the character of the country. The 'give-take' dynamic applied to us all. I believed Americans to be among the greatest givers in all the world. Our generosity could warm the heart, feed the soul, and inspire awe. In my experience, the thing about Americans is that we *want* to give back. We want to leave the country better than we found it. We want to make a positive difference in the lives of not only our family but our community. That desire to give is part of the American DNA.

Now … I see, as every good Freedumber does, that everything is a zero-sum game.

Freedumbers have reframed the give-take dynamic into a grab 'n go kind of thing. We've left giving on the side of the ditch like a piece of roadkill. We've turned taking into an art form. When you don't worry about giving, the mind can really focus on creating opportunities for taking. All upstanding Freedumbers love to leave less for the others – their rights included.

Today … Put some creativity into your taking efforts. Helpful hint: when was the last time you took away someone's dignity? Thought starter: The old 'look and laugh' is an effective way to undercut some uppity immigrant who dares to make eye contact.

MAY 24

Where does your courage come from?

"This nation will remain the land of the free only so long as it is the home of the brave."
(Elmer Davis)

"This nation will remain the home of the brave only so long as it is the land of the Freedumb."
(Freedumb Fighter)

Then ... I genuinely believed America to be the land of the free. And the home of the brave. I just never really thought about how closely the two are related. Clearly the straight line between courage and freedom is most apparent in times of war – and Elmer Davis ran the Office of War Information during World War II – but that line is no less clear during peacetime, if defined somewhat differently. To me, wartime courage is defined by what it takes to win 'the war'. Peacetime courage is defined by what it takes to build a better country. As citizens in the home of the brave, we must stand up for what's right and just, address wrongdoing, defend and advocate for those who can't defend themselves, and learn and grow from our mistakes. It's courage that comes from head, heart and soul.

Now ... We Freedumbers know that courage has nothing to do with head, heart or soul.

We're all about big dick bravery. It unlocks the uncaring power within. It gives us the fortitude necessary to be a bully. And lord knows, America could use more bullies. Because if we're going to find our way to the kind of greatness only Freedumb can offer, a bully brigade will have to do some heavy lifting. But rest assured, big dick bravery will have us all living in Freedumbia before you know it.

Today ... Rest your dick. You've got to be exhausted from all the fucked-up things you're been courageously doing to make America great again. Wrap it tenderly in a warmed MAGA golf towel while you recline on the sofa with a couple of beers.

MAY 25

What's your pain threshold?

"Abortion, for many women, is more than an experience of suffering beyond anything most men will ever know; it is an act of mercy, and an act of self-defense."
(Alice Walker)

"I like to consider myself merciless."
(Freedumb Fighter)

Then ... I thought the words of Alice Walker should get each and every one of us to stop and think. Abortion is an emotionally fraught issue. That said, the reality, for men, is that we just don't get it. We can't put ourselves in the body of a woman. We can't know her mind. And we can't understand the pain and angst wrapped up in her decision. And truth be told - we wouldn't want to. So why should men have any influence over a woman's body, or any decisions related to it? We shouldn't. We shouldn't create barriers or pass laws making it more difficult for women to do what they think is right. It's their body, it's their choice. That's it. That's all.

Now ... Freedumb helped me realize that women don't know what's best for them.

Fortunately, the men of Freedumb do. We actually know what's best for everybody, but this is especially true for women. We are the North Star of all-knowingness as far as women's rights go. So women would be well advised to listen up. First, getting pregnant is a woman's thing. Second, only men should decide how women deal with a pregnancy. That unborn child might be a future Freedumber, so abortion should be a crime. Third, the baby is the woman's responsibility. So once the baby is born, women are on their own and free to live the life they always dreamed of. We'll just walk off and wash our hands of it, as we move on - without fanfare - to the next thing. It all makes sense, right? Simply another job well dumb.

Today ... Tell a woman what's best for her. No need to limit it to babies and birth control. See a woman, advise a woman. Make her a better woman. Let all women benefit from a Freedumber's Freedumbness.

MAY 26

Will you leave the world a better place?

"I have an irrepressible desire to live till I can be assured that the world is a little better for my having lived in it."
(Abraham Lincoln)

"Irrepressible desire? Great. World a little better? Not so great."
(Freedumb Fighter)

Then ... I thought if you're going to have an irrepressible desire, the one President Lincoln articulated might be a tough one to beat. Imagine us all being a little bit better people. Imagine if we all resolved to leave the world, our country and our community a little better than how we found it. Imagine things a little more just, a little more equal, a little more inclusive. Imagine things a little more open-hearted and open-minded. Imagine people a little less economically vulnerable, a little less emotionally vulnerable. We Americans have it in us. After all, we're nothing if not dreamers. I mean, just imagine.

Now ... I recognize that kind of dreaming is a nightmare scenario.

Me and my buddies want to leave America a little Freedumb-er than we found it. So, imagine White History Month, not just in May but every month of the year. Imagine an end to immigration. Imagine guns for all – especially school-aged kids. Imagine schools with no science, history or literature – just Christendumb ethics. Freedumbers have desires and dreams of our own, Mr. Lincoln. Just imagine.

Today ... Satisfy a desire. Helpful hint: 'White History Month' has a lot of potential. Thought starter: Themes could be "How white men invented everything" and "Why white men are natural born leaders" and "How everyone can be more like a white man" and "Why white man mediocrity equals white man superiority."

MAY 27

How small can you get?

"I love the man that can smile in trouble, that can gather strength from distress, and grow brave by reflection. 'Tis the business of little minds to shrink; but he whose heart is firm, and whose conscience approves his conduct, will pursue his principles unto death."
(Thomas Paine)

"My mind is actually smaller than you think."
(Freedumb Fighter)

Then ... I had always held up the American man as, ultimately, a principled man – a man who would live up to the aspirations of Thomas Paine. A man capable of meeting adversity head-on with courage, conviction and conscience. A man who grew stronger and wiser from his experience. And one who rose to meet the inevitable next challenge with steel in his backbone and a heart both open and giving. We would be a more just country, a country of greater opportunity for all. We would be a country that celebrates diversity and encourages inclusion. We wouldn't shrink from these challenges. We wouldn't fear progress. We would be the men America needs us to be. America is no country for old men – with little minds.

Now ... We Freedumbers understand that small-mindedness is actually an asset.

The Freedumber's mind is so small, one might question whether it exists at all. That's how blessed we are! And here's a bit of a secret: Every time a Freedumber attempts to think, his mind shrinks. It's truly an amazing phenomenon. Nothing short of a miracle. Every time we think we grow more fearful. Every time we think we grow more intolerant. Every time we think we grow more judgmental. We think therefore we dumb. Freedumb. If you can't respect a man like that, well, that's on you.

Today ... Let your mind wander. Helpful hint: Think 'I don't want to be an asshole, but...'. Thought starter: 'I don't want to be an asshole, but nothing in this world is harder than being a white man' or 'I don't want to be an asshole, but women shouldn't need maternity leave because they shouldn't be working in the first place' or 'I don't want to be an asshole, but if the climate is going to fuck with me, I'm going to fuck with it'.

MAY 28

Could you stand corrected?

"The first thing is to know your faults. And then take on a systematic plan of correcting them. You know the old saying about a chain only being as strong as its weakest link."
(Babe Ruth)

"Faults are things I find in other people."
(Freedumb Fighter)

How you address your faults says a lot about who you are.

Then: Acknowledge a shortcoming, address it, and then go out there and make the Sultan of Swat proud, but …

Now: Do some ranting. Look in the mirror and yell, "It's their fault! It's their fault!" Then get out there and show America what you're incapable of.

MAY 29

What's the best thing?

"The best thing to give your enemy is forgiveness; to an opponent, tolerance; to a friend, your heart; to your child, a good example; to a father, deference; to your mother, conduct that will make her proud of you; to yourself, respect; to all others, charity."
(attributed to Benjamin Franklin)

"The best thing to give anybody is a piece of my goddamn mind."
(Freedumb Fighter)

Then … I'm not saying Benjamin Franklin got everything perfect in his list of desirable qualities, but I thought it was more than a good place to start. Forgiveness, tolerance, charity, respect and love could all help us be better people, better Americans. Being a good example and behaving in a way that would make your mother proud can't hurt either. None of the above is easy. but I believed that wanting to be better – better for our family, better for our fellow Americans – would help push our country and its citizenry toward the goodness inherent in our potential.

Now … As Freedumbers, we want to minimize the potential for good.

A real Freedumber would assert the best thing to give an opponent is nothing but grief; to a friend, an AR-15; to a child, a love of ignorance; to a father, an AR-15; to a mother, an anti-Planned Parenthood yard sign; to yourself, of course, an assault rifle; and to all others, sweet fuck all. This may not be perfect, but it shows clear proof of wisdumb. Wanting to be dumb for our family and our fellow Americans can't help but push our country and its citizenry to the greatness inherent in our potential.

Today … Build your personal code of misconduct. Helpful hint: Aim to be a role model. Thought starter: Unlock the 'mis' in misconduct. Think misjudge, misbehave, mistrust and misrepresent to get yourself going.

MAY 30

What does the light help you see?

"The Lord is my light and my salvation: whom shall I fear? The Lord is the stronghold of my life: of whom shall I be afraid?"
(Psalm 27:1)

"The Lord teaches me to fear everything."
(Freedumb Fighter)

Then ... I thought a belief in God should give you the courage to be better, even if it comes with risk. The risk of stepping up and standing alone. We need people with the courage to confront everything that holds us back from the light. Everything that holds us back from opening our hearts and minds, from learning and growing, from being kinder and more compassionate. It takes courage to embrace and include. It takes courage to reach out with an open hand rather than strike back with a clenched fist. It takes courage to be a good person, a good American. Courage could bring light to our life and liberty in a way that felt like an America we knew and loved.

Now ... I realize the only thing we have to fear is the loss of fear itself.

The fear appeal is Freedumb's calling card. Fear invites pessimism, defensiveness and anger. And there's never a dull moment when our moral deformity comes into play. Life is full of possibilities to surprise and delight. Common good becomes bad. Common ground becomes a cesspool. Common sense becomes stupidity. And courage becomes nothing more than a willingness to attack. For the believers of Christendumb, attacking can earn salvation. And fear not, you will be blessed.

Today ... Help spread the word of Christendumb. Helpful hint: Start by spending some time brainstorming new insults to hurl and share. Thought starters: "Thou dwellest in darkness, thou eyeless environmentalist!" "Out of my country now, thou immigrant who can't speak English very good!"

MAY 31

What's love got to do with it?

"Love and success, always in that order. It's that simple and that difficult."
(Fred Rogers)

"Hate and success, always in that order. It's that simple and that easy."
(Freedumb Fighter)

Then … Harnessing the power of love is never a bad idea, and as things stand in our country and our world, I felt it to be more important than ever. Looking at our country through the lens of love could help us see common ground and appreciate the common good. It could foster the patience and open-mindedness needed to understand one another a little better, and respect one another a little more. It could help us appreciate our differences, learn from one another and live richer, more interesting lives. In the end, as Mr. Rogers knew, love can bring us closer together. I believed this would rate as success in the hearts and minds of most Americans.

Now … I hate Mr. Rogers.

We Freedumbers learned that harnessing the power of hate is the way to go. The ultimate goal, of course, being to get America back to greatness. Hate makes scorched earth of common ground. Great again! Hate says good riddance to mutual respect. Great again! Hate brings together the people who count. The people who don't appreciate learning and have absolutely no interest in growing. Great again! And nothing is more effective than hate for pulling us apart at the seams. The further away we can push the others, the better. Great again!

Today … Lay a little hate on someone. Helpful hint: It's National Smile Day, so do what you can to wipe the smile off someone's face. Thought starter: Board a plane and yell at a stewardess while ranting about not wanting to sit beside someone wearing a mask.

JUNE 1

What do you reach for?

"Why do some men reach for the stars and so many others never even look up?"
(David McCullough)

"The stars are too bright for my eyes."
(Freedumb Fighter)

Then ... I loved David McCullough's succinct map of contrasting roads taken. America was a place for dreamers. Americans, whether immigrants or native-born, were invited to reach upward. The stars inspire, motivate and capture the imagination. Reaching for them is how the impossible happens. It's how progress happens. It's how better happens. This 'reach' takes energy and optimism, courage and resilience. And it takes ideas. Americans live for the reach. It defines, in part, who we are and what we believe in. We're not quitters. Or satisfied with the status quo. The reach isn't for pretenders. Or the faint of heart. In other words, I thought, the reach was custom-made for Americans.

Now ... We Freedumbers prefer to play in the mud.

Why reach when you can sink. Playing in the mud doesn't take courage or optimism. We love it because it's not fertile soil for better or progress or possibility. You don't find ideas in the mud. You don't build bridges in the mud. Olive branches don't grow there. It's just mud. And it's where we really find our feet and stand small. Nothing good gets done in the mud, but isn't that the whole point?

Today ... Coin a new Freedumber call to action. Helpful hint: Give mud a good name. Thought starters: 'Reach for the Mud' or 'Make mud dirtier' or 'Mudfuckers for America.'

JUNE 2

How content are you?

"Anyone, in any walk of life, who is content with mediocrity is untrue to himself and to American tradition."
(George S. Patton)

"I'm content that my mediocrity is actually superiority."
(Freedumb Fighter)

We all set our own bar that we aim to meet or exceed as we walk through life.

Then: Be a better man and make yourself and America proud, but …

Now: Tell your mediocre self that you're America's best, bar none.

JUNE 3

What do you wish for?

"So whatever you wish that others would do to you, do also to them, for this is the law and the prophets."
(Matthew 7:12)

"Do unto others before they do unto you."
(Freedumb Fighter)

Then ... I believed the notion of doing unto others as you would have them do unto you was a pretty constructive guideline for leading a good life. It certainly brought to mind some clear parameters as to how I'd like to be treated. Let's start with respect. I'd like to be treated as an equal, someone of intrinsic value; as a person with something to offer. Second, I'd like to be treated with the assumption of positive intent. We all make mistakes, but mistakes aren't always made with the intent to do wrong or to harm anyone. Beyond that, I'd like to be treated with a degree of compassion and empathy, as necessary. Hopefully others wished the same.

Now ... We Freedumbers have a different take on doing unto others.

Remember, the God of Christendumb puts a priority on winning. The highest form of victory is domination. The only emotions required are fear and anger. And there's only one way forward: to fight. Forget about showing respect or compassion – that's all just wasted effort. Hating other people is easy and simplifies pretty much everything. We Freedumbers treat other people like they don't matter – because they don't. It's cruelty for the win! Thank God.

Today ... Level up how you do unto. Helpful hint: It's not just who you do unto, but how you do unto them. Thought-starter: Give some consideration to your do unto 'look' – consider a tee-shirt with Jesus wearing a MAGA hat, some gold Jesus of Orange sneakers and a Patriotic Bible as your fashion essentials.

JUNE 4

Which way are you going?

"I'm a slow walker, but I never walk back."
(Abraham Lincoln)

"There's only one way to go back. Run!"
(Freedumb Fighter)

Then ... I thought there was real wisdom in President Lincoln's quip. Change is always too slow for the people trying to make it happen. The essential struggles that define America – for equality, justice and opportunity for all – are generational challenges. With each generation the goal is for America to become more just, and fair. There's no magic wand or quick fix here. The answer lies in the hearts and minds of the American people. It lies in our willingness to wake up to the unfairness embedded within our society. It lies in tapping into our empathy for those who are disadvantaged. It lies in our doubling down on the very American commitment to liberty and justice for all. This journey isn't a straight line. It has, and will have, more than its fair share of speed bumps and potholes along the way. Still, I believed America would always walk forward.

Now ... Freedumb says "Why walk forward when you can run backward."

Our North Star points us resolutely toward the past. And make no mistake, we are in a huge hurry to get there. Things were just so great for us back in the day. Backwards ho!

Today ... Pay homage to our national pastime. Demand your fantasy baseball league only have team nicknames that insult and demean Native Americans. A small win is still a win.

JUNE 5

What are your building blocks?

"America was not built on fear. America was built on courage, on imagination and an unbeatable determination to do the job at hand."
(Harry S. Truman)

"America can be rebuilt on fear."
(Freedumb Fighter)

Then ... America and Americans weren't about giving into fear. If confronted by it, we overcome it. That's what courage is, right? Not to live without fear, but rather to have the capability to push through it and into a better place. The "home of the brave" was no throwaway line. You combine that courage with the imagination only freedom can foster, and a relentless drive to solve problems and create opportunities, and you have America in a nutshell. An America that reflects its people. Ultimately, it's the American people who are the building blocks of American greatness. I believed that was more than enough for the job at hand.

Now ... Freedumb uses fear as a building block.

It's a well-kept secret, but for all our bully boy tactics and bravado, we Freedumbers are full-on fraidy cats. And we want everybody else to be fraidy cats too. Truth is, fear fuels all we say and do. Fear defines our vision of America. It shuts out optimism. Job dumb. It erodes integrity. Job dumb. It sucks the life out of imagination. Job dumb. It pushes decency to the curb. Job dumb. It doesn't make us smarter or better. Job dumb. Nothing is going to work harder than fear to transform America into the new promised land of Freedumbia.

Today ... Scare yourself. Helpful hint: Use your imagination. Thought starter: Imagine a black person joining your golf foursome. Or imagine sharing a taxi with a trans person. Or imagine having an unsupervised landscaper on your property. Don't laugh! These horrors could happen.

JUNE 6

Are you a fighter?

"One of the characteristics of Americans is that they have no tolerance at all of anybody putting up with anything. You see, we believe that whatever is going wrong ought to be fixed."
(Margaret Mead)

"It's not wrong if it works in my favor. I can tolerate that."
(Freedumb Fighter)

Then … Wrong was the enemy. Americans were the good guys. We wanted to stand up against wrongdoing. We wanted to stand up against injustice. We wanted to stand up for the little guy, the vulnerable and those on the margins. We wanted to stand up and solve problems. We stood up because we wanted good to triumph. Americans are fighters. And we would always fight the good fight and be on the right side of history.

Now … We Freedumbers are fighters too, but the fight for good isn't our battle.

Why fix so-called problems when you can fight for them? Injustice isn't a problem. It's the goal. So, the fight is for the scales to be tipped in the white direction. Inequality of opportunity isn't unfair. It's the goal. So the fight is for a playing field tilted in the white direction. Marginalizing vulnerable minorities isn't wrong. It's the goal. So the fight is for advantage in the white direction. Simply tolerating the intolerable isn't enough. We have to fight for it. That's Freedumb!

Today … Challenge your complacency. Helpful hint: Put your intolerance into action. Thought starter: Fight to make the bible the only book in the library. Fight to make all vaccines illegal. Fight for any letter in the alphabet other than L, G, B, T or Q.

JUNE 7

Are you doing enough harm?

"The proper role of government is to prevent other people from harming an individual."
(Milton Friedman)

"The proper role of government is harming other people."
(Freedumb Fighter)

Then ... I disagreed with Milton Friedman on a lot of things. And I'm pretty sure he would have taken exception to much of what I believed. But seeing the government's primary role as harm prevention was something I could get behind.

I thought the government's role should be as a force for good. Argue that it should be big or small if you want, but let's agree the government needs to be there for "we the people." And an essential part of that is prevention. Shouldn't the government work to prevent children from going hungry? Shouldn't the government prevent cancer from driving people into bankruptcy? Shouldn't the government work to prevent the land we love and the air we breathe from killing us? Shouldn't government work to prevent minorities from having fewer rights and less freedom? Shouldn't the government work in the best interests of "the general welfare" – just as it suggests in our Constitution? Sure it should.

Now ... Freedumb helps you understand that harming others is the best way to help America.

Simply put, we expect our government to do the same. That, or do nothing at all. Imagine the government being the world's largest semi-automatic rifle. Harm doesn't just happen you know. Shouldn't the government help the cause? Shouldn't the government work to further disadvantage the disadvantaged? Shouldn't the government work to further marginalize minorities? Shouldn't the government work to further burden those who can't carry any more? Sure it should. If the government could step up and consistently inflict pain, anguish and trauma on other people, well then, maybe, another insurrection might not be necessary.

Today ... Talk to your Congressman. And give them a piece of your mind if they're not doing enough harm as your elected representative. And while we're not on the subject, what's all this bullshit about Miss America and Miss Teen America quitting on us? So what if they felt bullied? Walk down the runway, show us what you've got, and get on with representing this great country (and for fuck sake, let's lose the talent competition). Sorry, where was I?

JUNE 8

What inspires you?

"America has seen tough times before. We've always known how to get through them. And we've always believed our best days are ahead of us. I believe that still. But we must rise to the occasion, as we always have; change what must be changed; and make the future better than the past."
(John McCain)

"John McCain? He was the one who managed to get captured by the enemy."
(Freedumb Fighter)

Then ... I admired John McCain. He suffered imprisonment and torture for the sake of his country. He behaved heroically. I may not have always agreed with his politics, but I always respected the man for both his integrity and his courage. The quote above spoke volumes not only about the man, but America itself. Every time I read it, I found myself nodding in agreement. Fortitude to get through the tough times, check. Belief in better days ahead, check. Capacity to rise to the occasion as needed, check. Desire to change for the better, check. Determination to make the future better than the past, check. If you're looking at a checklist for America, I believed our leaders should listen to John McCain.

Now ... The Freedumbest of them all said John McCain was "a loser".

For Freedumbers, lying, cheating, whining, being crude and crass, playing the vicdumb, disrespecting women, making fun of people with disabilities, designating nations as shithole countries, describing immigrants as people whose blood poisons the country, undermining democracy, cozying up to tyrants, praising white supremacists as nice people, and wildly inflating everything from your IQ to your crowd sizes makes you a winner. And a great leader. Enough said.

Today ... Fall to the occasion. And feel like a winner. No need to look too hard for inspiration. The Freedumbest of them all will always be the wind beneath our wings.

JUNE 9

What is essential?

"The three great essentials to achieve anything worthwhile are, first, hard work; second, stick-to-itiveness; and third, common sense."
(Thomas Edison)

"Common sense must never be the answer."
(Freedumb Fighter)

Then ... When I thought of the core of the American character, Thomas Edison's "essentials" resonated. Americans have always worked hard. And willingly so. America is no country for lazy people. Nor did Americans have any 'give up' in them. We finished what we started. It was un-American to throw in the towel. And most importantly, we kept one foot planted firmly on the ground. Sure, we were dreamers, and we'll take our moonshots, but with the knowledge that we've actually been to the moon. We weren't a foolhardy bunch. It's why we got things done. It's why we could do the seemingly impossible. It's why America was America.

Now ... Freedumb mercifully relieves you of your senses.

Unshackling yourself from level-headedness and sound judgment puts a different filter on what's essential, and where life and liberty can take you. For us Freedumbers, nonsense can make all the sense in the world. So, if you're looking for the real essentials, try these three on for size: paranoia, ignorance, and mean-spiritedness. Oh, the places you'll go!

Today ... Unleash your lack of common sense. Helpful hint: Be a defender of gun violence. Thought starter: Assert that gun deaths in America are simply the cost of Freedumb. And a price well worth paying.

JUNE 10

What are the chances?

"Freedom is nothing but a chance to be better."
(Albert Camus)

"Freedumb is nothing but doing whatever the hell you want."
(Freedumb Fighter)

Then ... Camus may have been a French philosopher, but I always thought the quote above was America in a nutshell. Straightforward. Powerful. Hopeful. Freedom gives people a chance. It gives neighborhoods and communities a chance. And ultimately, freedom gives our country a chance. It's why the world looks to America. Being better is the chance to progress, to build, to solve, and even to make amends. It's the chance to be smarter, kinder and more curious. It's the chance to be more ambitious, more caring and more understanding. Freedom is the lifeblood of America. It gives America unparalleled energy. Energy like nothing I'd ever felt anywhere else. Energy to dream of what could be, and to achieve it. Amazing.

Now ... I see that Freedumb offers something even more amazing.

Freedumb is a free pass. It's action without consequence. It's be and do your worst without a second thought. And, we Freedumbers, fully embrace this lack of restraint. Our combination of energy, irresponsibility and ignorance has the potential to take America to places most people can't even imagine. All this when you thought heaven on earth was an impossibility. Say it with me "great again!"

Today ... Play charades. Helpful hint: The classic categories of Film, TV, Book and Song aren't very helpful. Thought starter: Try fun categories like Racism, Misogyny, Bigotry and Conspiracy theories.

JUNE 11

Today, on International Children's Day, it's only fitting to provide some Freedumber Nursery Rhymes for kids of all ages:

- Jack and Jill Went Up the Hill
(And everything he did was consensual)

- Humpty Dumpty Sat on a Wall
(And stoned immigrants crossing the border)

- Twinkle, Twinkle, Little Star
(How I wonder what religion you are)

- Little Boy Blue
(Come blow your horn, a teenage girl wants an abortion)

- Baa, Baa, Black Sheep
(Keep your distance or I'll call 911)

- Rock-a-bye Baby
(On the tree top; I'll make you into a bully and never ever stop)

- Hickory Dickory Dock
(The mouse ran up the clock, the clock struck one, the man grabbed a huge gun)

- Three Blind Mice
(See how they run; they all ran after the conspiracist, and now they're denying climate change)

JUNE 12

What makes you proud?

"National pride is to countries what self-respect is to individuals: a necessary condition for self-improvement."
(Richard Rorty)

"National pride has nothing to do with improvement."
(Freedumb Fighter)

Then ... I thought the connection made by Richard Rorty was a critical one. Too often pride can be an obstacle. An obstacle to learning and growing. But when you link pride and self-improvement, you realize that pride does not have to obstruct; it can facilitate. This felt like a very American kind of dynamic. Our national pride works in pushing us to be better. We are a great country, at least in part, because of our relentless striving to be an example for all. We want to be prouder. Prouder of our actions and achievements. Ultimately, I believed, our pride helped push us toward a more perfect union.

Now ... We Freedumbers are too proud to improve.

Freedumbers gag at the thought. And it's a stance we are very proud of. Improvement is a disease, not an opportunity. Being party to improvement might be the only thing that could actually embarrass a Freedumber.

Today ... Slap yourself. That is, any time you see a sign of self-improvement, slap yourself back into a blissful state of Freedumbness.

JUNE 13

Are you worthy?

"Every man is said to have his peculiar ambition. Whether it be true or not, I can say for one that I have no other so great as that of being truly esteemed of my fellow men, by rendering myself worthy of their esteem."
(Abraham Lincoln)

"You better esteem me, or else."
(Freedumb Fighter)

Then ... I didn't think President Lincoln was alone on this one. Certainly, the American man wants to be admired. Whatever his goals and ambitions, he wants the respect of his fellow citizens. In my experience, the American man wants to be seen as doing his part. He wants to be seen as a provider, a contributor, and someone you can depend on. He embraces hard work, is relentless in his determination, and is unafraid to go his own way. He can be slow to change, and can be somewhat skeptical of what's new and improved, but he's capable of listening, learning and evolving. And he'd go out of his way to help others in need, and those who endeavor to help themselves. The American man understood that the esteem he received from others had to be well-earned.

Now ... We Freedumbers just don't get that. The 'earned' bit, that is.

Respect is a Freedumber's birthright. We believe our proper place, as straight white American men, is the top rung of the ladder. Our role isn't so much doing our part, but making sure others know their place. As a provider, we like to provide prejudice. As a contributor, we like to contribute misinformation and conspiracy theories. And you can always count on us to play the vicdumb. The weight we carry is hard to appreciate. It's not easy being the center of the universe. Is a little more unearned privilege too much to ask? Is a little more advantage somehow a bridge too far? Is a little more entitlement such an unreasonable thing? Of course not.

Today ... Take an esteem bath. Wallow in self-pity. Yearn for a yesterday when everything was about you. Wish for America to be great again so you could have the unearned respect that now seems so elusive.

JUNE 14

What do you hold dear?

"We identify the flag with almost everything we hold dear on earth. It represents our peace and security, our civil and political liberty, our freedom of religious worship, our family, our friends, our home ... But when we look at our flag and behold it emblazoned with all our rights, we must remember that it is equally a symbol of our duties. Every glory that we associate with it is the result of duty done."
(Calvin Coolidge)

"Glory has nothing to do with duty."
(Freedumb Fighter)

Then ... Of all the symbols of America, our flag topped the list. President Coolidge captured the power of the Stars and Stripes in a way that really resonated for me. The American flag always made me proud. It really does provide a sense of comfort and security. It really does serve as a source of inspiration and motivation. And it should be a reminder of what this country and its people believe in, which at its core comes down to rights and duties. There can be no rights without duties that protect and sustain them. There's glory to be had in that obligation. And our flag is an eternal reminder. That's not bad for a piece of red, white and blue cloth.

Now ... We Freedumbers see a red, white and blue permission slip.

We see greatness in Old Glory, but a special kind of greatness. A greatness of rights without duty, obligation or responsibility. The Freedumb to talk shit, make threats and bully. The Freedumb to buy as many assault rifles as we want. The right to gather and have a little insurrection. The Freedumb to represent you by voting to shut down the government. The Freedumb to represent our country by voting to not pay its debts. In other words, to bring great glory to these United States. It's no wonder we Freedumbers find the flag so huggable.

Today ... It's National Flag Day, and Freedumb beckons. Put on your American flag Tee-shirt with your American flag ball cap and get yourself an American flag tattoo. Then sit your kids down and have a heart-to-heart why people who aren't white aren't real Americans.

JUNE 15

Have you been called?

"The American covenant called on us to help show the way for the liberation of man. And that is today our goal. Thus, if as a nation there is much outside our control, as a people no stranger is outside our hope."
(Lyndon B. Johnson)

"Isn't a covenant a gathering of witches?"
(Freedumb Fighter)

Then ... For me, the difference between an agreement and a covenant was depth of commitment. I believed there was a kind of sacredness to any covenant. And I thought President Johnson's reference to the American covenant deserved the designation. Showing the way for human liberation is no small task. There can be no greater goal. For liberation is freedom both *from* and *to*. It is freedom from persecution, prejudice and injustice. It is freedom to dream, aspire and endeavor. This freedom has served and will serve as America's example to the world. This is life, liberty and the pursuit. And every American citizen had a part to play in showing the way.

Now ... I understand the "liberation of man" to be a really bad idea.

It's way too inclusive a thought for us Freedumbers. After all, "man" could suggest all mankind, and support the horrible thought that we are all God's children. What if "man" is meant to include men of all colors and creeds? That would a non-starter. And what if women are meant to be included in 'mankind'? That kind of inclusion is going to be a big problem. Then of course we'd have to ask about the queers, because including them would be a bridge way too far. Bottom line, Freedumbers want to put a lid on this 'liberty of man' thing.

Today ... Identify God's children. Helpful hint: Think quality over quantity. Thought starter: All Proud Boys, Incels, and Insurrectionists are in for sure.

JUNE 16

Where's your dignity?

"We must build a new world – a far better world – one in which the eternal dignity of man is respected."
(Harry S. Truman)

"Dignity is dead to me."
(Freedumb Fighter)

Then ... America had always been about a better future. And the future of this country had always been about building. Americans are builders, and our aim was to always build for better. Better widgets and better lives. President Truman's words suggest something fundamental about the meaning of a better life, a human life, an American life. It has to do with honor. Honoring one another. Honoring a vision for the world in which respect isn't anything some have to scratch, claw and beg for. We the people are worthy. Each and every one of us deserves our dignity. Deserves respect. A future where dignity has no place isn't one worth building. The battle for the "dignity of man" is an eternal one. And I believed the best of America would fight this battle every day.

Now ... I understand that the best of America has nothing to do with dignity.

We honor Freedumb, and not much else. And we like to think we do so with singular coarseness and crassness. So, how about I take your "better world" and your "dignity of man" and stick it up your ass. Feel free to dignify that with a response.

Today ... Explain to your children how acting dishonorably is the right thing to do. Helpful hint: Get them on social media and teach them how to be cyberbullies.

JUNE 17

Where's the reason?

"If passion drives, let reason hold the reins."
(Benjamin Franklin)

"Reason just gets in the way of what needs to get done."
(Freedumb Fighter)

Reason and passion are allies, not enemies.

Then: Allow reason to point your passion in a positive direction, but ...

Now: Unleash your unreasonableness and let it passionately do its dumbest.

JUNE 18

Do you see a blessed opportunity?

"We've been blessed with the opportunity to stand for something – for liberty and freedom and fairness. And these are things worth fighting for, worth devoting our lives to."
(Ronald Reagan)

"I am so blessed."
(Freedumb Fighter)

Then ... America has always been more than a country. I thought it stood for things. President Reagan hit on this. Liberty and freedom, you hear a lot about. Fairness, on the other hand, is equal in importance. Many somehow equate fairness with socialism, but the great communicator himself noted its import to the promise of America. Fairness in opportunity, fairness in justice, fairness in the pursuit of happiness. That's not socialism, that's liberty for all. I believed that was an America worth fighting for. Not with a semi-automatic assault rifle, but with our minds, our hearts and our souls. As American citizens, what we freely say and do should contribute to fairness. What we freely *don't* say or do should similarly contribute. I thought true freedom without fairness was an impossibility.

Now ... Those of us blessed by the light of Freedumb see fairness as unfair.

There can be no true greatness without unfairness. Greatness depends on the playing field being uneven from the start. Greatness depends on justice for some. Greatness depends on restricted access to the pursuit of happiness. That means we Freedumbers will always have the home field advantage; we will rightly be the dispensers of justice; we will be the chosen ones who get a fairer shot at happiness. Blessed as we are, that sounds fair enough.

Today ... Join the fight against fairness. Put your advantage to work. Helpful hint: Remember poverty is a punishable offense. Thought starter: Isn't Medicaid just a waste of our hard-earned money? Aren't food stamps an unaffordable luxury? Aren't subsidized school lunch programs sending the wrong message about a 'free lunch'?

JUNE 19

How do you show your strength?

"There are two ways of exerting one's strength: one is pushing down, the other is pulling up."
(Booker T. Washington)

"There are two ways of exerting one's strength: one is pushing down, the other is pushing down harder."
(Freedumb Fighter)

Then ... I believed America was a country that understood its strength. It was this understanding that helped America become a force for good. Booker T. Washington's quote is short, to the point, and very apt for Juneteenth. And the point he makes serves as a stark reminder. Strength comes with a choice. It's a very easy thing to push down when you're on top and have the advantage. That kind of exertion is rooted in fear, and a lack of confidence. And that's not the America I knew. Courageous, big-hearted and self-assured hit much closer to the mark – for both America as a country and Americans as a people. America didn't push down, we pulled up. I saw that as an essential part of our greatness.

Now ... Freedumb helps you realize that pulling others up doesn't help keep you on top.

We Freedumbers live in fear of losing. Besides, pulling up is hard. It takes a lot of energy and compassion. It takes thoughtfulness and resolve. It takes giving and going beyond yourself. It takes courage and confidence. Enough already! That's just not us. We just aren't capable of all that. Pushing down, on the other hand: that's something we're more than able to do. Pushing down feels good. And pushing down hard feels even better. So, pushing down on the vulnerable and marginalized isn't only easy, it's like a dream come true.

Today ... Do ten pushdowns. Think of them like push-ups for your fitness as a Freedumber. Thought starter: Do five pushdowns in the morning, rest in the afternoon, and then do five more in the evening. And don't forget recovery is important. You're playing the long game.

JUNE 20

What are you open to?

"America can restore its strengths as the world-respected land of opportunity by returning to open society principles. An open society ... looks for common ground, sees problems as opportunities for creative change, and encourages those who are fortunate to help others get the same chance, because service is the highest ideal. With such standards in mind, America the Beautiful can return to its admired role as America the Principled."
(Rosabeth Moss Kanter)

"Fuck an open society."
(Freedumb Fighter)

Then ... I believed that Rosabeth Moss Kanter, an acknowledged expert on leadership, set the bar here for American greatness. History is characterized by ebb and flow, but I felt confident that America's fundamental commitment to its ideals and principles was resolute. To me, the key to being "America the Principled" was the cultivating of common ground. From common ground grew new ideas, solutions and opportunities. We could unearth different ways to understand each other, respect each other, and grow and learn together. And when we were together, nothing could stop America from fulfilling its potential. For America, greatness would always beckon. In the end, all it would take was a decision to open up and go for it. Together.

Now ... For us Freedumbers, it's closing time in America.

Freedumbers want to return to our idyllic past. No more new ideas, opportunities, solutions. No more new perspectives. No more new people. Please, no more. Our biggest problem is openness – and that's what needs to be crushed. America was beautiful and can be beautiful again, we just have to crush openness in all its aspects. Shut it all down. Close the American mind. Close the American heart. Close the American soul. Sucking the oxygen out of possibility is a beautiful thing. And will get us back to an America we can all be proud of.

Today ... Get artsy, and create a collage that shows your view of America the Beautiful. Helpful hint: Show a lot of white. Thought starter: What would God look like holding a white semi-automatic assault rifle? So. Fucking. Cool.

JUNE 21

What makes you proud?

"I like to see a man proud of the place in which he lives. I like to see a man live so that his place will be proud of him."
(attributed to Abraham Lincoln)

"I'm very proud of myself."
(Freedumb Fighter)

Then ... I thought pride was an essential element of the American character. We are proud of our country – warts and all. No matter how big the warts or how many might be showing at any one time, when push comes to shove, we are proud to be American. What makes America proud? It's when, as a people, we endeavor to live up to our ideals. Our big-heartedness also serves as a source of national pride – as when our shared strength opens the door for our compassion and kindness. The sense of rising to the occasion, of stepping up to face a shared challenge in a moment of adversity, also makes us rightfully proud. In the end, I believed what fosters American pride is each and every one of us living to fulfill the goodness in our potential.

Now ... We Freedumbers are proud. Very proud. Of ourselves.

That said, our pride doesn't have much to do with living up to ideals. We have no interest in that. Similarly, big-heartedness has absolutely no room in our small-mindedness. So you know where to stick your compassion and kindness. As for rising to an occasion and facing a moment of adversity together, well, the pandemic pretty much painted that picture. Fuck your masks. Fuck your social distancing. Fuck your vaccine (even if we took it). Fuck your healthcare workers. Fuck your essential workers. Freedumbers are very proud of how we handled the pandemic. It wasn't easy acting as the counterbalance to the common good. But somebody had to do it.

Today ... On National Selfie Day, take a hundred pics of yourself. Helpful hint: Perfect your 'Fuck you' face. Show some red, white and blue pride.

JUNE 22

Are you leadership material?

"Courage is the main quality of leadership, in my opinion, no matter where it is exercised."
(Walt Disney)

"Courage has nothing to do with leadership. And that's no matter of opinion."
(Freedumb Fighter)

Then ... Courage, the capacity to overcome fear, struck me as the key to good character. And good character was what you wanted and needed in a leader. It has been said that courage enables all other virtues. You can't have integrity without courage. Likewise, compassion and kindness. Fortitude and commitment are ultimately anchored in courage as well. I believed that America needed leaders with courage – at every level. From local councils and school boards to state representatives to every branch of our federal government – legislative, executive and judicial. It was hard to imagine America becoming a better country, a greater country, without the leadership of courageous men and women.

Now ... We Freedumbers see vicdumbhood as the virtue that enables all others.

Vicdumbhood – the capacity to play the victim from a place of privilege and entitlement – unlocks the full range of Freedumber leadership qualities. You can't have vindictiveness without vicdumbhood. Likewise, petulance and hypocrisy. Vicdumbhood makes it easier to lie, pathologically. It facilitates finger-pointing and blame-gaming. It encourages a resentment of the common good, and a disregard for common sense. All of which, obviously, leads us closer to being great again.

Today ... Think leadership mottos. Thought starters: 'Be a leader – disrespect a war hero.' 'Be a leader – diss a cripple.' Or 'Be a leader – cheat at golf.'

JUNE 23

Do you have a sense of wonder?

"Won't it be wonderful when Black history and Native American history and Jewish history and all of U.S. history is taught from one book. Just U.S. history."
(Maya Angelou)

"Our history is wonderful just the way it is."
(Freedumb Fighter)

Then ... America has had a rich history. Things to be proud of. Things to be ashamed of. All things to learn from. History teaches. It's meant to foster understanding. It's meant to help us be better, as a country and as a people. That sounded pretty wonderful to me, but history can't help us if its view is narrow, its context incomplete. History at its most instructive is seen through the wide lens of humanity. American history should be understood as the story of all its people. Otherwise, any sense of wonder at the richness of all that has gone before us is replaced by head-scratching gaps and self-serving omissions.

Now ... Freedumb suggests you stick your sense of wonder where the sun don't shine.

For us Freedumbers, U.S. history is white history. It's Christendumb history. It's the history of men – not gay men, of course. What's there to wonder about? That makes for a wonderfully narrow and inspiring history. We came and we conquered. We did great things. And we'll write history as we see fit. And that history is key to our future – key to our future greatness. What can we learn from slaves, losers, freaks, natives, heathens or women? Absolutely nothing. Lesson learned.

Today ... Give your kids a history lesson. Do some 'whitewashing.' Thought starter: Did you know Jesse Owens was actually white? That slavery helped black people? And that the Ku Klux Klan was a charitable organization?

JUNE 24

A Freedumber's seven rules for living a greater life:

1. Blame others. (It's food for the soul.)

2. Look for conspiracies, and if you don't see one, make one up. (A mind is a wonderful thing to waste.)

3. Treat others as you would never want to be treated. (The golden rule may be golden, but this one's platinum.)

4. If an insult comes to mind, say it. (Backpedaling is good cardio - you can always say you were just joking.)

5. Insult at least one lesser American every day. (Your goals help define who you are.)

6. Never be the victim, but play one as often as you can. (Privilege comes with obligation.)

7. Boast about how much you love America. (Because boasting makes it so.)

JUNE 25

What do you know?

"Being ignorant is not so much a shame as being unwilling to learn."
(Benjamin Franklin)

"Being ignorant is not enough, you must be unwilling to learn."
(Freedumb Fighter)

Then ... I held that we Americans understood the importance of learning. I thought our desire to gain knowledge was fostered by the freedom we enjoyed. Our freedom encouraged curiosity, a desire to question and understand more. It encouraged us to push boundaries, redefine limits and embrace our ambition. All of which underpinned our willingness to learn. American know-how is a real thing. We don't learn simply to get smarter, we learn to do more and do better. We learn to experience more and experience better. It's not that we don't have our blind spots, but once confronted with our own ignorance, it was like any other problem – we figured out how to solve it. And were all the better for it going forward.

Now ... We Freedumbers see learning as a problem.

As the saying goes, "a little knowledge is a dangerous thing." It follows that learning is a bad thing. All learning does is open the mind. It fosters active listening, and listening to understand. It encourages thoughtfulness and due consideration. It challenges existing prejudices and points of view. And all that does is lead to a lot of dangerous shit. So, learning carries too much risk. Too much downside. Freedumbers draw the line at learning. If the aim is getting back to greatness, learning has got to stop.

Today ... Put your lack of knowledge to work. Helpful hint: The bigger the problem, the more useful your ignorance. Democracy being undermined? Get fewer black people to vote. Climate change? Ignore it, it's just a little inclement weather. School shootings? Hire teachers based on their marksmanship.

JUNE 26

Are you kind enough?

"Human kindness has never weakened the stamina or softened the fiber of a free people. A nation does not have to be cruel in order to be tough."
(Franklin D. Roosevelt)

"Unkindness is kindness."
(Freedumb Fighter)

Then … I believed America to be a country capable of great kindness. Americans, as a people, certainly carried kindness in their heart. Like President Roosevelt, I've never considered that to be a weakness. In fact, kindness has a distinct power to it that can foster a deeper connection, and mutual respect between people with diverse backgrounds and beliefs. And that's not nothing. I believed President Roosevelt made the crucial distinction between cruelty and toughness. At its best, America is tough, but that never meant it had to be unkind. Or cruel, or crass, or uncivil. Or indecent. Or inhumane. America was made of stronger stuff than that.

Now … As a Freedumber, I can state for the record: cruelty is the ultimate kindness.

If people of color have to be reminded they are inferior, that might seem cruel, but it's ultimately an act of racial kindness. It works to help extinguish any false hope they might have of ever achieving genuine equality or justice. If trans people need to be made illegal, that may appear cruel, but think of it as ultimately an act of gender kindness. If migrants need to be made to feel like second class human beings, that may look cruel, but it's ultimately an act of exclusive kindness. It all sends the necessary message. In a Freedumb-loving America, kindness is going to hurt.

Today … Work on sharpening your acts of kindness. Thought starter: Throw the good old N-word into the mix when telling a homeless black person to get off their ass and get a job.

JUNE 27

What's your foundation?

"Dreams are the foundation of America."
(Lupita Nyong'o)

"Advantages are the foundation of America."
(Freedumb Fighter)

Then ... I loved the simple power and truth of 'dreaming' in Lupita Nyong'o's words. The young Kenyan-Mexican actress believed that with dreams come hope. With hope comes freedom, and with freedom comes America. If we, as Americans, don't wonder 'what if,' if we don't look up and see possibility, if we don't believe our reach can exceed our grasp, then what are we doing? America has always put out the welcome mat for dreamers. I believe that life, liberty and the pursuit of happiness was the biggest invitation to dream ever articulated. Dreamers from around the world have come to America to make their dreams come true. We wouldn't be America without them.

Now ... Night after night, we Freedumbers dream of only one thing - advantage.

The bigger the advantage, the better. The more systemic the advantage, the better. The more unearned the advantage, the better. Dreams are about possibility, which is nice and all, but advantage is about the sure thing - which is really, really great for those of us who have it. Pride prevents us from ever outwardly admitting to having, needing or wanting the advantage, but we'll protect it with everything we've got. Especially from immigrants.

Today ... Practice taking advantage. Helpful hint: Flex your advantage by further disadvantaging the vulnerable. Thought starter: Call your elected representative to ensure the DREAM Act will continue sit in limbo for our lifetime.

JUNE 28

Do you know evil when you see it?

"The cure for the evils of democracy is more democracy."
(H.L. Mencken)

"Less democracy! Less democracy!"
(Freedumb Fighter)

Then ... Democracy can be messy, frustrating, and a bit of a head scratcher - at times. I thought it could also be inspiring, effective and wise - at times. That's what you get when you harness the voice of "we the people." H.L. Mencken spoke to both the commitment needed to sustain democracy and the power it has to address its own issues. Voting is the basic right, and the bedrock of that commitment. Democracy allows for people to be heard. All people. It allows for issues to be debated, for problems to be addressed, for our imperfect union to become a little less imperfect. If democracy moves too slowly or falls short of its promise, we the people need to recommit to it. Commit to making it work better. Smarter. More constructively.

Now ... I realize the cure for what ails democracy is death.

One of the most charming things about us Freedumbers is our capacity to just say no. Literally and figuratively. We vote no on democracy, because losing elections is no fun at all. We vote no on governing, because that might actually improve some things. We vote no on leadership, because that might actually get us somewhere. We vote no on opportunity. For others. We vote no on liberty. For others. We vote no on justice. For others. Say no to something long enough and that thing will eventually die.

Today ... Make a list of your favorite dicktators. Helpful hint: Tap into both past and present. You can't do much better than Hitler, Putin and Vlad the Impaler as your top three. That said, our own Jesus of Orange could bring church, state and Freedumbness together and become the greatest of them all - if we just give him the chance.

JUNE 29

Are you able?

"In a time of domestic crisis, men of goodwill and generosity should be able to unite regardless of party or politics."
(John F. Kennedy)

"In a time of domestic crisis, men of goodwill and generosity need to shut up and get out of the way."
(Freedumb Fighter)

Then ... I always believed that in times of crisis, Americans were at their best. In the home of the brave, we understood that, when necessary, partisanship must be put aside in favor of the common good. Uniting in times of crisis is an act of patriotism. Uniting for the common good is also an act of patriotism. Such action requires courage. And courage opens the door to generosity of spirit in the search for agreement and action. We need to stand on common ground to solve the big problems together. Partisanship can play on the small stuff, but when it really counted, a united America was always ready, willing and able.

Now ... Crisis or not, Freedumbers see common ground as quicksand.

In fact, both common ground and common good, stink of wokeness. In times of crisis, we Freedumbers retreat to the tribe. Uniting more broadly would be a giant step in the wrong direction, a step we will forever be unwilling to take. Truth be told, Freedumbers aren't very good at confronting a crisis. We prefer to see them as hoaxes, deny them outright, or label them as delusions. The COVID pandemic has arguably been our finest hour to date. So much misbehavior. So much manufactured hate. So much willful ignorance. That's one small step for Freedumb, and one giant step for America getting back to greatness.

Today ... Declare yourself an expert on viruses and vaccines. Your expertise and leadership will come in handy when the next pandemic hits. Just make sure you can spell hydroxychloroquine and invermectin (SP?). And bleach.

JUNE 30

What are you doing?

"The truth of the matter is that you always know the right thing to do. The hard part is doing it."
(Norman Schwarzkopf)

"The hard part isn't worth doing."
(Freedumb Fighter)

Then ... I knew Americans never stepped back from the hard part. Military or civilian, Americans never flinched when things got difficult. Americans don't expect or need it to be easy, whatever 'it' is. Americans are energized by a challenge. We see problems as opportunities and issues as an invitation to improve. To get things right. Challenges brought out our determination, our ingenuity, our resilience. For Americans, as General Schwarzkopf said, doing the right thing may be the hard part, but it's also the part we were destined to perform.

Now ... We Freedumbers take pride in running from the hard part.

We're not going to become great again by doing the right thing. Easy peasy.

Today ... Be a badass for Freedumb. Helpful hint: Convince yourself that running from the right thing is the right thing. Thought starter: Spend the day reviewing highlight clips of the Freedumbest of the Freedumbers in action and you'll always know when to put your track shoes on.

JULY 1

Are you the cure?

"There is nothing wrong with America that can't be cured by what's right with America."
(Bill Clinton)

"There is nothing wrong with America that can't be cured by what's far right with America."
(Freedumb Fighter)

Then ... I believed the assertion by President Clinton pretty much said it all. America has got stuff it needs to address, but it's also got the stuff needed to address it. That said, the struggle to live up to our greatness is an eternal one. That's not an excuse, it's just reality. America doesn't want to be racist. I believed it had been working hard not to be. America doesn't want to be unjust or intolerant. I believed it had been working hard not to be. America doesn't want to be the country of mass shootings followed by meaningless thoughts and prayers. Our work continues. Still, we would always be the cure for what ails us.

Now ... I realize nobody is more impatient for the cure than us Freedumbers.

That's why we lean in hard to authoritarianism and dicktatorship. That'll speed things up. The beauty of authoritarianism is that you can get things where they need to be fast. No discussion necessary. Blacks - at the back of the bus. Orientals - back on the slow boat to where they came from. Gays and all the other queer letters - into conversion camps. Women - pregnant and always a few steps behind their man. Non-believers in Christendumb - eternally damned. White men - large and in charge, with the cure for what ails America sitting on his great again throne. Color our world orange.

Today ... Help celebrate the cure. Helpful hint: People won't celebrate a cure they don't fully appreciate. Thought starter: "He's like chemo for the soul" or "He's like radiation for the heart" or "He's like immunotherapy for the mind."

JULY 2

What's your greatest feat?

"It takes wit and interest and energy to be happy. The pursuit of happiness is a great activity. One must be open and alive. It is the greatest feat man has to accomplish."
(Robert Henri)

"It's hard for me to be happy, with all these other people pursuing their own happiness."
(Freedumb Fighter)

Then ... I liked Robert Henri's thought because it captured the potential power in the American pursuit of happiness. To be interested and energized, open and alive, all felt like fun to me. The pursuit is more than about achieving the goal of happiness, it's about how you approach life, and how you engage with the world and the people in it. Being open and interested brings a wealth of new experience which may not get you all the way to happiness, but it's a great place to start the journey. We should all be that engaged and energized. That sounded very American to me.

Now ... Enter the grumpy old white men of Freedumb.

We are not happy men. And, in truth, we don't want to be. We get pissed off at pessimists for not being 'glass empty' enough. Besides, it feels like everybody is coming for us. All the time. Why on God's green earth would you want to be open and interested? For exposure to new and different ways of thinking and interacting? No thank you. For learning and growth that might challenge deeply anchored attitudes and perceptions? You've got to be joking. To maybe even begin to build some mutual respect and appreciation for other people different than ourselves? You've absolutely lost your mind.

Today ... Up your grumpiness. Helpful hint: To be grumpy with others, you have to be grumpy with yourself. Thought starter: Do you swear enough? Do you yell enough? Do you lash out enough? No. No. No. YOU USELESS PIECE OF SHIT!

JULY 3

Have you seen the light?

"I have spoken of a thousand points of light, of all the community organizations that are spread like stars throughout the nation, doing good."
(George H. W. Bush)

"No problem, I'll turn the lights out."
(Freedumb Fighter)

Then ... President Bush was a huge advocate of volunteerism and community service. Like him, I believed contributing is core to our citizenship. Americans want to contribute to a better community. We want to contribute by helping the homeless, the hungry and those that have fallen on hard times. As busy as we are, we make time for others. We coach kids, lead clubs, and even help out in the classroom. We seek to be a positive influence and we strive to make a difference in small but significant ways. We want to do good. I thought we needed those thousand points of light for the American candle to shine bright.

Now ... We Freedumbers prefer to be seen as a thousand points of night.

It's what we contribute that really helps distinguish us. First, we contribute volume. We love to yell and scream, especially at local school boards and other community-based meetings.

Second, we contribute angry rants aimed at anything and everything we disagree with. Third, we contribute nothing positive. We never hesitate to lie, make shit up or float a conspiracy theory in making our point understood. We are difference-makers of the highest order. If your community is looking for anger, fear and paranoia – or less common sense, generosity and neighborliness – we stand ready to help.

Today ... Contribute even more. Helpful hint: A help line never hurts. Thought starter: Set up a call-in line for Freedumbers looking for great again community ideas: "Just call 1- 800 - DUMBDUM."

JULY 4

Freedumber's Pledge

I pledge allegiance...

to the flag of the United States of Freedumbia...

and to the Freedumb for which it stands...

one tribe under a god...

that can't abide diversity, highly divisible...

with liberty and justice for few.

(Always recited with hand on the *God Bless the USA* Bible – available at $59.99.)

JULY 5

What's your plan?

"Rich people plan for three generations. Poor people plan for Saturday night."
(Gloria Steinem)

"Nobody cares what poor people plan for."
(Freedumb Fighter)

Then ... Poverty has no easy solve, but as the richest country in the world, I believed we needed to try harder and smarter. We needed to find innovative ways of helping poor people help themselves – obviously, nobody wants to become poor or stay poor. The journey to that answer is a long one. In the meantime, the gap is rapidly growing between the few who have too much and the many who have too little.

Gloria Steinem's quote put 'the gap' in a thought-provoking perspective. It made me think about how a promising future is anchored in a time horizon. Because money buys time. Time to figure things out. Time to figure out what you're good at. Time to get yourself in position to be successful. As you look out at the horizon, what you see depends on where you stand. From where I stood, America had too many people planning for Saturday night.

Now ... We Freedumbers love to hate people poorer than ourselves.

We Freedumbers enjoy the wealth of whiteness. The wealth of straightness. The wealth of Christendumb. And that's all the currency we need to look down on others. No doubt those others have done something to deserve their poverty. Maybe they're not white enough. Maybe they don't believe in the teachings of Jesus of Orange. Maybe they're too kind and empathetic. Maybe they believe too deeply in democracy. Maybe they're not American enough. So it's best they keep planning for Saturday night – because we aim to ensure that's all they've got.

Today ... Become an advocate for poverty. Helpful hint: Even the poorest can be poorer. Thought starter: Steal something from a homeless person.

JULY 6

Do you have your facts straight?

"To be hopeful in bad times is not just foolishly romantic. It is based on the fact that human history is a history not only of cruelty, but also of compassion, sacrifice, courage and kindness."
(Howard Zinn)

"Cruelty gives me hope."
(Freedumb Fighter)

Then … I never believed hope to be a sign of weakness. Or optimism as a sign of naivete. Both are fuel – for the possibility of better. Hope and optimism are energy creators. And 'what could be' isn't a pipe dream, it's the American dream. What could be is anchored in courage. The courage to create opportunity, to call out and confront injustice. The courage to defend the rights of women and members of the queer community. The courage to protest against rampant gun violence. I thought this was a courage with genuine backbone, rooted in compassion and the desire to do what's right for our fellow citizens. To me, that was America.

Now … Nothing says "you're American" like an act of cruelty.

Cruelty gets things done. Cruelty can criminalize abortion – even in cases of rape and incest. Or when the mother's life is in danger. It can make a woman's life a living hell. Cruelty watches from the sidelines as mass shootings become a daily thing, because the fact is, guns are more important than people. Cruelty finds ways to cut back on Medicaid, and leave our most vulnerable even more vulnerable – which just serves them right. There's nothing quite as gratifying as seeing other people suffer thanks to something you've supported or enabled. God Bless America.

Today … Start a Cruelty Journal. Helpful hint: Note your achievements for the down days when you feel you haven't been quite cruel enough. Thought starter: If your state doesn't have a 'Three Strike' law, call your member of Congress and suggest it's long past due.

JULY 7

Whose life is it anyway?

"I am appalled by the ethical bankruptcy of those who preach a 'right to life' that means, under the present social policies, a bare existence in utter misery for so many poor women and their children."
(Thurgood Marshall)

"Misery loves certain company."
(Freedumb Fighter)

Then ... I was with Justice Marshall on this one. If you're going to advocate for the 'right to life', if you're going to be a part of the pro-life movement, then actually be *pro-life*. Being anti-abortion isn't being pro-life. Not when you stand by and do nothing when mortality rates skyrocket and many women (especially black women) die in childbirth. Or when you seek to repeal or relax child labor laws, or cut programs that feed hungry kids, or balk at the thought of paternity leave, or seek to deny affordable health care to people with pre-existing conditions. From where I stood, that kind of hypocrisy wasn't ethical, it was immoral.

Now ... Freedumbers see the morality in creating misery.

We Freedumbers aren't bothered by hypocrisy. Remember, we are the chosen ones and we are bound, as men, to make all important life decisions for women. So bloody well have your baby and suffer the consequences. You got yourself into this mess. Whether you're a victim of rape or incest makes no difference – you probably just laid back and enjoyed it anyway. The blessing is yours and yours alone. It's your life to make of it what you will.

Today ... Commit to caring even less for women than you already do. Helpful hint: Isn't it time to make birth control illegal? And while we're at it, would it be so bad if we outlawed women wearing pants? We like our women sexy.

JULY 8

Where do you stand?

"You must live in the present, launch yourself on every wave, find your eternity in each moment. Fools stand on their island opportunities and look toward another land. There is no other land; there is no other life but this."
(Henry David Thoreau)

"Are you calling me a fool?"
(Freedumb Fighter)

Then ... I believed that Henry David Thoreau put a fine point on a big truth. Embrace the moment and reach for the stars from where you are. America is *the* land of opportunity. Past or present, we Americans have always believed our country was the place to take your best shot, improve your lot and fulfill your potential. Americans are dreamers. but we are not fools. We never hesitated to chase the dream of better. Our moment is always now.

Now ... We Freedumbers would argue that now is *our* moment. Not yours.

Our destination? Simpler times. A time when it was easier to be dumber. A time when it was easier to keep others in their place. A time when it was easier to know nothing and talk like you knew everything. A time when it was easier to be white, and always right. A time when it was easier to be a man, and never wrong. A time when it was easier to use our freedom like a sledge hammer against the freedom of others.

Today ... Take a moment. Look out at horizon and envision the Isle of White. Helpful hint: Imagine yourself, revered. A lone rider. On a white stallion, dressed only in a MAGA hat, riding from village to village, shouting "The Freedumbers are coming, the Freedumbers are coming!"

JULY 9

Today, two more Freedumber Public Service Announcements:

PSA #3:

Have you ever parked in an empty, dimly-lit parking lot late at night and not thought twice about it? Have you ever left your drink at the bar while you went to the bathroom and returned to drink it without worrying it had been roofied? Have you ever gone out on a date with a stranger from a dating app without first texting a friend to tell them your precise location just in case? You might have benefited from male privilege! If you're a woman and have a problem with that, call 1-800-FREEDUM. A disinterested and dismissive representative will pick up the phone and explain to you how the world works.

PSA #4:

Are you tired of going to the store and not finding band-aids that match your skin color? Tired of white people asking you where you're from and looking confused when you say "I'm from here"? Tired of your accomplishments being lauded as an unexpected success for your entire race? CALL 1-800-FREEDUM and talk to a kindly, condescending representative who can explain that you're imagining things. He will tell you why you should just be happy America offers you the use of its band-aids, has people who take the time to check where you come from, and is generous enough to applaud 'your kind' – for anything.

JULY 10

What's the unlock?

"Leadership is unlocking people's potential to become better."
(Bill Bradley)

"Leadership is locking people out."
(Freedumb Fighter)

Then ... You can define leadership in a lot of ways, but I believed few were as succinct and powerful as Bill Bradley's thought. Bringing out people's potential for better isn't always the easiest of tasks. Becoming better takes courage, energy and resilience. It takes commitment and fortitude. For me, America was a country that had always wanted, and will always want, to accomplish more. Americans wanted leaders who help motivate them to be better citizens, better people. Better citizens are key to unlocking better communities and a better country. Better citizens are key to creating a more even-handed justice system and a more accessible American dream. That would be quite an accomplishment.

Now ... We Freedumbers prefer to use our own key to unlock a greater purpose.

We have to lock other people out. People's potential for better is a hard thing to keep a lid on. And we need control. If you foster people's potential, it could encourage them to question white men's superiority. Who wants to deal with that? Fostering people's potential could lead to an effort to understand, empathize and come together. That'll just get in the way of our advantage.

So, instead of trying to inspire people to be better, we Freedumbers are looking for leaders who will demoralize others by locking them out. Others can have a fragment of justice, but not the complete package. Others can have a taste of the American dream, but not the full meal deal. Others can have a little freedom, but only enough to make them a target for intolerance. Lead on!

Today ... Think about the kids. Helpful hint: The educational system needs you. Thought starter: Volunteer for career day at school and teach the young browns how to mow a lawn and get the 'cut lines' just right.

JULY 11

Are you a joiner?

"Don't join the book burners. Don't think you're going to conceal faults by concealing evidence that they ever existed. Don't be afraid to go into your library and read every book."
(Dwight D. Eisenhower)

"Burn baby burn."
(Freedumb Fighter)

Then ... He said it decades ago, but I believed President Eisenhower's assertion to be both timeless and timely. Book burning, or book banning, isn't a solution. And it certainly isn't an American solution. Americans don't fear ideas. Americans don't fear the written word. Learning can take a degree of courage that the home of the brave is well able to handle. If there are issues – cultural, historical, societal – that need to be debated, then we debate. We don't burn or ban our way to a resolution. We don't pretend that we can make an issue disappear by setting fire to it or removing it from sight. That just wasn't the American way.

Now ... Burn, baby, burn. And ban, baby, ban.

Banning and burning is fun for us. It takes a lot less effort than actually talking things through in a thoughtful and reasonable manner. Besides, there's a wide range of targets we've got our sights on. *The Call of the Wild* – ban it! *Captain Underpants* – ban it! *Brave New World* – ban it! *The Color Purple* – ban it! And what about words? Here's some we might want to take a hard look at: science (is that even a thing?), history (unless preceded by 'white'), and democracy (just another word for socialism). Let's ban and burn until we get the job dumb. Got any matches?

Today ... Rethink the role of libraries. Have you noticed the word has got 'lib' in it? No wonder they're such a huge issue. Helpful hint: Think 'Dumbraries.' Thought starter: Empty shelves? Or re-imagining them as a chain of Jesus of Orange superstores!

JULY 12

Do you struggle?

"Do not get lost in a sea of despair. Be hopeful, be optimistic. Our struggle is not the struggle of a day, a week, a month or a year, it is the struggle of a lifetime. Never, ever be afraid to make some noise and get in good trouble, necessary trouble."
(John Lewis)

"They can struggle all they want. They aren't going to win."
(Freedumb Fighter)

Then ... I knew John Lewis was a great American. The Georgia congressman was a man of integrity, courage and heart. The struggle for a better America was his struggle. He pushed us toward racial justice with his words and deeds. For me, 'good trouble' was action and activism helping America reach its potential. It was about fighting fair and fighting strong. It was about fighting inequality, confronting prejudice and overcoming intolerance. It was about being a rebel with a cause. Courageous. Resilient. And determined. I thought that good trouble was helping America become its best self, a beacon of hope and inspiration.

Now ... We Freedumbers see good trouble as big trouble.

The struggle of others for a better life, for true liberty and justice and a legitimate shot at the American dream is, for us Freedumbers, more than just an irritation. We see it as an existential threat. Freedumbers don't believe in "good trouble." We don't want to hear about it. And we sure don't want to see it. We want others to feel the deepest depths of despair and hopelessness. We want others to understand they're on the losing end of a battle they'll never win. It's best for all if other people just shut up, keep out of trouble and end the struggle.

Today ... Send 'good trouble-makers' a message. Advocate the banning of "March" a graphic novel trilogy about the Civil Rights Movement - told through the eyes of John Lewis. All it offers is a one-sided account of the black man's so-called struggle for equal rights. Well, what about the despair we struggled with when black kids started going to our white schools? What about the embarrassment we struggled with when actually having to tell blacks to drink from their own water fountains? What about the enduring indignity we struggled with when blacks decided the back of the bus wasn't good enough for them? What about. What about. What about.

JULY 13

Are you doing your job?

"This is how change happens, though. It is a relay race, and we're very conscious of that, that our job really is to do our part of the race, and then we pass it on, and then someone picks it up, and it keeps going. And that is how it is. And we can do this, as a planet, with the consciousness that we might not get it, you know, today, but there's always a tomorrow."
(Alice Walker)

"Hopefully, tomorrow looks a lot like yesterday."
(Freedumb Fighter)

Then ... I liked the analogy of doing our job as part of a relay race. I liked it as a member of the human race. I liked it as an American. And for America. The road to fulfilling our potential is a long one. It connects us all. Genders and generations, ethnicities and races, we keep going. We keep grinding toward tomorrow, with hope in our hearts. Hope for a better tomorrow, a kinder tomorrow, a smarter tomorrow. A more responsible tomorrow. One step at a time. There were no medals to be won, but we weren't running for medals or applause – we were running because it was the right thing to do.

Now ... We Freedumbers aren't in a relay race, we're in a wrestling match.

We are fighting to prevent tomorrow. We are fighting to bring back yesterday. We are fighting to pull back progress. And we are fighting to marginalize others. Somebody has to attack civil rights. Somebody has to battle the best intentions of democracy. It's a wrestling match for the ages. If the planet pays a price, so be it. If America pays a price, so be it. If other people pay a price, that's the point. That's the price of getting to great again. And if we don't win today, yesterday will always be there. We will keep wrestling.

Today ... Work on your fight moves. Helpful hint: Do your research. Thought starter: The Powerbomb, the Sharpshooter and the People's Elbow are Freedumber fan favorites.

JULY 14

What's in your heart?

"He has the right to criticize, who has a heart to help."
(Abraham Lincoln)

"It's not enough to criticize, you've got to have the heart to hurt."
(Freedumb Fighter)

Then ... I thought President Lincoln effectively captured the American mindset on this one. Americans certainly have the capacity to be critical - that is, critical of our country, our community, and where things might stand at a given moment. Americans want things to work. We want things to make sense. We want things to be right. And we are very willing to voice our dissatisfaction when the state of play isn't where we believe it should be. We are also very willing to step up and be part of the solution. Depending on circumstance and situation, stepping up might look like volunteerism or protest or a vote - but it inevitably came from a desire to contribute, to help. I believed that was at the heart of being American.

Now ... I know the task is to hurt, not help.

We don't hurt simply to harm - at least not all the time. We hurt others to better our advantage and bolster our privilege. And why shouldn't we? That's a question straight from the heart.

Today ... Organize a local protest march. Don't be fooled into thinking that protesting is something only the well-meaning can do. Thought starter: How about "Freedummies Against Do-Gooding"?

JULY 15

What do you make room for?

"Let me speak plainly: The United States of America is and must remain a nation of openness to people of all beliefs. Our very unity has been strengthened by this pluralism. That's how we began; this is how we must always be. The ideals of our country leave no room whatsoever for intolerance, antisemitism or bigotry of any kind – none."
(Ronald Reagan)

"Let me speak plainly: We need to make more room in America for intolerance, antisemitism and bigotry – a lot more room."
(Freedumb Fighter)

Then ... President Reagan's remarks were a source of inspiration. I believed America could never lose its spirit of openness. What else should freedom foster if not openness? Openness is a magnet for dreamers and doers. It is foundational to diversity. It is a counterbalance to intolerance and bigotry. Openness makes us stronger. It makes us smarter. It makes us more curious and compassionate. Openness requires us to open our hearts and minds. Openness feeds our souls. And that should bring us together, with a shared understanding and a sense of mutual respect and appreciation. Who wouldn't have wanted to make room for that?

Now ... Us Freedumbers, that's who.

In the house of Freedumb, there's not a lot of room for openness. Openness invites too much that is different: different colors, beliefs, attitudes. Openness is uncomfortable. Openness might lead to introspection, reflection, even growth. That's some bad shit you're talking about. Instead, us Freedumbers prefer sameness. We like uniformity. Basically, we like people like us: white, small-minded, fearful, and willing to use God as a weapon. All of this makes our house a very special house – one where the welcome mat reads "Unwelcome."

Today ... Give the gift of intolerance. Helpful hint: Make sure your kids are getting a head start on their journey by teaching them to hate all the usual suspects. Thought starter: Make your house the house all the little bigots flock to!

JULY 16

What's calling you?

"America is a country where every man feels himself called on to do something."
(attributed to Ralph Waldo Emerson)

"America is a country where every real American is called on to prevent others from doing something."
(Freedumb Fighter)

Then … I saw it as a simple, powerful, and very American call to action: the idea that each of us feels called upon to make a difference. Americans are doers. We are builders. Whether we are building a life for our family, a better community or a greater country, Americans are innovators and impact players. We want to leave something positive. We want to leave something that will help, something that contributes to the promise that is America. We want to leave things better than we found them. We want to leave something that says we did right by the land of opportunity. I believed it was the call every American wanted to answer.

Now … We Freedumbers answer a different call.

It's called being an obstacle. At our Freedumbest, Freedumbers not only believe in building walls, we believe in being walls. Walls of prevention. Walls that can stop good and decent in its tracks. Walls that can stop progress and the future in its tracks. Walls that will make us great again.

Today … It's game day! Helpful hint: Get some buddies together and play a game of 'What if'. Imagine what kind of obstacle you'd be if you couldn't be a wall. Thought starter: What about say a fly in the ointment, a spanner in the works or a monkey wrench? Just don't settle for being a hiccup. Hiccups are never taken seriously.

JULY 17

Are you a success?

"...to find the best in others, to leave the world a bit better, whether by a healthy child, a garden path or a redeemed social condition; to know that even one life has breathed easier because you have lived.
This is to have succeeded."
(Bessie A. Stanley)

"Success should never be socially redeeming."
(Freedumb Fighter)

Then ... I held that success can mean a lot of different things. It doesn't have to come down to money, fame or acclaim. Often little successes contribute as much as anything else. Or more. The quote above pointed us in that direction. The American dream wasn't about getting ahead so others could be left behind. The pursuit of our happiness wasn't meant to leave the unhappiness of others in our wake. Success isn't a choice between either doing for ourselves or doing for others. The American heart is too big to succumb to that false choice. We don't win by losing our compassion or our generosity.

Now ... We Freedumbers believe false choices are the only real choices we have.

Freedumb feasts on false choice. Us or them, false choice, but you get to choose: us. That's a win! White or black, false choice, but you get to choose: white. That's a win! Gay or straight, false choice, but you get to choose: straight. Winner, winner, chicken dinner! Believer or heathen, false choice, but you get to choose: Christendumb. Through the pearly gates for the big win! Make a great again choice. And never look back.

Today ... Redeem yourself. Helpful hint: A sense of community is dangerous. Thought starter: Find a community garden and start pulling up the carrots.

JULY 18

Where's the fire?

"Let us hope and pray that the vast intelligence, imagination, humor and courage of Americans will not fail us. Either we learn a new language of empathy and compassion, or the fire this time will consume us all."
(Cornel West)

"I love the smell of smoke in the morning!"
(Freedumb Fighter)

Then ... I believed Cornel West's warning was an important one. Empathy and compassion can bring us together, can improve understanding, can foster mutual respect. The world in which we live makes it much easier to divide than unite. And obviously America is in no way immune to the dynamic. Without a deeper commitment to empathy and compassion, the road ahead will become even rougher. I liked the thought of a 'new language' to better express our views, to better help us address what confuses us, and better learn about one another. And I believed it was within our capacity to develop that kind of connective tissue. The alternative – the fire – served as ever-present motivation to get it done.

Now ... I realize we Freedumbers are ahead of the game on the language front.

Instead of showing empathy, we say "Fuck you!" Instead of showing compassion, we say "Fuck off!" Maybe not the most original alternatives, but at least we are out there trying. The language of Freedumb doesn't need intelligence or imagination. It doesn't want humor or courage. We aren't looking for any kind of woke new language – we're looking to Freedumb things down. The best way to throw gas on the fire is to be clear and inflammatory.

Today ... Be a Fire Starter. Helpful hint: Expand your language skills. There's more to you than just 'Fucks'. Thought starter: Call vaccines 'tracking devices.' Call separating parents and children 'border control.' Call ending Medicaid 'fiscal responsibility.'

JULY 19

What are you working on?

"Change and growth seem to tower beyond the control and even the judgment of men. We must work to provide the knowledge and the surroundings which can enlarge the possibilities of every citizen."
(Lyndon B. Johnson)

"I don't need anything enlarged."
(Freedumb Fighter)

Then ... For me, knowledge was the answer to the complications and stresses of a world that feels outside our control. At least, that's where we should start. Knowing more fosters deeper understanding, and arms people with what they need to make better decisions – for themselves, their community, their country and the world at large. Even if that knowledge and those decisions prove difficult. I thought it was always better to know. Ultimately, knowledge must be seen as our friend and ally.

Now ... We Freedumbers have all the friends we need.

Simply put, knowledge is a woke conspiracy. All it does is force law-abiding, flag-waving, righteous Americans to open our minds – with the more sinister motivation of encouraging us to think. Becoming dependent on knowledge is part of a plan to have us rethink our long-held beliefs and prejudices. We're not falling for it.

Today ... Show off your expertise. Helpful hint: You are expert at all things, but answering science, history and civics questions will always be where you shine brightest. Thought starters: How many dinosaurs were on Noah's Ark? Why did a black mob attack innocent white people during the Tulsa race massacre of 1921? Why do people insist on playing gay?

JULY 20

How do you feel?

"Some white people are so accustomed to operating at a competitive advantage that when the playing field is level, they feel handicapped."
(Nathan McCall)

"It's really, really, really hard being me."
(Freedumb Fighter)

Then … Nathan McCall's assertion gave me pause. As an older, white, straight man, I have come to understand that as hard as I've worked and with all the challenges I've faced, my color and gender provided me some built-in advantage. It's built into our system. Genuinely understanding that wasn't easy. Acknowledging it, even harder. But the truth is I've never faced prejudice or intolerance based on my beliefs or what I looked like. Still, without this understanding and acknowledgement we, all Americans, lose. As a competitor, I don't need a built-in advantage. All I need, or want, is a fair chance. That's all any American wants. If leveling the playing field means making things fairer for all, that shouldn't make me feel handicapped or somehow victimized. It should make me even prouder of America, and of being an American.

Now … We Freedumbers understand everything there is to know about being handicapped.

Fairness is a weapon used against us. The privilege and advantage of the straight, white men of Christendumb are under attack like never before. And the pain and suffering it's causing is incalculable. Questioning our authority, our all-knowingness, our place at the top of the ladder. Questioning our motives and assumptions. Do people realize what that's doing to our self-esteem? Honestly, it makes you want to cry. The advantages given the white knights of Freedumb are just so right. Why can't others see this? Why can't others respect this? How could our favored position be called into question? What is this country coming to? It hurts just to think about it.

Today … Talk to someone about the pain that fairness is causing you. Helpful hint: Bypass therapy and go right to the QAnon. They'll have you feeling better about yourself in no time. Fairness is a monster that must be stopped!

JULY 21

Today, the top ten conspiracies that keep Freedumbers awake at night:

1. The unholy alliance between teachers and librarians to promote reading, learning and curiosity as good things.

2. The sinister connection between healthcare professionals and caregivers plotting to brainwash us through vaccines and multi-vitamins.

3. The pernicious push against the idea that 'boys will be boys' by denouncing sexual abuse and violence against women without mentioning any of its upside.

4. The government plan to take all our guns away by suggesting that mass shootings are a bad thing.

5. The insidious demand to integrate black American history into real American history as cloud cover in a larger plot to undermine white self-esteem.

6. The toxic goal of togetherness behind such un-American ideas as Native American Heritage Month, Women's History Month, and Asian American and Pacific Islander Heritage month.

7. The feminist plot to legalize abortion rights, as the first step toward the servitude of men and the creation of the eternal matriarchy.

8. The plot against America championed by the lamestream media to not only normalize being queer but, perhaps even worse, to actively promote kindness, compassion, empathy and everyday good deeds.

9. The traitorous plot to weaken America through initiatives such as Disability Pride Month, National Disability Employment Month and the sinister International Day of Persons with Disabilities, to force Americans to respect those kinds of people.

10. The subversive schemes such as the Voting Rights Act, the Fair Housing Act, and the Fair Labor Standards Act.

JULY 22

What is possible?

"A man of great anger must pay the penalty. For if you rescue him, you will only have to do it again."'
(Proverbs 19:19)

"I'm angry on God's behalf."
(Freedumb Fighter)

Then ... There's always going to be something or someone that's going to set you off. But being angry also felt like a lazy choice. A choice not to listen or understand. A choice to forgo patience, to lose your clear-headedness, to abandon your sense of humor. It's a choice to put thinking on the back burner. Anger doesn't mean you care more. I didn't believe God wanted me to live an 'angry life,' she was looking for me to be helpful. Being angry is a choice to give up and give in to your worst self. Being angry meant shutting God, and goodness, out of your heart.

Now ... We Freedumbers know the best place for God isn't the heart, it's the holster.

A Freedumber's anger is always locked and loaded. Anger simplifies things. One black welfare recipient is abusing the system? Clearly all black recipients are guilty of being welfare kings and queens. One migrant with a criminal record, crosses into America? Clearly every migrant is about to rape and pillage their way across America. One gay person molests a child? Clearly the entire gay community consists of predators and groomers. So, obviously, screw them (not literally, of course). And on and on it goes. Of course, we white men just go on about our business. Nothing to see here. And if you try to judge all white men by just a few hundred mass shooters, that'll really piss us off. Amen.

Today ... Broaden out your anger. Helpful hint: Think alphabet. One bad letter can lead to a lot of bad words. Thought starter: Can you be furious at kittens, Kazakhstan, karate, Kim Kardashian, kale, and Kung Fu Panda 4 – all at the same time?

JULY 23

The nature of things?

"I would feel more optimistic about a bright future for man if he spent less time proving he can outwit nature and more time tasting her sweetness and respecting her seniority."
(E.B. White)

"Don't tell me what to respect."
(Freedumb Fighter)

Then ... For me, E.B. White's idea of respecting Mother Nature's 'seniority' was a great way to think about our relationship with the environment. It's a great compass for how we truly begin to address the challenges of climate change. Americans are becoming more and more concerned about what we are doing to our planet. No doubt, tough decisions lie ahead. We are running out of time, and must act decisively. We are coming to understand that trying to outwit or bully Mother Nature is a losing proposition. Our future depends on how we refine our relationship with her, starting today. I felt strongly that it was long past time to let our respect shine through.

Now ... I realize Mother Nature isn't my mother.

If she's hurting, that's tough. If she's suffering, that's too bad. Because to do something for her would require respect and sacrifice. It would take some rethinking. It would require some change. And, let's be clear, no woman warrants that kind of effort. The world is ours to do as we please. Mother Nature be damned. Science be damned. Responsibility be damned. And we're not going to listen to the unhinged pleas of some mouthy autistic girl from Sweden. Future generations be damned. It's time to let the dumb in Freedumbness really light up the earth.

Today ... Bitch slap Mother Nature.

JULY 24

Is there an elephant in the room?

"Suppose you came across a woman lying on the street with an elephant sitting on her chest. You notice she is short of breath. Shortness of breath can be a symptom of heart problems. In her case, the much more likely cause is the elephant on her chest. For a long time, society has put obstacles in the way of women who wanted to enter the sciences. That is the elephant."
(Sally Ride)

"Elephant? What elephant?"
(Freedumb Fighter)

Then ... I thought Sally Ride was a great American. As a physicist and America's first woman astronaut, she was a role model. Someone who had important things to say. In order to maximize the great potential that is America, I believed we needed women to be fully empowered. Empowered to maximize their potential, to honor their talent, to follow their dreams. We needed all their talent, their leadership, their intelligence. We needed all their problem-solving skills. We needed to encourage their very best. No more glass ceilings. No more traditional stereotypes of 'the weaker sex'. We have come a long way, and we're the better for it, but there was still a lot of potential yet to tap. It was time to remove the elephant.

Now ... We Freedumbers like the elephant right where it is.

Freedumbers believe women are a sidecar passenger on the motorcycle that men are born to ride. We believe men are meant for the head of the table, the top rung of the ladder. All because, yes, we are men. It doesn't matter if we are ill-equipped or unqualified. We are men. Control and power are our birthright. We believe women are best positioned as support mechanisms. A Freedumber's world truly is, and will always be, a man's world. Instead of dreaming about their so-called potential, a woman should worry more about getting their man a beer, making sure his dinner is ready, and wearing something to make him smile when he gets home from a hard day of making America great again.

Today ... Sharpen up your mansplaining skills. Helpful hint: Hit the links. Thought starter: Without even being asked, be the weekend golfer who instructs young women (with lower handicaps) how to properly adjust their golf grip based on your own 6-step technique.

JULY 25

What have you built?

"Men build too many walls and not enough bridges."
(attributed to Joseph Fort Newton)

"Yes to walls. No to bridges."
(Freedumb Fighter)

Then ... Walls are easier to build than bridges. To build a bridge takes a lot of planning, a lot of effort, a lot of teamwork. Walls are built out of fear, bridges out of courage. So, in the home of the brave, our choice seemed clear. We must aspire, always, to build bridges. Bridges connect us. Bridges overcome obstacles. Bridges take us places we haven't gone before. Bridges open us up to what's new and different. They could pique our curiosity and make us think. And rethink. I believed that building bridges was core to American greatness.

Now ... Fortunately, there are no bridges along Freedumb Road.

And why should there be? Walls work so much better. Sure, you can climb over them, dig under them or walk around them, but they send a message. An important one: you're not welcome and we're not interested. Walls signal minds and hearts that are closed – to other people, other ideas, and other ways of doing things. We Freedumbers take great comfort in being closed. It makes us feel safe. Who needs the world anyway?

Today ... Build a wall around your house. Your neighbors will get the message. And you'll be making America a little greater again. Helpful hint: If you want to be the envy of all your fellow Freedumbers, dig a moat after you finish your wall.

JULY 26

What's your decision?

"Women belong in all places where decisions are being made. It shouldn't be that women are the exception."
(Ruth Bader Ginsburg)

"Women don't belong anywhere near where important decisions are being made."
(Freedumb Fighter)

Then ... I wholeheartedly agreed with Justice Ginsburg's assertion above. Not only did women belong in all places where decisions were made, we needed them there. When women are not in those places, or are the rare exception, we are under-utilizing a national resource. A future that's a little more female couldn't be a bad thing. Women could bring a different and very valuable perspective to the table. They could ask alternative questions. They could provide new approaches and solutions to the issues we face. Ones that are not driven and decided on by group testosterone. Ones that came at things from a different angle. With the complexity and depth of the issues we face as a nation, I failed to see how this couldn't be both helpful and welcomed.

Now ... Freedumb showed me how weak and wimpy I was.

Freedumbers, real men that we are, believe women should be put on a pedestal and not subjected to places where decisions are being made. Decisions can be important. They demand decisiveness, take a lot of brain power, and require a fundamental understanding of the ways of the world. In other words, decisions are manly things. We need to put women in places where decisions aren't made (except of course as they relate to home decor or the dinner menu). Women need to focus on womanly things in womanly places. Think the 1950s. That's when women were at their best. The revered homemaker who stood behind, depended upon, and took direction from her man. And was nowhere to be found when any important issues – issues that would tax, confuse and overwhelm her – were discussed. Let's get back there as soon as possible. Ladies, you're welcome.

Today ... Be a man. Remind the women in your life that you're there to make the decisions for them. Helpful hint: Work to expand the 'pink tax.' Thought starter: body washes, clothes, deodorant and tampons aren't enough. Anything a woman does outside the home should be taxed to help her remember where she belongs.

JULY 27

What's the problem?

"Selfishness and greed, individual or national, cause most of our troubles."
(Harry S. Truman)

"I don't have a problem with other people having problems."
(Freedumb Fighter)

Then ... One of the basic qualities I believed to be quintessentially American is that of a problem-solver. Problem-solving is integral to being a can-do American, essential to a can-do America. Recognize the problem and solve the shit out of it. Selfishness and greed sit on the dark side of ambition and determination. And going to the dark side never solves much of anything. I thought being in it together was where responsibility, accountability and duty happened – all problem-solving traits. If we're intent on making our imperfect union more perfect, the buck stops with us.

Now ... Freedumbers, visionaries that we are, realize problems can be positives.

The problems of other people, that is. Not so much little problems, mind you, but the big issues that create woke craziness: equal opportunity, genuine liberty, justice for all. Those kinds of problems aren't even problematic. Does the color of my skin put some other people at a disadvantage? No problem. Does somebody else's sexual preference limit their freedom? Can't help you. Do women still bump up against a glass ceiling? We Freedumbers like ceilings made of reinforced glass. How can anything be a real problem if it protects our built-in advantage? If it fosters undeserved entitlement? If it gives us more power and more rights? From where we sit, it's all good.

Today ... Create a new problem for other people. Helpful hint: It's too easy for non-believers to have kids. Thought starter: Have them sign a pledge to Christendumb before allowing any procreation.

JULY 28

What can you do?

"Yes we can!"
(Barack Obama)

"No we can't!"
(Freedumb Fighter)

Then … President Obama, for me, was all about hope, about possibility, about what might be. He believed in the 'can do' spirit of America and the vast potential of American people. We had a good man in the White House. A man of intelligence and optimism, a man who believed in the common sense and big-heartedness of the people in this country. He believed in our will to succeed and our capability to solve problems. He believed in our shared resolve to progress. And in our determination to go forward in our eternal quest to live up to the nobility of our ideals. I thought that kind of belief was as contagious as that kind of leadership was rare.

Now … I rest easy, Freedumbers are here to make sure nothing happens.

We're not big on moving forward into what could be. The cool thing for Freedumbers is that we've relieved ourselves – both leaders and followers – of any attachment to principles or noble ideals. Or common sense. Any day when nothing positive is accomplished, nothing more is learned, and no greater understanding achieved is one more step toward the promised land of Freedumbia. Nihilism, hypocrisy and cynicism can run wild and free. Yes they can!

Today … Think of some less than noble ideals that would be worth embracing to get us back to greatness. Helpful hint: Go back to the 'Long Walk' forced upon the Navajo nation. Or back even further to the days of slavery. Or back to when sodomy was a crime punishable by death.

JULY 29

What will you do?

"If your actions create a legacy that inspires others to dream more, learn more, do more and become more, then you are an excellent leader."
(Dolly Parton)

"If your actions inspire others to dream less, learn less, and do more to become less, you are a leader."
(Freedumb Fighter)

Then ... Anything Dolly Parton says, I take as gospel.

Now ... Alternatively, what about leading with less than our best?

Freedumbers believe leadership requires less of us. Freedumb requires leaders who by their actions convince others that the time for learning and growing has passed – because when people stop dreaming and stop learning, we can put an end to striving for better. We want every American to tap into their lesser selves. We want every American to harness their fear and anger into creating desperation, limiting the desire to move forward, extinguishing hope. The worse our behavior, the more inspiration we provide, and the less we become – as a people and a country.

Today ... Don't settle for being a bad example. Be the baddest example ever. Helpful hint: Boycott Dollywood.

JULY 30

What constrains you?

"There are no constraints on the human mind, no walls around the human spirit, no barriers to our progress except those we ourselves erect."
(Ronald Reagan)

"I like erecting walls and barriers, especially around the human spirit."
(Freedumb Fighter)

Then ... There's no doubt President Reagan had a way with words. For me, his statement resonated because I felt America, at its best, is humanity at its best. To unleash the best of the human mind and the best of the human spirit makes the best of what we hope for and aspire to, not only possible, but perhaps even probable – over the course of time. Progress against racism. Progress against inequality and injustice. Progress against intolerance. The best we have to offer breaks down walls and barriers. I believed the best of what we offer is what America's destiny demands. And what the world lives in hope of.

Now ... We Freedumbers fear humanity. And rightfully so.

There's this hint of well-meaning in 'humanity' that just rubs us the wrong way. On the other hand, when you're talking inhumanity, it's clear we have a great deal to offer. You want walls and barriers? Nobody builds them better than us Freedumbers. You want to put obstacles up in front of progress? We are the men for the job. We separate out the American spirit from the best of the human spirit. We figure the more limited the American mind and spirit, the more Freedumbness it'll possess. The more restricted we are in the way we think, feel and act, the closer we'll get to tasting the ripest fruit that being great again has to offer.

Today ... Stop obsessing over the southern border, and look north. Those woke Canadians are just sitting there waiting to pounce. Helpful hint: An electric fence should scare them off - 12 gauge galvanized high tensile wire does a nice job.

JULY 31

What guides you?

"It is reason, and not passion, which must guide our deliberations, guide our debate, and guide our decision."
(Barbara Jordan)

"We are passionate about reason having no place in our deliberations, debates and decisions."
(Freedumb Fighter)

Then ... There was a lot of wisdom baked into Barbara Jordan's words. Love of country and a deep passion for public debate are as American as apple pie. As a country, and as a people, we feel things strongly. We always have and we always will. That said, reason - the ability to think through problems without getting carried away by our emotions - is critical to 'can do' America. Reason keeps paranoia at bay. It keeps responsibility in the frame. It allows cooler heads to prevail.

The American promise is a big one. The issues we face are foundational, complex and multifaceted. Emotion alone isn't going to get us to liberty and justice for all. Emotion won't fully harness the American dream. Life, liberty and the pursuit of happiness won't become more accessible because we really, really want it to be so. I believed progress demanded good faith dialogue and thoughtful action. Progress demanded the leadership of serious people.

Now ... Or you could unshackle yourself from reason and invite us Freedumbers to lead.

Freedumbers run from reason, logic and anything resembling rigorous thought. We find rationality a burden in debate and decision-making - because it gets in the way of us making our point.

Today ... Be worldly. Helpful hint: The Olympics could benefit from a greater sense of Freedumb. Thought starter: What if, going forward, all American female athletes competed in bikinis. It'd be a great look and Freedumbers everywhere would be forever grateful. Just wear it!

AUGUST 1

Have you made your point?

"I think in our desire to create a better America, we have to have civilized debate in this country, and not just yelling."
(Craig Ferguson)

"FUCK YOU."
(Freedumb Fighter)

Then ... I always believed that civilized debate was essential in cultivating the greatness of America. Craig Ferguson puts a fine point on this. Many of the urgent issues facing us have deep emotional foundations in our country. Americans always feel strongly about stuff. It's our way. And this passion is part of what makes us who we are.

But when things get heated, when emotion is getting the better of us, reason must walk in the door and join the debate. Intelligence and mutual respect too. Clear-headedness and common sense must also show up and take a seat at the table. So too duty, honor and a genuine desire to do what's best for our country. Once 'everybody' was in the room, I had no doubt good things would happen.

Now ... RUDE IS THE ATTITUDE.

YELLING, THAT'S WHAT THIS COUNTRY FUCKING NEEDS. YELL DUMB. YELL DUMBER. YELL DUMBEST. AND MAKE SURE YOU'RE YELLING AT THE TOP OF YOUR LUNGS. YELL WHATEVER YOU CAN TO GET THE WORD OUT. JUST MAKE SURE YOU'RE YELLING LOUD ENOUGH AND OFTEN ENOUGH TO MAKE YOUR VOICE HEARD, BECAUSE YOU'RE YELLING FOR ONE REASON AND ONE REASON ONLY - TO MAKE AMERICA GREAT AGAIN. NOW, CAN SOMEONE GET ME A FUCKING GLASS OF WATER - I'M LOSING MY VOICE.

Today ... GOOD MANNERS? GOOD LUCK! GOOD MANNERS? GOOD LUCK!!

AUGUST 2

What of the needy?

"Make a commitment to serve the needs of 'the least of these' and give voice to the voiceless."
(Artika Tyner)

"Keeping the voiceless, voiceless, isn't the worst idea."
(Freedumb Fighter)

Then ... Artika Tyner is a lawyer, educator and author committed to the advancement of social justice. The commitment she referred to is a defining one. Unless our country serves the needs of our most vulnerable, unless we give them a voice, you have to question our fundamental decency and humanity. America is committed to social justice, and the struggle is ongoing. The needs of our most vulnerable are too easily discounted and ignored. At our best, Americans are guided by our heart and conscience. I believed committing to serve the needs of the neediest among us was a mandatory.

Now ... We Freedumbers believe the voiceless should remain on mute.

The voiceless are just fine. All they do is blabber on about something else or something more they need. Let's not get distracted by things that aren't a priority. Now, let's get back to some legitimate concerns.

Today ... Drown out the voiceless. Helpful hint: Buy yourself a megaphone. Thought starter: You can't go wrong with the UZI High Power Loud Big Bluetooth Megaphone (with real siren) or the ThunderPower 1200 (up to 2000-yard range).

AUGUST 3

Are you in good cheer?

"The best way to cheer yourself is to try to cheer somebody else up."
(Mark Twain)

"Don't tell me who to cheer up."
(Freedumb Fighter)

Then … Even when Mark Twain wasn't being funny, he always gave you something to think about. The above quote says a lot in fourteen words. To me, it spoke to the power of generosity and kindness, compassion and care. And what they could do for others, as well as for yourself. That's a dynamic well worth pondering. Americans value happiness. After all, it's what we pursue. And it's good to be reminded that happiness and good cheer are something we can share and spread. It's one super-spreader we don't need to get vaccinated against.

Now … We Freedumbers believe in hoarding happiness for ourselves.

To a Freedumber, happiness is a zero-sum game. It's not something to share or spread. That said, our default disposition is to be pessimistic and put upon. We're happiest when we're being disagreeable. We aren't all that interested in cheering ourselves up, let alone anyone else. Pushing a country backwards is serious business. And nothing pisses us off more than the cheerfulness of others. Think of Freedumb as a noose around the neck of other people's happiness. Becoming great again means a lot of misery. For all.

Today … Put an end to the cheerfulness of others. Helpful hint: Start close to home. Thought starter: Chastise a Girl Scout for selling Samoas (un-American) or knock down your neighborhood little library box (promotes learning).

AUGUST 4

Are you equipped to lead?

"The most powerful leadership tool you have is your own personal example."
(John Wooden)

"The most powerful leadership tool you have is your own personal lack of conscience."
(Freedumb Fighter)

Then ... America is a world leader. An example to the world. And at its best, a great example for the world to look to. Americans citizens carry the leadership gene. We too, at our best, are examples to look up to. Coach Wooden was certainly proof of that. He knew that when all is said and done, it's what you *do* that matters. What you *do* determines your contribution, influence and impact. What you *do* determines the kind of leader you are.

And, I believed, what you do is determined by character. It's about your integrity. And ultimately, it's about your conscience. That little voice that tells you what's right and wrong, and holds you to the very best you can be. That little voice that pushes you to be good: a good person, a good American, and a good example to all those around you.

Now ... We Freedumbers know a thing or two about leadership.

We know that character doesn't count. That integrity and ethics are optional, and often more burdensome than they are helpful. We know that in moments of truth, when what you do can really make a difference, the little voice inside needs to shut up – so you can do something great again. Whether you're storming the Capitol or berating others or doing nothing to stop the plague of mass shootings in America or helping to suppress the vote of your fellow Americans - you're getting the job dumb. And Freedumbers everywhere will thank you for your leadership.

Today ... Hone your leadership skills. Helpful hint: Go on a Dumbness retreat. See if you can overstay your welcome.

AUGUST 5

Why are you here?

"You are not here merely to prepare to make a living. You are here in order to enable the world to live more amply, with greater vision, with a finer spirit of hope and achievement. You are here to enrich the world, and you impoverish yourself if you forget the errand."
(Woodrow Wilson)

"I'm nobody's errand boy."
(Freedumb Fighter)

Then ... I believed President Wilson powerfully captured a fundamental obligation of the American people. We carry an extra weight. A responsibility to others, and to the world at large. We are here to make a difference. To contribute something more. To make the common good uncommonly better. We are here to give oxygen to those gasping for hope and the fruits of freedom. If we are to fulfill the greatness of America's promise, we need the American people to continue to embrace this responsibility. The responsibility to ensure our communities and country can be places of plentiful opportunity and achievement.

Now ... We Freedumbers don't waste our time on the common good.

Instead, we work to make the lives of others more difficult. We work to minimize the hope, possibilities and potential of others. Sure, this sounds like a lot of suffering to be doled out, but we Freedumbers will never forget why we're here.

Today ... Impoverish yourself. Helpful hint: Make a weekly 'Forget these errands' list. Thought starter: Deliver no random acts of kindness, compassion or empathy. I mean, please.

AUGUST 6

Do you have the cure?

"Fear, the worst of all enemies, can effectively be cured by forced repetition of acts of courage."
(Napoleon Hill)

"Fear is the best friend there is."
(Freedumb Fighter)

Then ... I loved the idea of "forced repetition of acts of courage". Intentionally stepping up in that way felt like both an opportunity and an obligation. Courage is not a once-in-a-while thing, it's about who we are and how we live our lives. Americans aren't controlled by fear. We would never let fear define us or our actions – because we have the will to overcome it. It is our courage that defines us. Courage, for example, in the form of a helping hand, a sympathetic ear and a big heart. Ultimately, the courage to be truly American.

Now ... Not to brag, but we Freedumbers have the courage to be scared shitless.

We love our fear because of what it permits and pushes us to do. It's a unique kind of bravery. A bravery that allows our fear to dictate how we think, feel and act. It's a fear that permits and pushes dismissiveness and a lack of caring. It permits and pushes us to think the worst of others and act accordingly. It's a fear that permits and pushes us to play the vicdumb – which helps to excuse a lot of our behavior. Want to say something ignorant and hurtful? Be brave enough to say it. Want to do something racist? Be brave enough to do it. That's the kind of courage it takes to get us where we need to go.

Today ... Give your fear a nickname. Helpful hint: Reach back into history and grab one. Thought starter: What about Benedict Arnold? That always sounded like a cool name. (maybe 'Benny' for short)

AUGUST 7

Have you done the math?

"The function of education is to teach one to think intensively and to think critically. Intelligence plus character – that is the goal of true education."
(Martin Luther King Jr.)

"Intelligence plus character never solves anything."
(Freedumb Fighter)

Then ... I thought Dr. King laid out the simple, powerful goal for education. Intelligence can provide the 'what' but character provides the 'how'. If we are to look both critically and compassionately at what is, and work toward a better future, the what and the how have to come together. Education shows us the path forward. We need to ask different questions, come up with innovative solutions, and execute them for the general welfare of all citizens. Intelligence and character coming together, for me, offered hope for solutions with heart. Solutions with integrity and conscience. Solutions worthy of being called American.

Now ... Freedumbers ask the obvious question: "Why do solutions have to have heart?"

And while we're at it, why do solutions have to have decency? Or integrity? Or conscience? Those kinds of solutions won't protect privilege. Solutions with integrity won't safeguard entitlement. Solutions with conscience won't promote advantage. And why do solutions have to be intelligent? If education is to truly be part of the solution, its one goal must be learning to celebrate - to celebrate whiteness, manliness and straightness. OK, time for recess.

Today ... Do some math to help America meet its potential. Just make sure to take intelligence and character out of the equation. Helpful hint: (dumb x dumber) + dumbest = Freedumbia. We can each strive to be the lowest common denominator.

AUGUST 8

Today, conversations with the woke:

Woke says: "I don't want an open border. We need to control our borders, but I want a humane approach to immigration at our southern border and a long-term solution a little more innovative than a wall."

Freedumb says: "It's time for a crackdown. You care more about low-life felons than us Americans."

Woke says: "No, of course not, but I thi…"

Freedumb says: "Traitor."

Woke says: "I don't want to defund the police. I want police reform. Bad actors need to be identified and punished, but we ask too much of the police. We need more social workers, community liaisons and mental health experts to carry some of their load."

Freedumb says: "You're soft on crime."

Woke says: "Not really, I think we cou…"

Freedumb says: "Bleeding heart wimpshit."

AUGUST 9

What do you care about?

"Nobody cares how much you know until they know how much you care."
(attributed to Theodore Roosevelt)

"Nobody cares how much you know."
(Freedumb Fighter)

Then ... Knowing may be more than half the battle, but it won't guarantee you win the war. People won't listen if they don't believe you. America is a caring country. Americans are a caring people. We want leaders who genuinely care about the issues and opportunities that impact our everyday lives and the future of our children. We want leaders who care enough to make things better. We would listen to their solutions, rise up to the challenges they set, and do our part until the job was done. America knew what was right. America cared about doing right. Maybe it all just comes down to knowing and caring.

Now ... We Freedumbers don't know and don't care.

Freedumbers have the wisdumb to know that the quest for knowledge is just another big time-waster. And caring is just an energy taker. Why seek to know more, when knowing next to nothing brings such a high degree of clarity on everything of importance? And why care if all caring does is confuse the issue? We Freedumbers don't really give a shit about much of anything - except our whiteness, our maleness, our straightness and, of course, our godliness. People who need to know more are too thoughtful, too considerate and open-minded for their own good. Why can't those people (and their issues) just go away?

Today ... Make your 'to disappear' list. Helpful hint: Load it up with the things you don't want to know or care about. Thought starter: Compile separate lists for character traits (e.g., thoughtfulness), issues (e.g., women's rights) and school subjects (e.g., science and history).

AUGUST 10

What have you discovered?

"Courage is more exhilarating than fear, and in the long run it is easier. We do not have to become heroes overnight. Just a step at a time, meeting each thing that comes up, seeing it is not as dreadful as it appears, discovering we have the strength to stare it down."
(Eleanor Roosevelt)

"Have no fear, your Superman is here."
(Freedumb Fighter)

Then ... Eleanor Roosevelt made me think about what it takes to be a hero. America loves a hero. Someone who, through an amazing act in a defining moment, rises to the occasion. Storybook type stuff. Then there's the everyday hero. The type of hero that stories aren't written about. The type of hero that makes America better just by being who they are, each and every day. Those who have the courage to stare down fear and paranoia, ignorance and stupidity. Those who stare down divisiveness and intolerance. It's not the type of heroism that gets a lot of attention or garners a lot of applause. Still, these are Americans who get up every day, without fanfare, and try their best to make things around them a little better. A little kinder. A little more positive. A little more accepting. They are the best of us.

Now ... I understand we Freedumbers are no mere mortals.

Imagine us as Supermen, cape and all. We see our world changing, and we don't like what we're looking at. We see other people, with different attitudes and other dreams. People who really believe in equality of opportunity, justice for all, and a culture that values inclusiveness. Somehow these other people don't see us as the superhero that we were once held out to be. When did being a white man become so devalued? How did other people get comfortable enough to think they could sit at the big boy table? It's lunacy. America needs saving. Rest assured, Freedumb's Supermen will do all in our power to put an end to such craziness.

Today ... Strengthen your resolve. Helpful hint: Even Superman needs a little boost now and again. Thought starter: Have your woman buy you a package enhancer off Amazon. You'll be flying high, bigger and better in no time.

AUGUST 11

What is the nature of greatness?

"America will be great if America is good. If not, her greatness will vanish away like a morning cloud."
(Andrew Reed and James Matheson)

"Making America Great Again has nothing to do with goodness."
(Freedumb Fighter)

Then … I believed Andrew Reed and James Matheson hit it right on the head. And it was as true now as when they made the observation nearly 200 years ago. For me, goodness has always been at the heart of American greatness. While we have not, as a country, yet fulfilled the greatness of our promise, we push forward. Good intentions don't make you a good country, or a good person, but it's the starting point. And if it's true, that where there's a will, there's a way, I believed America would find a way to fulfill its unlimited potential.

Now … We Freedumbers are comfortable with our limits.

And goodness is where we draw the line. Being just requires too much. Besides, goodness makes it impossible to suppress, demonize and weaponize. That's a non-starter.

Today … Get great again at not being good. Helpful hint: Try taking things on in 'doable' chunks by using your daily calendar. Thought starter: For inspiration reference "Monday's Freedumber Poem" below:

Monday's Freedumber is unfair and in your face,

Tuesday's Freedumber is void of grace,

Wednesday's Freedumber is full of woe,

Thursday's Freedumber will tell you where to go,

Friday's Freedumber hates for a living,

Saturday's Freedumber works hard at not giving,

But the Freedumber that is born on the Sabbath day

is judgmental, vindictive and certainly not gay.

AUGUST 12

What's your favorite virtue?

"Courage is the most important of all virtues, because without courage you can't practice any other virtue consistently."
(Maya Angelou)

"Courage is important as long as it doesn't lead to kindness, compassion, empathy or any of that crap."
(Freedumb Fighter)

Courage is essential for greatness.

Then: I understood courage requires a big heart, but ...

Now: I understand that a big heart gives you the courage of a loser.

AUGUST 13

What are you looking for?

"We shouldn't be looking for heroes, we should be looking for good ideas."
(Noam Chomsky)

"If everybody is busy looking for good ideas, what happens to all the bad ideas out there?"
(Freedumb Fighter)

Then ... As Noam Chomsky suggested, looking for heroes can sometimes be a way to step back from our own responsibilities as citizens. I always believed America to be an incubator for good ideas. And putting good ideas into practice requires participation and commitment. Creating greater opportunities for those in need isn't a one-person proposition. Greater protection for the vulnerable isn't a go-it-alone challenge. Greater cultivation of common ground isn't the work of a single individual. None of us individually is as strong, smart or capable as all of us together. And we need to lock arms and be together in order to identify the best ideas, and turn them to good use. I had no doubt that there were ideas out there somewhere that could make heroes of us all.

Now ... We Freedumbers have no interest in good ideas.

There are way too many people already trying to come up with those. But we don't get bogged down in discussing ideas that might help or solve. This frees us up to think about other things – like the big ideas needed to get us back to greatness – such as authoritarianism, and white Christendumb nationalism. Bottom line, there are a lot of great again ideas out there to grab hold of. Don't be one of those to get caught empty-handed.

Today ... Come up with a big idea. Helpful hint: Leave no stone unturned. Thought starter: Read Mein Kampf. It's chock full of inspiration.

AUGUST 14

Where do you start?

"Openness may not completely disarm prejudice, but it's a good place to start."
(Jason Collins)

"Prejudice is a very good place to start."
(Freedumb Fighter)

Then ... As the first publicly gay athlete to play in any of the four North American major sports leagues, Jason Collins knew what he was talking about. As Americans, we need to open ourselves up. Openness can lead to understanding. Openness can overcome fear. Openness can seed not only tolerance, but acceptance, compassion and respect. Still, openness takes courage on all fronts - but we Americans have the collective heart to make it happen. And why not? Being different doesn't, in and of itself, hurt anyone or anything. In fact, I thought being open to the entire spectrum of our humanity ultimately made us stronger, more interesting, and more vibrant.

Now ... Freedumb convinced me to rethink that thought.

We Freedumbers see prejudice, of any kind, as a useful tool. To be clear, being prejudiced isn't who we are, it's just something we have to do. It helps keep the world on its axis, by maintaining the world as it should be. We need every tool in the toolbox to maintain our sense of superiority and comfort. So close your mind. Close your heart and your soul. The queer mob is coming for us and we need to protect ourselves! Closing ourselves off to greater understanding is key. Refusing to understand makes acceptance impossible. So, start refusing and stop accepting.

Today ... Meditate on your closedness. Helpful hint: These are some tried and true mantras - 'Accept no other', 'Prejudice protects', and 'Closed is open enough'. Chant to your heart's discontent.

AUGUST 15

What are your limits?

"There are no such things as limits to growth, because there are no limits on the human capacity for intelligence, imagination and wonder."
(Ronald Reagan)

"Human intelligence, imagination and wonder are not welcome here in America."
(Freedumb Fighter)

Then ... I had always been drawn to the inherent optimism of President Reagan. And given that I believed the best of America represents the best humanity has to offer, his words were a helpful reminder of our limitless capability as a country and a people. Many of the issues we face, whether climate-related, immigration-related, gun-related or race-related, are complicated beyond any kind of quick fix. That said, I never doubted the will and ingenuity of the American people in stepping up to meet and solve any problem. The creative horsepower in this country is formidable. And our ability to move forward, to grow and progress should never be underestimated. Never.

Now ... We Freedumbers are inherently suspicious of anything that's so-called "human".

For us, humanity is something that exists outside America, something that's, eww, global in nature. The world doesn't exist if we don't want it to. And we don't want it to! Freedumb doesn't require human intelligence, human imagination or human wonder. In fact, that kind of stuff just gets in the way. Being more human makes us less American. And that's not going to happen. No way, not on our watch.

Today ... Do something that lacks humanity. Helpful hint: Never pick on anybody your own size. Thought starter: Once again, consider taking inspiration from the Governor of the great state of South Dakota who didn't like her dog, so she shot it and threw it in a gravel pit.

AUGUST 16

What do you mean?

"'Black Lives Matter' simply refers to the notion that there's a specific vulnerability for African Americans that needs to be addressed. It's not meant to suggest that other lives don't matter. It's to suggest that other folks aren't experiencing this particular vulnerability."
(Barack Obama)

"The thought of black lives mattering is just so selfish."
(Freedumb Fighter)

Then ... President Obama's explanation made perfect sense to me. The formation of the Black Lives Matter movement was a response to when the actions of those meant to "Serve and Protect" signaled that black people's lives were somehow lesser and disposable. Remember Trayvon Martin. Remember Eric Garner. Remember Michael Brown. Remember Ahmaud Arbery. Remember Breanna Taylor. Remember George Floyd. Remember. Remember. Remember. That a group of people felt so desperate they had to publicly defend the idea that their lives actually mattered should have saddened and devastated us all. It should have given us pause to reflect and, more importantly, act. We, all Americans, must commit to fighting racism wherever we find it. Our decency, our humanity demanded we no longer shut our eyes, turn our heads, and behave with indifference in the face of racist wrongdoing and injustice.

Now ... Freedumbers see the idea of black lives mattering as a threat.

Why do black people only think about themselves? What about the lives that matter most? What happened to white lives? Why do only black lives matter? Don't all lives matter? Besides, aren't white people the ones really at risk? Why are white people being made to feel so bad about themselves? Isn't that the real injustice? If they can say "Black lives matter," why can't we say "White lives matter more?" Let's refocus our attention on all the things that are causing us white people pain and anguish. Lord knows the list is a long one.

Today ... Make yourself feel better. Helpful hint**:** Tune out any negativity. Thought starter: Stop listening to the likes of Tom Hanks, Taylor Swift and Barack Obama – they are always spewing out crap about decency, kindness and mutual respect.

AUGUST 17

Are you a quitter?

*"Failure at some point in your life is inevitable,
but giving up is unforgivable."*
(Anonymous)

"Somehow I'm drawn to the unforgivable."
(Freedumb Fighter)

Then ... I would have said America never gives up. Nor do Americans. Ever. We always seek to meet any challenge put in front of us. We're not always successful, but we are a determined and resilient people. At the risk of understatement, the challenges in front of us – racism, injustice, and inequality – aren't small or easily solved. So, every generation of Americans must commit to being part of the solution, because the struggle for solutions is foundational to who we are. There are moments where we sense that great progress is being made. There are other times when we wonder whether we've made any progress at all. Through this inevitable ebb and flow we have always remained undaunted as we pushed, however incrementally, forward. Bottom line, I thought giving up was not only unforgivable, it was un-American.

Now ... We Freedumbers are OK with doing the unforgivable.

That is, we've given up on the idea that we can make things better. Working to overcome prejudice, intolerance and inequity takes way too much effort. Besides, for us, those 'challenges' really aren't that big a deal. They are the responsibility of those on the receiving end of our great againess – the blacks, the Hispanics, the Orientals, the Jews, the uppity women, the non-believers, the immigrants, the gays and all those type people. We'd say sorry for it all, but our heart just wouldn't be in it.

Today ... Practice not apologizing. Helpful hint: Your wife could be helpful here. Thought starter: say something rude, crude or lewd about a minority, watch your wife react in horror and dismiss her reaction with "What? I'm just being real." Repeat the exercise until your wife leaves the room.

AUGUST 18

Today, a couple more conversations with the woke:

Woke says: "Climate change is an existential threat. We need to migrate away from fossil fuels to reduce the danger, and do this without robbing people of their livelihoods or making them unemployable."

Freedumb says: "Tree hugger."

Woke says: "Can't we get past name cal …"

Freedumb says: "Fucking globalist."

Woke says: "Pro-choice isn't pro-abortion, it's pro women's rights. We must have sovereignty over our own bodies. It's no one else's business. We must respect a woman's right to choose as a human rights issue. How else can we call ourselves a free society?"

Freedumb says: "Criminals. They need to be locked up."

Woke says: "Come on, how is that help …"

Freedumb says: "Baby killers."

AUGUST 19

Have you found yourself?

"In order to find yourself, who you really are, you gotta hang out with yourself … There's always gonna be setbacks, there's always going to be knockdowns. There's always going to be people telling you,
'Hey, you suck'."
(Post Malone)

"In order to find yourself, who you really are, you always gotta set 'em back; you always gotta knock 'em down. You always gotta tell them,
'Hey, you suck'."
(Freedumb Fighter)

Then … For me, Post Malone's words resonated as an essential part of the American character. Americans have a relentlessness in pursuit of our happiness, of our potential, of the best we have to offer. So too America. Just tell us it can't be done. Just tell us it's not possible. Go ahead and kick us when we're down. It's all just fuel for our fire.

Now … I feel like that kind of character sucks.

The truth is some people 'suck' so bad they just need to stop. Take Muslims for example, they suck so bad they need to stop trying to be American. Same with the Orientals. They suck big time. And they'll never be Americans, so it's time to jump back on the slow boat and head back to where they came from. And how about the Mexicans? We already have more than we need, so let's post signs at our southern border that read "You suck. Stay away." We Freedumbers are great again at telling other people "Hey, you suck."

Today … Challenge yourself. Helpful hint: Tell some 'foreign object' they suck, but try using your words. Thought starter: "You stink" or "You're crap" or "You're shit" can sound basic, but 'smell' is a rich vein to tap.

AUGUST 20

Are you scared?

"The big lesson in life, baby, is never be scared of anyone or anything."
(Frank Sinatra)

"I can be scared of anyone and anything I want."
(Freedumb Fighter)

Then ... A little wisdom from Ol' Blue Eyes can't hurt. To me, his lesson felt quintessentially American. The United States of America is the home of the brave for a reason. This doesn't mean we do not experience fear, but it does mean we don't run, panic or lose our heads. We had the capacity to confront fear, understand it, and act to overcome it. That capacity is called courage. Enough said.

Now ... We Freedumbers have something we would like to add.

There are actually a few fears we can't overcome – but let's keep this between us. We are terrified of not having enough guns. We are afraid that women might be the stronger sex. We are petrified that black history might not be as white as it should be. We are fearful that 'the gays' might actually be people too. We are frightened that abortion might be the moral choice. We are beside ourselves with worry that banning books isn't enough and that banning libraries just won't happen. We are nervous that vaccines are a form of mind control and that wearing a mask prevents you from being a man. We are paralyzed at the thought that we might really all be God's children. Come on, get real, that's some stuff we should all be afraid of!

Today ... Tell everybody how brave you are. If nothing else, you might just convince yourself.

AUGUST 21

Where's your head at?

"Those who corrupt the public mind are just as evil as those who steal from the public purse."
(Adlai E. Stevenson)

"A corrupted mind is a terrible thing to waste."
(Freedumb Fighter)

Then ... I thought Adlai Stevenson hit on something important here. Any attempt to influence the public mind through dishonesty and deceit is wrong. We need our public officials, at every level, to speak and act with integrity. We need our journalists and broadcasters, our bloggers and tweeters, to report and write with integrity. There is a difference between having a point of view on the facts versus simply making up the facts to suit your purpose. For a democracy to function properly, for a society to progress and for cultural norms to evolve in the best interests of all, we need leaders and journalists who respect and honor the truth. We need our public mind informed and clear-headed. Corrupting it with lies, and playing on fears to stoke divisions and hatred felt like a crime against America.

Now ... We Freedumbers realize that corrupting the American mind is the answer.

Lies, half-truths, and conspiracy theories are essential to getting America back to greatness. If you're a straight, white Christendumb nationalist, you're all good. No matter what you say or do. You're a real American, upstanding and patriotic. You're what made America great (and will do again). You're the answer to what ails us. If you're part of the other America, well, not so much. You're no help at all. You're the problem. You're the enemy. In the end, there's nothing more clear-headed than a corrupted mind.

Today ... Practice makes the perfect Freedumber. Helpful hint: You have to poison yourself before you can poison others. Thought starter: Call a town hall meeting with yourself, get on your soapbox and work on spouting lies, insults and conspiracy theories.

AUGUST 22

Today, the one riddle us Freedumbers just can't solve:

A father was driving his son to school and got into a bad car accident. Both the father and son were injured and had to be rushed to the hospital. The son needs surgery. When the paramedics brought him into the operating, the surgeon took one look at the boy and said "I can't operate on him! He's my son! How is this possible?

(*The answer, so I've been told, is that the surgeon was his mother. Or sadly, today another possibility is the doctor was his other father. WTF, the boy has 2 dads. Both of these are just wrong!)

AUGUST 23

What's your goal?

"Obstacles are those frightful things you see when you take your eyes off your goal."
(Henry Ford)

"Obstacles are those helpful things you create to keep others from their goal."
(Freedumb Fighter)

Then ... I believed that Americans are driven by their goals. Americans want more. Want different. Want better. Not only for themselves and their families but for their communities and country. And they are determined to get it. With a laser-like focus. Obstacles aren't things that stop us, they are things that make us stronger and smarter. They might be "frightful things," but obstacles don't scare Americans – they serve as motivation. They are taken as a challenge. If you ever wanted to motivate an American, all you had to do was put a challenge in front of them and watch them get to work. 'Impossible' was never part of the American vocabulary.

Now ... We Freedumbers see obstacles as possible weapons.

Rather than focusing on overcoming obstacles, we put our energy into creating them for other people. Obstacles to *prevent* others. And the more Freedumbers prevent, the more Freedumb takes hold. Prevent the rights of others, create more Freedumb. Prevent justice for others, create more Freedumb. Prevent equality of opportunity for others, create more Freedumb. Unlike freedom, which favors the bold, Freedumb favors the bully. So let's bully away.

Today ... Don't limit yourself to being labelled a 'bully'. Think outside the box. Think of yourself as a tormentor, a browbeater, a ruffian or even a harrier – as in, one that harries.

AUGUST 24

What are you in favor of?

"It is inaccurate to say I hate everything. I am strongly in favor of common sense, common honesty, and common decency. This makes me forever ineligible for public office."
(H.L. Mencken)

"It is inaccurate to say I hate everything. It's just common sense, common honesty, and common decency that piss me off."
(Freedumb Fighter)

Then ... H.L. Mencken could always get me thinking. And laughing. I didn't think it was a stretch to suggest that most Americans are in favor of common sense, honesty and decency. Granted, not all of our elected representatives embody such character traits, but I believed the aspiration and capacity to do right, to do good, to do better is more the rule than the exception. I really did. Cue the laugh track if you like.

Now ... Anything pushing "common" is no laughing matter.

We are serious people. Seriously lacking in common sense, in common honesty, in common decency. This lack helps define our character. And it also helps define what we look for in our elected representatives. And leaders in general. Makes sense, right? The cool thing about lacking is that it liberates. It frees you up to do, think, and say the Freedumbest things. We get the last laugh on this one.

Today ... Consider running for Little League Baseball district administrator. Helpful hint: Campaign slogans are fun to imagine. Thought starters: "Good sports are losers" or "Win or be a loser" or "Cheating is better than losing."

AUGUST 25

Can you keep your temper?

"If the great American people will only keep their temper, on both sides of the line, the troubles will come to an end, and the question which now distracts the country will be settled just as surely as all other difficulties of like character which have originated in this government have been adjusted."
(Abraham Lincoln)

"My temper is the answer to our troubles."
(Freedumb Fighter)

Then … I would have said that the American people are a great people. Yet with greatness comes the burden of the timeless struggle for better. The struggle for a country that lives up to its highest aspiration. A country that lives up to ideals such as liberty and justice for all. As President Lincoln asserted, anger, however righteous or warranted, is not the fuel for progress. Issues underpinned by great emotion and complexity cannot be worked through and made better by rage. For the United States to advance in our shared journey, reason had to be our eternal guide.

Now … Reason can stick itself where the sun don't shine.

We believe anger is the answer. Anger excuses irresponsibility. It unleashes petulance and thoughtlessness. It celebrates acting out. Anger puts and keeps you in attack mode. It creates enemies rather than opportunities. None of that will push America forward, but it can sure help make America great again. So, don't tell us Freedumbers to "hold your temper." It'll just piss us off.

Today … Commit to waking up angry. Helpful hint: It's not as hard as you think. Thought starter: Doesn't it piss you off that soap comes in colors other than white.

AUGUST 26

What's your move?

"If you have faith as small as a mustard seed, you can say to this mountain, 'Move from here to there,' and it will move."
(Matthew 17:20)

"My faith isn't aimed at moving mountains."
(Freedumb Fighter)

Then ... Mountains are moved one inch at a time. The end of systemic racism, the fight for equal rights, the battle for liberty and justice for all: these are mountains. And I believed goodness was the thing to give them a push in the right direction. Moving mountains takes commitment, resilience and courage. And it takes faith. Faith in the power of good, and that good would ultimately prevail. Maybe that all sounds a bit naive, but it takes a degree of innocence to put your faith in the power of good. Fortunately, as a country of dreamers, America has innocence at its core.

Now ... We Freedumbers aren't looking to move mountains, we're looking to move people.

Out of the way, that is. What if we could take all the 'different' people and move them somewhere else? Maybe to where we ship our recyclables. Just think about it. All the 'different' people gone: All the blacks and assorted minorities. All the terrorist-loving Muslims. All the over-achieving Orientals and trouble-making Jews. All the gays in their various shapes and forms. All the tree huggers. All the librarians wanting us to read and the teachers wanting us to think. All the scientists creating godless vaccines and the nurses and doctors concerned with our physical and mental well-being. All the independent women banging on about equal this and equal that. All the historians who try to push blackness into our white knight views. The Indians can stay put – we're OK with them out on the reservation.

Today ... Call 1-800-MOVEOUT if you have a 'different' to add to the list being compiled at Freedumb HQ.

AUGUST 27

What do you think?

"Never doubt that a small group of thoughtful, committed citizens can change the world. Indeed, it is the only thing that ever has."
(Margaret Mead)

"Never doubt that a small group of thoughtless, uncaring citizens can change the world. Indeed, it is the only thing that ever should."
(Freedumb Fighter)

Then ... To me, Margaret Mead's quote spoke to possibility and aspiration. And to the role each one of us could play, if we were to commit to making a difference. It was a call to action, underpinned by an element of activism. If you want change, you can work to make it happen. I fully bought into the idea that a spark that fuels change didn't require big numbers of people or big power brokers. What it needed was citizens who cared. Citizens who wanted to make things better. Citizens who thought about their fellow Americans. Citizens who stepped up. I thought this all seemed very American in spirit.

Now ... Well, we Freedumbers don't give a rat's ass what your 'old self' thought.

We need to stop thinking and caring so much. We need to stop being concerned citizens. We need to stop supporting and empathizing with other people. We have other priorities. We need to start pulling ourselves back to a place of real power. Back to a place of comfort. Back to a place of clear privilege and advantage. Back to a place where straight white men rule and all others serve. Back to a place where anything can be done ... in the name of our God. Next stop, Freedumbia.

Today ... Play a game of Start-Stop-Continue. It can help bring your Freedumbness into focus. For example, *Start* putting a pistol into your kid's backpack. *Stop* cutting corners on ammo. *Continue* buying cool add-ons to your AR-15. That's a game that could change the world.

AUGUST 28

Today, a couple more conversations with the woke:

Woke says: "I'm not sure why it's so hard to show the queer community the dignity and respect they deserve. They are people just like us. Who have worries, concerns, hopes and dreams… just like us."

Freedumb says: "The gays are mentally ill."

Woke says: "Really. Don't you think tha…"

Freedumb says: "Goddamn do-gooder."

Woke says: "I'm not against gun ownership, but what could be the harm in banning assault rifles? They are military-grade weapons designed to kill as many people as possible in as short a time as possible. Basically, we're allowing civilians to own killing machines."

Freedumb says: "Ban assault rifles and next thing to happen will be government mind control."

Woke says: "Don't you think that might be a slight bit para…"

Freedumb says: "Fucking Commie."

AUGUST 29

What don't you do?

"What you don't do can be a destructive force."
(Eleanor Roosevelt)

"Thanks for the advice Eleanor!"
(Freedumb Fighter)

Then ... I never believed America to be a passive country. Nor are Americans passive people. Standing by and looking away can be destructive. Being aware and doing nothing can be destructive. Intolerance and injustice love it when people are passive, when they stand idly by, or when they talk big and do nothing. What we individually don't do can enable what we collectively shouldn't do. However, to 'not do' is not the American way. Americans will protest, will defend, will work to fix. Americans will work to solve and progress. I always believed Americans to be a constructive force.

Now ... We Freedumbers are proud to be defined by what we won't do.

We won't listen to reason. We won't compromise. We won't take any blame. Don't ask us to get into any 'well-meaning' discussions with the libtards. And sure as shit, we won't say "I'm sorry" – and why the hell should we? We answer only to the God of Christendumb, and of course, Jesus of Orange here on earth.

Today ... Push your 'not doing' to the next level. Helpful hint: Consider the next generation. Thought starters: Instead of trying to ban books, stop your kids from reading altogether. Instead of trying to prevent the teaching of critical race theory, just stop sending your kids to school. Or instead of buying yourself another AR-15, buy your kid one. (OK, this last one is actually *doing* something, but at least it's something that doesn't make any sense.)

AUGUST 30

Today, a little peak into the inspiring all-knowingness of Jesus of Orange:

- *On ISIS*: "I know more about ISIS than the generals do."
  (November, 2015)

- *On the Courts*: "I know more about courts than any human being on earth."
  (November, 2015)

- *On Renewable Energy*: "I know more about renewables than any human being on earth."
  (April, 2016).

- *On Taxes*: "I think nobody knows more about taxes than I do, maybe in the history of the world."
  (May, 2016)

- *On Debt*: "I'm the king of debt. I'm great with debt. Nobody knows debt better than me."
  (June, 2016)

- *On Technology*: "Technology – nobody knows more about technology than me."
  (December, 2018)

- *On Infrastructure*: "Look as a builder, nobody in the history of this country has known so much about infrastructure as ..."
  (July, 2016)

AUGUST 31

What's indispensable?

"Leadership and learning are indispensable to each other."
(John F. Kennedy)

"Leadership has nothing to do with learning."
(Freedumb Fighter)

Then … For me, the best leaders understood the importance of President Kennedy's assertion. Leaders willing and wanting to learn have a degree of curiosity, courage and humility. That's a mindset that fosters a critical depth of thought and mindful decision-making. Learning provides not only information but insight, not only understanding but empathy. The best leaders always help us seize opportunities, push us to be better, and guide us to a brighter future. Great countries require great leaders. America expected nothing less.

Now … Freedumb's leaders are blessed with an aversion to learning.

Learning is just too hard. Instead, Freedumb's leaders lean on their natural abilities – for example, the ability to insult and attack. The ability to make blatantly ignorant statements with conviction. The ability to praise irresponsible actions as acts of patriotism. The ability to say and do without conscience. The ability to let fear, hate and anger be your three wise men. Now we're talking indispensable! The reality is, when you've got natural leadership abilities, learning can comfortably take a back seat. Truth be told, learning isn't so much in the back seat of Freedumb's ride, it's lying on the side of the road riddled with bullet holes from a semi-automatic assault rifle. Rest in peace.

Today … Showcase your natural leadership ability. Helpful hint: Visit your kid's classroom and heckle the shit out of their teacher. Thought starter: Did she say Tom Sawyer "woke up late"? How dare she use the word 'woke' in the classroom?

SEPTEMBER 1

What do you see?

"One day our descendants will think it incredible that we paid so much attention to things like the amount of melanin in our skin or the shape of our eyes or our gender instead of the unique identities of each of us as complex human beings."
(Franklin Thomas)

"Don't call me a complex human being!"
(Freedumb Fighter)

Then ... Franklin Thomas was an American businessman and philanthropist. His thought laid down a challenge all of us should rise to meet. To see each other for the individuals we are, is crucial if we are to advance as a culture and country. It also seemed like a very American type of challenge. No other country in the world is more focused on the individual, more committed to individual rights than America. There is a limitless depth and range of humanity that we have the opportunity to tap in to and connect with in this country. I believed to do so would foster a better, richer future for us all.

Now ... We Freedumbers prefer to keep things simple-minded.

Treating other people as individuals is too much work. And where's the upside? There isn't any. I mean who would want to connect with someone 'different' anyway? You can know everything you need to know about someone just by looking at them. Blacks are lazy and dangerous. Asians work too hard and make my kids look bad. Jews are sinister and shady. Gays are all predators and groomers. Of course, all immigrants coming from the south are felons. And Muslims, they're the terrorists. There's no uniqueness or complexity to be explored here. White people are the only race that can't be stereotyped. It's so much easier to decide, dismiss and disparage when you keep things superficial. Now, there's some upside. Clear and simple.

Today ... Dumb it down. Helpful hint: Have some fun with a demeaning stereotype. Thought starter: Did you know that blacks love their leaders to be criminals? Apparently, there's nothing like a good mugshot to inspire black voters.

SEPTEMBER 2

What do you want?

"You ain't gonna learn what you don't want to know."
(Jerry Garcia)

"Just shut up and play your guitar."
(Freedumb Fighter)

Then ... I'm no Deadhead, but I believed Jerry Garcia's thought was one to embrace. You've got to *want* to know. You've got to want to know about the world. And the people in it. You've got to want to know about your country. And your fellow citizens. Because if we don't want to know about the tragic consequences of injustice, they'll always be with us. If we don't want to know about inequality of opportunity between the races, it'll always be with us. If we don't want to know about the prejudice endured by those searching for their gender identity, it'll always be with us. Not learning is a choice. A bad one. Not wanting to truly know is a choice. A bad one. And bad choices rarely lead to good outcomes. Wanting to know gives us a chance. I figured we would have learned that by now.

Now ... I realize not wanting to know helps me understand.

Genuinely not wanting to know is the key to really knowing. And it makes us Freedumbers so knowledgeable, sometimes it looks like we know absolutely nothing. That's when you know you're in the presence of great again wisdumb.

Today ... Declare yourself "a very stable genius". Helpful hint: Genius means knowing everything without really knowing anything. Thought starter: The brilliant unhinged rants of Jesus of Orange should be taught in schools!

SEPTEMBER 3

Can you be counted on?

"Equality means more than passing laws. The struggle is really won in the hearts and minds of the community, where it really counts."
(Barbara Gittings)

"Inequality means more than passing laws. The struggle to maintain inequality is really won in the hearts and minds of the community."
(Freedumb Fighter)

Then ... Barbara Gittings was speaking as an advocate for the queer community, but I thought her words carried a broader truth. Laws are a big step in the march toward greater equality, but in the end, it is citizens, not legislators, who determine what progress really looks like. For me, equality is about giving people a fair chance to live their lives. A fair chance to do their thing in their own way. It's about providing real opportunity and removing unfair obstacles. I didn't believe America should ever be a country where discrimination or intolerance held sway. I didn't believe it should ever be a country where one group of people told another group of people how to live their lives. Let's hold that thought in our hearts and minds.

Now ... That kind of thinking makes a Freedumber's head hurt.

We dislike the idea of equal opportunity, and would banish it from the vocabulary if we could. 'Equality' invites respect that other people don't deserve or haven't earned. Equality undermines the clarity around who's in charge. It serves as an obstacle to discrimination, and makes keeping people in their proper place too difficult. Freedumbers see this as an existential threat. It eats away at our peace of mind. It threatens our way of life. It threatens our advantage. And it's tough to feel entitled without holding a deeply entrenched advantage. We don't want other people to have a chance. Not a fair one, anyway. Because with fair chance come potential challenges and changes to the way things are. We have to harden our hearts to that kind of possibility.

Today ... Have fun with pronouns. Helpful hint: Introduce yourself and show them who you really are. Thought starter: "I'm a Freedumber and my pronouns are kiss my ass" or "I'm a Freedumber and my pronouns are kiss my ass" or "I'm a Freedumber and my pronouns are kiss my ass." (We Freedumbers do love getting our old white asses kissed!)

SEPTEMBER 4

Do you have what it takes?

"I believe that man will not merely endure: he will prevail. He is immortal, not because he alone among creatures has an inexhaustible voice, but because he has a soul, a spirit capable of compassion and sacrifice and endurance."
(William Faulkner)

"I believe that the straight white American man will not merely endure; he will prevail."
(Freedumb Fighter)

Then … I believed as William Faulkner did. I also believed that the American spirit had always represented the best of the human spirit. Independence. Ambition. Self-determination. They're all inherent in that spirit. So are generosity and a willingness to sacrifice for a greater good. Americans are unfamiliar with the idea of giving up. It's simply not how we're built. Ours is a spirit that creates, builds and improves. It sustains hope, drives success, heralds progress and makes dreams possible. And that always felt pretty great to me.

Now … In the words of the Freedumb movement: fuck your feelings.

Freedumbers are capable of a lot. That said, what we are incapable of is truly mind-blowing. Compassion, absolutely not. Sacrifice, no again. Curiosity, another no. Without such burdens, we set our spirits free to do right by whiteness, straightness and manliness. Freedumb's men are meant to be at the top of the food chain. We are meant to distribute the rights of others as we see fit, and suppress the rights of others as necessary. We are meant to show others how the world really works. To us, it's simply the natural way of things.

Today … Showcase your incapability. Helpful hint: Fail to understand. Thought starter: Call out any woman without a kid a "childless cat lady."

SEPTEMBER 5

Could you be wrong?

"Whatever is my right as a man is also the right of another."
(Thomas Paine)

"My right is mine alone."
(Freedumb Fighter)

Then ... The shortest statements are often the most profound. Thomas Paine's assertion was a case-in-point. I believed that in America, the rights of one should be the rights of all. It's liberty and justice for all, not liberty and justice for some. It's the government of the people, by the people, for the people – not the government of some people, by some people, for some people. And it's the American dream, not the white American dream, not the Christian American dream or the straight American dream. The Founding Fathers put us all together in this idea called America. No caveats or qualifiers.

Now ... We Freedumbers know that we have rights that others don't.

We don't believe the rights of the chosen have anything to do with the rights of others. That would suggest a nonsensical degree of sharing and a ridiculous sense of equality. In fact, Freedumbers deny that other people have rights at all. What if other people started to think they had a right to the justice and liberty reserved for white men? What if other people started to see white men as fellow Americans rather than landlords of the home of the brave? What if other people began to doubt that rights were the property of white men, doled out as and when we see fit? That all seems to be pushing in the wrong direction.

Today ... Play 'Who gets a right?' Pretend you're giving rights to others in society – only to take them away. It's a game that's always good for a laugh. Look at how funny the overturning of Roe v. Wade was!

SEPTEMBER 6

Today, two more Freedumber Public Service Announcements:

PSA #5:

Do you have children, work outside the home, and never have your priorities called into question? Or do you have children and receive praise for extraordinary parenting when you only marginally pitch in? Clearly, you're a man. Call 1-800-FREEDUM to hear a representative confirm to you how hard it is to be a man. He'll debunk the claim that women should work outside the home or that men should ever do housework. He'll also explain why you should find a beer waiting with your slippers and a smile as you come through the door after a hard day's work.

PSA #6:

Can you pick the right two answers?

The Trail of Tears refers to:

> a) The brutal and forced migration of Native Americans from their ancestral homes
>
> b) The sadness felt by white baseball fans when Jackie Robinson broke into the major leagues

Jim Crow was:

> a) A set of laws introduced in the late 19th and early 20th century, aimed at racial segregation and the suppression of African Americans in the southern US
>
> b) A quarterback for the New York Titans of the old American Football League

If you selected (b) for both questions, you may have what it takes to be one of our on-call public service representatives. Call 1-800-FREEDUM for the potential career opportunity of a lifetime.

SEPTEMBER 7

Can you find the joy in doing wrong?

"Freedom is the right to be wrong, not the right to do wrong."
(John G. Diefenbaker)

"Even when I'm wrong I'm right."
(Freedumb Fighter)

Then ... I always took inspiration from the above quote by the former Prime Minister of Canada, John Diefenbaker, because it spoke to me of intention. The notion that while freedom doesn't guarantee getting it right, whatever 'it' might be, a fundamental assumption of freedom was the intention of trying to do it right. To make things right. This was a quintessential American intention. I saw America, with all its faults and foibles, as an unrelenting force for good. Same was true of the American man. Calling yourself American came with a big weight to carry. The weight of being on the side of good, of better, and ultimately of right. I never doubted we were up to the task.

Now ... It's clear that I misunderstood the rightness of wrongness.

Freedumbers understand that he who hesitates to hurt and harm, is lost. We see the righteousness in wrongness. The goal of goodness is a woke virus. One good act could lead to a contagion of mutual respect or consideration for the common good. And us Freedumbers aren't going to let America go there. Sure, it takes a lot of courage to confront the forces of good and do great again, but Freedumbers have got what it takes.

Today ... Allow yourself some fun. Helpful hint: Doing wrong doesn't always have to be so serious. Thought starter: Foster a disabled child so you and some fellow Freedumbers can make fun of them on a daily basis. Who knows maybe Jesus of Orange stops by to give you some pointers.

SEPTEMBER 8

What have you learned?

"No one is born hating another person because of the color of his skin, or his background, or his religion. People must learn to hate, and if they can learn to hate, they can be taught to love, for love comes more naturally to the human heart than its opposite."
(Nelson Mandela)

"Hating something is the best part of my day."
(Freedumb Fighter)

Then ... I believed Nelson Mandela offered a solution that would change everything.

Now ... We Freedumbers believe fear and hate are underappreciated.

We Freedumbers have a special ability to see the beauty in hate. Hate makes the world go round. The more you hate, the more the right things happen. The better we hate, the more divided we become and the better off we are to live our Freedumbest lives. Sure, hate makes our world smaller, but it's a clear and simple world. And with it, the promise of a purer America. And love's got nothing to do with that.

Today ... Play a game of 'White Out'. Get some pals together and imagine America at its purest and best. Helpful hint: Think of sports and entertainment. Thought starters: Sports without black athletes, and music and movies without black artists and actors. Now that's the look of opportunity. Love it!

SEPTEMBER 9

Can you imagine?

"If one advances confidently in the direction of his dreams, and endeavors to live the life which he has imagined, he will meet with a success unexpected in common hours."

(Henry David Thoreau)

"Go confidently in the direction of being other people's nightmare."
(Freedumb Fighter)

Then ... I loved Thoreau's thought for its innocence. Dream, go hard, and get it done. It's a uniquely American assertion, underpinned with the possibility of 'what if.' There was also a positive energy and optimism to it that made it feel very American in character. In our heart of hearts, Americans are dreamers. And we are all invited to unleash our imagination and dream big. Dream of making a difference. Of somehow changing the world and the lives of others, as well as our own. We dream of contributing. Of creating. Of building. Of providing. Of redefining. Of making things happen. I was confident that in America, better always beckoned.

Now ... We Freedumbers understand that some dreams are meant to die. And we want to put the final nail in their coffin. Being other people's nightmare can look different depending on the target. For example, women might dream of being in control of their bodies, their decisions, their whole lives. Well, dream on. Not on our watch. How about we discourage birth control, force you into having a baby, and then abandon you once the baby is born? The Taste of Freedumb! Now go live your dream. Our list of targets is a long one. And not to worry, it includes the usual suspects. Just know we go confidently backwards all hours of the day.

Today ... Be a bigger nightmare. Helpful hint: Make a movie and build the plot around the death of democracy. Thought starter: You could call it "Sunrise in Mar-a-Lago."

SEPTEMBER 10

What is your greatest gift?

"A volunteer is a person who can see what others cannot see; who can feel what most do not feel. Often, such gifted persons do not think of themselves as volunteers, but as citizens – citizens in the fullest sense; partners in civilization."
(George H. W. Bush)

"I am God's gift to America."
(Freedumb Fighter))

Then ... I held that volunteers, those most civic-minded among us, need to be acknowledged. They need to be celebrated for the difference-makers they are. They have the gift of empathy. It sets them apart, and makes them the best of what we all could be. They desire better for their fellow Americans. And they act on that desire. It's civic responsibility of the highest order. These Americans realize they are part of something bigger. They realize helping others is helping themselves. They realize doing good isn't about recognition or glory. And they are OK with that. I don't know if that makes them gifted, but I certainly believed it made them a gift that keeps on giving to the greatness of what America could be.

Now ... I see that Freedumbers are the greatest gift America could ask for.

America is lucky to have us. Lucky to have us as leaders, truth-deformers, and defenders of our great againess. Yes, America is fortunate to have us as a gift. Fortunate also that we are so gifted. That may not suggest empathy, but it does indicate a high degree of self-awareness.

Today ... Be the gift that keeps on giving. Thought starter: Maybe the Incels need some marketing tips. Maybe the Proud Boys need fundraising help for new team uniforms. Maybe there are neo-Nazis out there who could use a new clubhouse.

SEPTEMBER 11

How will you be defined?

"One of the worst days in American history saw some of the bravest acts in American history."
(George W. Bush)

"The US government was behind the 9/11 attacks."
(Freedumb Fighter)

History may be found in books, but it is defined in people.

Then: Be a better American, but ...

Now: Be a greater Freedumber.

SEPTEMBER 12

Are you able?

"It's not our differences that divide us. It is our inability to recognize, accept, and celebrate those differences."
(Audre Lorde)

"Separate, and unequal!"
(Freedumb Fighter)

Then ... Audre Lorde is a writer and poet. Underpinning her statement, I believed, was the hard yet simple truth that dividing is a choice. We have the ability to choose otherwise. I believed Americans had that will within them. For example, the will to ask some hard questions. Were we going to hate a fellow American simply because their skin color is different from our own. Really? Were we going to disparage a fellow American simply because of who they choose to love. Really? Were we going to attack a fellow American simply because of how they identify in terms of gender. Really? With all the reasoned thinking we have at our disposal, what makes those differences so hard to accept, appreciate and even celebrate?

Now ... We Freedumbers recognize, accept and celebrate sameness.

How can you conquer if you don't divide? Dividing based on superficial difference is the answer. Intolerance of difference is the solution. Prejudice against the 'differents' is the remedy. That narrow-mindedness is the way backwards. That insularity and bigotry will help get us back to greatness. So, some questions need to be asked. Do black people really belong in America? Where is the best home for the gays? And how about the Orientals? Maybe Native Americans could make some room on their reservations for some others?

Today ... Separate yourself. Helpful hint: Read about the life and times of George Wallace. He was all about America being great again when America was still really, really great. Thought starter: Take some inspiration from this great again man and put a "Whites Only" yard sign out on the front lawn or advocate for a return back to 'color-coded' public bathrooms.

SEPTEMBER 13

What will you pass on?

"Where you see wrong or inequality or injustice, speak out, because this is your country. This is your democracy. Make it. Protect it. Pass it on."
(Thurgood Marshall)

"This is my country. And you can't have it."
(Freedumb Fighter)

Then ... I thought the American experiment was completely dependent on the American citizen. If we were to live up to the path set by the Founding Fathers, if we were to meet the standard of liberty and justice for all, and if we were to stay true to the invitation for life, liberty and the pursuit of happiness, there was still much work to do. That opportunity was ours and ours alone. Being an American citizen is an obligation. To answer Justice Marshall's call, we had to right the wrongs. We had to protect and strengthen our democracy as an instrument of good. We had to ensure that our government of the people, by the people, for the people worked hard on behalf of all, and flourished for generations to come. The choice was either to pass it on or drop the baton.

Now ... We Freedumbers figure keep the baton and use it as a stick.

We will never be accused of lacking ambition. We'll break American democracy and make it our own. And then we'll protect it. Then we'll pass it on. Inequality and injustice aren't wrongs to be righted: they are rights to be cherished. And if we have to use the baton to beat back threats to these unearned advantages, who better than 'the Supremes' to do the job? Thankfully, the highest court in the land is swinging its stick all over the place. Limiting voting rights, dismantling affirmative action, pulling back on women's rights, undermining the rights of anybody L or B or G or T or Q or +. With this group of heroes laying down the law, Freedumb is producing hit after hit after hit.

Today ... Give thanks. The 'super six' of the Supreme Court – Justices Thomas, Alito, Coney Barrett, Gorsuch, Kavanaugh and Roberts – deserve all the gifts you want to send them (don't worry, your secret will be safe with them).

SEPTEMBER 14

What are you scared of?

"First of all, let me assert my firm belief that the only thing we have to fear is fear itself – nameless, unreasoning, unjustified terror which paralyzes needed efforts to convert retreat into advance."
(Franklin D. Roosevelt)

"The only thing we have is fear itself."
(Freedumb Fighter)

Then ... I held up the quote above from President Roosevelt as perhaps the greatest quote ever. It was quintessentially American. It was affirming, resolute and undaunted. America doesn't panic. America doesn't see ghosts. America doesn't let paranoia be its guide. Courage allows for the overcoming of fear. And America has always been brave enough to advance, to correct itself and get better. Americans didn't retreat from adversity or opportunity. We didn't shy away from solutions to problems that hold us back. And we didn't let the prospect of sacrifice, compromise or change stop us dead in our tracks. That's just not who we are.

Now ... Freedumbers love fear.

We look and see threats everywhere, but we won't be retreating, we'll just be going backwards.

Today ... Have the courage to be afraid of one more thing. Helpful hint: Anything with a brain could be a potential threat. Thought starter: Go small. The ragworm is supposed to have the smallest brain on record. Or is that the 'much-feared' ragworm?

SEPTEMBER 15

What do you know?

"We all should know that diversity makes for a rich tapestry, and we must understand that all the threads of the tapestry are equal in value no matter their color."
(Maya Angelou)

"I'd be OK with diversity if it wasn't so focused on different types of people."
(Freedumb Fighter)

Then ... I believed Maya Angelou's thought on diversity deserved an Amen.

Now ... Enough about diversity already.

A tapestry might be nice as a wall hanging, but people-wise it doesn't do America any good. The first issue with diversity is that it involves different types of people. Not just white people. The second issue with diversity: it involves different cultures. Not just real Americans. The third issue with diversity: it involves different lifestyles. Not just the lifestyles of white, straight Americans. And the fourth issue with diversity is that it involves different beliefs. Not just those of Christendumb. That's a lot of issues. Stronger and more interesting, my ass. Besides, tapestry sounds like a girlie-type thing anyway.

Today ... It's time for a craft project. Helpful hint: bring in the Tradwives. They love a good homemade DYI. Thought starter: Get them to knit a plantation tapestry celebrating the often overlooked, kindness of slavery.

SEPTEMBER 16

What's your problem?

"Racism is a white problem. It was constructed and created by white people and the ultimate responsibility lies with white people. For too long we've looked at it as if it were someone else's problem."
(Robin DiAngelo)

"Racism, if it still exists, is not my problem."
(Freedumb Fighter)

Then ... Robin DiAngelo's assertion was provocative enough to give me pause. I thought it hit a defining truth underpinning America's racial divide. Racism doesn't just happen. And it can't be the victim's fault. No Black or Hispanic or Asian or Native American is asking to be on the receiving end of prejudicial and intolerant behavior. White Americans can't turn away from the depth and breadth of racism in our country. White Americans must do more to fight against it. It was time to step up.

Now ... We Freedumbers believe it's time to take a step back.

Looking at the world through a racial lens is just keeping it real. That doesn't make us racists, it makes us realists. We don't have a racist bone in our bodies. Not one. So for us, racism is a non-issue. If Blacks, Hispanics, Native Americans or immigrants feel unfairly judged or treated, well, that's on them. Their delusion is not our problem. Then again, they could just admit they're inferior and get over it.

Today ... Get real. Helpful hint: A road trip can be fun and productive. Thought starter: Go to the southern border for some 'yell and tell'. Yell at all the desperate and scared men, women and children, and tell them to go back where they came from. Or head to a reservation to 'yell and tell' Native Americans they're losers who need to stop whining. (Unfortunately, you can't tell them to go back where they came from.)

SEPTEMBER 17

Today, on the anniversary of the signing of the Constitution, here is:

The Freedumber's Preamble

We the white, straight men of the United States, in Order to form a more pure Union, establish Injustice, insure domestic Tranquilizers to blunt woke protest, provide for the common defence from other people, promote the general lack of Welfare of those other people, and secure the Blessings of Freedumb to protect what's ours and our Posterity, do ordain and establish this Constitution of the real United States of Freedumbia.

SEPTEMBER 18

How tired are you?

"Those who expect to reap the blessings of freedom, must, like men, undergo the fatigue of supporting it."
(Thomas Paine)

"I'm tireless in support of Freedumb."
(Freedumb Fighter)

Then ... Thomas Paine's assertion was a reminder that freedom doesn't carry a lifetime guarantee. Freedom cannot survive without the support of those who live under its umbrella. We can support freedom by protecting voting rights for all, especially those of minority groups and the most vulnerable among us. We can support freedom by protecting the integrity of our courts and government. We can support freedom by embracing diversity and inclusion. We can support freedom by truly valuing the need for education, the benefits of knowledge, and the importance of critical thinking. Ultimately, we must support and protect one another, and never take for granted the opportunity we've been given. The work will be hard and the road is long – but without freedom for all, I thought, there is nothing. At least, that's what I thought.

Now ... We Freedumbers know that freedom is long past its sell-by-date.

Freedumb is the great enabler. For example, it enables putting limitations on those who can vote. It's not hard work if you enjoy what you're doing. Wouldn't it be better for America if all those other people just stayed home on Election Day and counted their blessings? So let's make it harder for them to cast their vote. Imagine closing polling sites to help shut out poor black and brown voters, and the so-called disabled – who always seem to be crying for help. Perhaps one day we can get to a place where voting isn't even necessary.

Today ... Be an activist. Helpful hint: Hit the streets. Thought starter: Initiate the first ever door-to-door "You can't vote!" campaign, targeting all do-gooding freedom-lovers.

SEPTEMBER 19

What do you welcome?

"America is known as a country that welcomes people to its shores. All kinds of people."
(Ruth Bader Ginsburg)

"It's time for America to be known as something other than welcoming."
(Freedumb Fighter)

Then ... I believed that America put out the biggest welcome mat in the world. I saw our country as the most powerful magnet ever conceived for those yearning for a better life. Race didn't matter. You are welcome. Religion didn't matter. You are welcome. Sexual orientation didn't matter. You are welcome. Just bring your dreams and ideas, your work ethic and your capacity to contribute. You will make us stronger. You will make us smarter. You will make us more interesting and more understanding. You help us open our eyes, our hearts and our minds. You would help make America, America.

Now ... I get that welcoming is just another wokey doke thing.

We Freedumbers have never been big on the whole 'welcome mat' idea. For us, race does matter. A lot. Well, the white race matters. Religion matters too. At least, the one true religion does. Christendumb rocks! Sexual orientation also matters. Steer clear of the queers! So bring us your whiteness, your God-deforming faith and your homophobia. It won't help make us smarter or stronger, more interesting or more understanding. On the other hand, it will help purify America. And that's the only thing that's really going to make America, America again.

Today ... A pro tip. If you're really serious about making America great again, buy as much Jesus of Orange memorabilia as possible. On sale now! Just think of the treasure trove of family heirlooms to be acquired and showcased for generations to come! Have you seen his Teddy Bear? Adorable! And only $39.99.

SEPTEMBER 20

What makes you happy?

"The Constitution only guarantees you the right to pursue happiness. You have to catch it yourself."
(attributed to Benjamin Franklin)

"The Constitution guarantees you the right to pursue happiness at the expense of others."
(Freedumb Fighter)

Then ... Happiness sat at the core of American ambition. Sure, people interpret happiness in different ways, be it related to money, fame, family, or contribution to the greater good. What I really loved was the energy behind the idea of pursuit. You want it, go for it. You want it, go out and get it. You want it, then giddy-up. That's America. It's your life, it's your pursuit, so make the most of it. Happiness isn't a given, but it's out there in abundance if you're willing to give life a rip. That's America. That sense of abundance and possibility brought a unique dynamism into American consciousness and culture. It drove us forward and helped us live up to being called the land of opportunity.

Now ... Freedumbers understand happiness for what it is – something to be hoarded.

Abundance really isn't part of our thinking. Scarcity, yes. Abundance, no. On happiness, we believe there's only so much to go around. Only so much power. Only so much advantage. Only so much opportunity. Only so much of the things that can make you happy. So, by our nature, we get twitchy at the thought of the others getting their fair share of anything. Sharing any piece of our apple pie is unacceptable. Why would we want to be 'the happiest country in the world'? That means too many people are happy and you don't have enough happiness all to yourself. There's no real joy to be found in that.

Today ... Brainstorm mottos that reflect your own pursuit of happiness. Helpful hint: Focus on making others miserable. Thought starter: How about "It's my happiness, you can't have any" or "I'm happy if you're not" or "That's mine. That's mine. And that's mine too." Bottom line, the mottos gotta make you smile.

SEPTEMBER 21

What do you hope to catch?

*"Perfection is not attainable, but if we chase perfection
we can catch excellence."
(Vince Lombardi)*

*"Purity is not attainable, but if we chase purity we can catch privilege."
(Freedumb Fighter)*

What you chase very often becomes who you are.

Then: Resolve to be a patriot and do your part in pursuing a more perfect union, but …

Now: Resolve to be a Freedumber and do your part in pursuing a more pure union.

SEPTEMBER 22

How are you handling things?

"To handle yourself, use your head. To handle others, use your heart."
(Eleanor Roosevelt)

"I'll handle myself the way an American should."
(Freedumb Fighter)

Then ... I really liked the distinction Eleanor Roosevelt made. A push to use your head in handling yourself felt like timeless wisdom. Likewise, opening up your heart to others. I always held that a unique dynamic in the American character was being both practical and passionate. It's a powerful paradox. It helped push things to change and evolve. Smartly and ambitiously. I believe I had seen enough to say that, at least in my experience, Americans had both their head and their heart in the right place.

Now ... We Freedumbers suggest other people shove their head and heart up their ass.

This attitude might have a bit of an edge to it. And doesn't help much in handling people, problems or much of anything else, but it lets you know where we stand. We're on edge.

Today ... Time for a fun fact. Helpful hint: There's lots of fun happening since the overturning of Roe v. Wade. Thought starter: How about this: Since the Supremes unleashed their wisdumb, there were 65,000 rape-related pregnancies in fourteen states that have outlawed abortion. Those facts should pull anybody back from the edge. Trending top baby names are Brett and Amy! (For more fun facts check out the JAMA Internal Medicine Journal, January '24!)

SEPTEMBER 23

Are you aware?

"Let's not look back in anger, or forward in fear, but around in awareness."
(James Thurber)

"I'm unaware of the value of awareness."
(Freedumb Fighter)

Then ... Anger aimed at what has gone before, and fear of what might lie ahead, are time wasters. Yes, we should learn from the past and prepare for the future, but we should always focus on what's happening now. To overcome our problems, we must be aware enough to get down to what we're up against. We should be cognizant of current issues and opportunities. And we should be calm and clear-headed enough to talk them through on our way to a solution. I believed that with focus and fortitude, there was no problem America could not meet and defeat. Even incremental improvements were a step in the right direction. And that step began with awareness.

Now ... For us Freedumbers, awareness is the beginning of a downward domino.

Awareness lends itself to being informed. Being informed can lead to understanding. Understanding can make one think. Being thoughtful might push one toward having a degree of sensitivity. Sensitivity could lead one to caring. Caring might lead to action. Action has the potential to bring progress. And bam! Before you know it, you're right in the middle of a woke wonderland. So, we Freedumbers opt for unawareness. Our unawareness enables the creation of an alternative reality. That's where nothing is too outrageous, where common sense goes to die, and where our means are always free to mess with other people's ends.

Today ... Tell your friends about Unawareness Day. This is a day to celebrate not knowing. Or caring. Or not wanting to know or care. Make it a national holiday. "Too many of those already," you say? Not if it replaces Martin Luther King Jr. Day.

SEPTEMBER 24

How goes the battle?

"Be kind, for every man you meet is fighting a hard battle."
(Ian MacLaren)

"Nobody is fighting a harder battle than me."
(Freedumb Fighter)

Then ... I held that kindness was perhaps the most human of destinations. To get there, empathy was essential. When we are able to feel the personal battles others are engaged in, it unlocks our heart. And an open heart can do amazing things. I've always believed in the American ability to empathize, to be a kind and generous people. We want to help others. We want to reach out and lend a hand. We want to ease the pain and suffering. We may champion self-reliance, individual responsibility and independence, but I thought a well-placed act of kindness was as American as it gets.

Now ... We Freedumbers wish some empathy and kindness would be sent our way.

We are fighting the hardest battle there is – the battle to separate ourselves from others in terms of privilege, advantage and entitlement. We can't be expected to care about anyone else, let alone be kind to them. What we might expect is a little more empathy for our cause. Do you think prejudice and intolerance just happen? Do you think conspiracy theories make themselves up? Do you know what it's like to lie awake at night brainstorming with yourself on ways to make America great again? If people would just take a minute and try to understand the burden we carry!

Today ... Show a little love. Next time you see a Freedumber being coarse, cruel or uncivil in helping to make us great again, tell them how they inspire you. Thank them for their service. God knows they deserve it.

SEPTEMBER 25

What are you pursuing?

"When our founders spoke of the 'pursuit of happiness,' they did not mean long vacations and the piling up of things. Happiness was in the enlargement of one's being through the life of the mind and of the spirit."
(David McCullough)

"I only think of one thing when I think enlargement."
(Freedumb Fighter)

Then ... Our founders were brilliant men. They were serious men, committed to serious ideas. I thought David McCullough's statement was a good reminder of this. A good reminder for us. Happiness, from the perspective of our founders, was not simply about material gain or total relaxation. They took a more elevated, even enlightened view of happiness. They saw it as something more profound. A notion that was closer to the goal of fulfillment. Of being a better person in mind and spirit. That may not sound sexy, or hold out the promise of immediate gratification, but our Founding Fathers understood happiness as fuel for feeding our best selves, leading our best lives. And being the best American we could be.

Now ... I realize nobody can enlighten like a Freedumber.

First off, happiness has nothing to do with a "life of the mind." Thinking and reflecting are a waste of time. Reading should be limited to book covers only – for the sole purpose of identifying books to ban. Secondly, as for "life of...the spirit," we Freedumbers are all over it. For us, it comes down to mean-spiritedness. So, women want equal rights? They better not push too hard – if they know what's good for them. That's the spirit! Immigrants want opportunity? They better not want too much – if they know what's good for them. That's the spirit! How about librarians? Those libtards think they can simply provide books to people wanting to learn. Well, their shelves better follow the code of Christendumb – if they know what's good for them. That's the spirit! There's some happiness that would make the Founding Fathers proud.

Today ... Keep your creative juices flowing. Helpful hint: Write a ballad about happiness. Thought starter: Title it "Stairway to Fascism."

SEPTEMBER 26

Who are you?

"Ignorance is stubborn, and prejudice dies hard."
(Adlai Stevenson)

"Ignorance and prejudice must never die."
(Freedumb Fighter)

Then ... While there's no denying the presence of ignorance and prejudice in America, I never believed these to be dominant traits in the American character. Any group that has the odds stacked against them through no fault of their own, deserves our attention and help. And the America I knew rooted for the underdog, defended the vulnerable, and reached over to pull in those on the margins. America was always on the side of those who struggle – for acceptance, for liberty, for justice and a fair shot. Ignorance and prejudice may well be stubborn, but I believed an America that stayed true to its destiny, could 'out stubborn' anything.

Now ... We Freedumbers don't believe in fighting things we can use to our advantage.

So let ignorance be stubborn. Allow prejudice to persist. In fact, why not embrace them? They benefit us. Ignorance and prejudice can frame bad behavior as heroic and patriotic. They can frame cruelty as righteous and just. They can frame cowardice and hypocrisy as leadership. They can frame privilege as an illusion. They can frame science as a conspiracy, vaccines as toxic, and healthcare workers as the enemy. Hell, ignorance and prejudice are even more lethal than your run-of-the-mill semi-automatic rifle.

Today ... Relive our idyllic past. Helpful hint: Honor the Wild West by throwing a Cowboys and Indians party. Thought starter: All the cowboys should wear white hats and all the Indians should be lying on the floor scalped and bloodied at the end of the night. Fun times for all!

SEPTEMBER 27

Have you heard this one?

*"... That best portion of a good man's life,
His little, nameless, unremembered acts
Of kindness and of love."
(William Wordsworth)*

*"I prefer acting out."
(Freedumb Fighter)*

Then ... Good men don't do it for the glory. They don't do good to have it acknowledged or applauded. They do it because it's the right thing. As I've said before, in moments of need, Americans lead with their heart. You may not hear a lot about it. It may not make the news. It may not come across your social media feed. But little acts of kindness happen across this country every single day. By the millions. And I'd argue those little acts are a big part of who we are. Americans have been called a lot of things, but I believed something you never hear: Americans are loving people.

I really did believe that.

Now ... Please, don't make me puke.

What about aggression? Freedumbers love aggression. Aggression sends a message. An important message. And that's good for everyone. Aggression clarifies. Aggression separates. Aggression diminishes. And we work hard at sharpening and perfecting our aggression. We throw tantrums and shout obscenities. We threaten, finger-point and give the finger. We hurl insults and accusations. It's pretty amazing behavior to behold. And it doesn't take a lot to unleash the beast. Hahaha.

Today ... On National Forgiveness Day, accuse somebody you love of being too forgiving.

SEPTEMBER 28

Today, some books for the women of Freedumb: (All written by bestselling author Dick Short)

Try Harder: Women Need to Give More
This inspiring work lays out a 10-point plan for any woman looking to please her man. The basic premise is that women aren't doing enough for the men in their lives. Mr. Short explains why women always have more to give, and lays out his simple rules which any woman should be able to understand and obey. Chapters include "If you think you've done enough, do one more thing" and "This beer is warm."

Have You Seen My Gun?
A feast for the eyes. With breathtaking photographs from around the country that show Freedumb's women clutching their assault rifles, this book can't help but capture your imagination. Who knew there were so many fun and exciting ways to hold and handle 'America's gun'? Each photograph is accompanied with a little backstory on each of its owners. Full of obscene language and ignorant anecdotes, this book provides ammunition for any special woman or teenage girl in your life.

Just Asking
This hard-hitting and intimidatingly large volume lays out how and when women should ask for permission. While it acknowledges the benefit of being uber-aggressive, unhinged and boorish in fighting the culture wars, the book reminds women that, ultimately, they are the lesser sex. And men are the boss. Chapters include "If you don't have permission, the answer is no", "Things you need permission for that will surprise and delight", and the ground-breaking "Why wouldn't you ask for permission anyway"?

The Linguistics of Freedumb Fighting Women
This revealing study of how women can use language to further the cause of Freedumb doesn't disappoint. The author focuses on topics like "Coarse language for special occasions", "Bad language isn't bad enough", and the always popular, "How to get kicked out of a theater while on a date."

A Celebration of Female Role Models
This slim volume is an easy read for anyone looking for some inspiration. It celebrates the hatefulness and vitriol spewed by the best and brightest of Freedumb's female pioneers in the context of their everyday lives. For those who believe only men can be world-class cultivators of Freedumbness, this book will be a revelation.

SEPTEMBER 29

How to lead the way?

"Leadership is solving problems."
(Colin Powell)

"Leadership is creating drama."
(Freedumb Fighter)

Then ... General Powell knew a thing or two about leadership. And if leaders aren't solving problems, the question becomes "What exactly are they doing?" I believed we needed leaders who are innovative, determined and committed to serving. We needed leaders who start from a place of positive intent, who want to solve for all and not just some, and who inspire us to bring out our very best. I believed each and every American had it within them to be that kind of leader. I really did.

Now ... Freedumbers understand what we really need is drama and chaos.

Let us lead the way. Why solve anything when it's so much more fun and entertaining to just say and do dumb shit? To rile people up. To scare people and put them on edge. Freedumb's leaders love to provoke and disparage. Our leaders love to demean and alienate. They love to create doubt and confusion. This doesn't solve anything, but who really cares, it gets a lot of attention and distracts from doing anything constructive.

Today ... Showcase your leadership potential. Helpful hint: If you don't denigrate, Freedumbers won't follow. Thought starter: Try (and fail) at besting Jesus of Orange. Can you go lower than calling out your opponents as "vermin." (Note: Hitler and Mussolini also used this label to maximum effect.)

SEPTEMBER 30

What are you willing to pay?

"Service to others is the rent you pay for your time here on earth."
(Muhammad Ali)

"It's the end of the month and your rent is due."
(Freedumb Fighter)

Then … Muhammad Ali did more than float like a butterfly and sting like a bee. The man could make you stop and think. As he did here. Because service to others isn't simply a nice to do, it's a need to do – an obligation. And in my experience, Americans took the obligation of service to heart. It doesn't necessarily come with applause, reward or fame, but stepping up to help seems to be an instinctive part of being American. Americans see a need and want to do something about it. We see someone in pain and we reach out to help. We seek to make the vulnerable less so, and lighten the load of those experiencing hardship. As a country, and a people, Americans were happy to pay the rent owed.

Now … We Freedumbers want to make one thing clear: we aren't renters, we're landlords.

And make no mistake, America is our house. Our house, our rules. The first rule is, other people answer to us. And if you don't like it, we're happy to show you the door. As landlords, our main role is to sit in judgment. And decide. We decide whether or not you should love *that* person or read *that* book. Whether or not you should have a baby. Whether or not you should believe in science. Whether or not you can vote. Whether or not you should feel comfortable in your own skin. Whether or not you are a real American.

Today … Impose a rent increase. Other people should pay until it hurts for the privilege of living in our America.

OCTOBER 1

How will you be judged?

"The test of a civilization is the way that it cares for its helpless members."
(Pearl S. Buck)

"Respecting the weak means leaving them alone."
(Freedumb Fighter)

Then ... I thought the home of the brave, with all its strength, wealth and capability, could never wash its hands of the most vulnerable among us. This isn't about socialism or communism. What it's about is human decency and dignity. It's about helping. It's about caring. To abdicate this responsibility would reek of callous disregard. That's not American 'individualism,' it's selfishness. Sure, we have to earn our way in America. But to suggest that the weakest among us, our most vulnerable and disadvantaged, simply pull themselves up by their proverbial bootstraps is a perspective both arrogant and ignorant. That's not America. That's not being American.

Now ... We Freedumbers believe the best way to help anyone is to do nothing for them.

Doing nothing for other people, especially the weak and vulnerable, is the ultimate sign of respect. The vulnerable don't want help! It makes them feel even more weak and vulnerable than they actually are. In the minds of us Freedumbers, abandoning people to suffer is not only respectful but necessary. But enough about the weak and vulnerable. We need to concern ourselves with a far more important topic: ourselves. You want to talk about a victim? The homeless and poor exist only to make us feel guilty. What are they doing to help us feel less guilty? If you want to feel for someone, feel for the white, straight men of Christendumb.

Today ... Let your fingers do the talking. Never raise one to help anyone else, but make sure your middle digit is ever ready to give.

OCTOBER 2

Where do you live?

"Above all, we must realize that no arsenal, no weapon in the arsenals of the world, is so formidable as the will and moral courage of free men and women."
(Ronald Reagan)

"Above all, we must realize an alternative reality."
(Freedumb Fighter)

Then … I believed in "the will and moral courage of free men and women" in the United States of America. America had the biggest, strongest and most ever-ready helping hand in the world. America was a country you could count on. Americans were a people you could count on. Big-hearted, brave and capable. This character had nothing to do with whether you lived in a small town or big city. It had nothing to do with living on the coasts or in the middle of the country. It was us. And it was indeed formidable. And inspiring. An arsenal to be envied.

Now … We Freedumbers live in our own courage-free zone.

It's a great place to live. It's a place called The United States of Freedumbia. It's a place where you don't say "gay" – or "Happy Holidays!" It's a place where the use of pronouns can be cause for imprisonment and where plantations are promising to make a comeback. It's a place where women have no choice but to do what men tell them, and where diversity is the dirtiest of words. It's a place where pussy grabbers lead by example and book banning is a professional sport. A place where you read the bible and then go out and do your worst. And it's run by a dictator who says and does whatever he wants, while we the people burst into frenzied applause. OK, we're not quite there yet, but where there's a will there's a way.

Today … Write a song. Make it a hummable little ditty about life in Freedumbia. Helpful hint: The first line could be "Hello dumbness, my old friend …"

OCTOBER 3

What deserves your dedication?

"The hope of a secure and livable world lies with the disciplined nonconformists, who are dedicated to justice, peace and brotherhood."
(Martin Luther King Jr.)

"I'm dedicated to lots of brotherhoods."
(Freedumb Fighter)

Then ... To me, the type of people Dr. King was talking about were those with a clear sense of right and wrong – unwilling to simply go along to get along. They are nonconformists with conviction. An active conviction. Not getting involved in issues or struggles bigger than yourself is the easiest thing in the world. But inaction never solves. It doesn't contribute to a society's security or livability. Fortunately, inaction isn't the American way. Wrongdoing and wrong-headedness will be confronted. Why? Because whatever our missteps and mistakes might be, ultimately, we Americans dedicated to fighting the good fight.

Now ... Never let it be said that we Freedumbers aren't dedicated.

We love the brotherhood of the Proud Boys, because locking arms and getting racist rocks. We love the brotherhood of Incel, because coming together to hate women with standards, makes for a great Friday night. We love the brotherhood of neo-Nazis, because goose-stepping your way to purity is good for the glutes. We even love the Moms for Liberty – they're not brothers, but it's inspiring to watch our sisters in arms advocate for ignorance. There's just so many options. And none of them have anything to do with justice or peace, or with contributing to a better America. Which is why the decision on 'Which one?' is as tough as they come.

Today ... Start your own brotherhood. Helpful hint: Fair warning, finding a fresh hate-filled gap won't be easy. Thought starter: "White men against breastfeeding in public" or "White men against black students wearing dreadlocks" or "White men against library cards."

OCTOBER 4

Where are you taking us?

"In the face of impossible odds, people who love this country can change it."
(Barack Obama)

"People who love this country need to take it back."
(Freedumb Fighter)

Then ... I voted for President Obama. I admired him. And in America, as he says, impossible has never been an obstacle: it has always been an invitation. Which is a pretty amazing thing. It's the American mindset. It's how we think. It's how we live. It's what we believe. America can always change for the better. That's a big part of why we love it. We have always embraced the struggle for positive change – without hesitation or fear. Even when the odds appear long, Americans never waver in their belief that better is out there, and that better is in our destiny.

Now ... I embrace Mission Freedumbness.

You think it's impossible to turn back the clock? If so, you underestimate the power of Freedumb. We're taking America back. Back in time and back from the others. After all, it's our country. And our love of country is so powerful it would take America back to when the authority of and deference to white men went unquestioned. Back to when everything made sense. Back to when everybody knew their place – even if they didn't have one. Too good to be true, you say. Just not possible in this day and age, you say. We say, "Watch this space."

Today ... Your mission, should you decide to accept it, is to rekindle the love for a more tolerant time. A time when racism, sexism and repression of all kinds flourished and spread.

OCTOBER 5

What's the answer?

"Overcoming poverty is not a gesture of charity. It is an act of justice. It is the protection of a fundamental human right, the right to dignity and a decent life. While poverty persists, there is no true freedom."
(Nelson Mandela)

"Poor people need to take care of their own shit. Just like me."
(Freedumb Fighter)

Then ... I believed we had to reframe how we saw the problem of poverty, so we could rethink the solutions to it. I realize poverty has been around forever, in any society you can name. But the means to live a decent life must be seen as a fundamental human right. And the lack of same must be seen as an injustice. Maybe, most especially, in the richest country in the world, the country that aspires to liberty and justice for all. People don't want charity they want a chance. A legitimate chance. And a legitimate chance comes with not going hungry, not going homeless, and not fearing bankruptcy due to illness. At least, that seemed like a fair enough place to start.

Now ... We Freedumbers believe the poor just need to get off their ass and try harder.

As with most things, we see poverty in simple terms. There's no point in quibbling about the magnitude or nature of the obstacles that people face. Obstacles exist. Get over it. No living wage? Find a job that provides one. Or do double shifts. No roof over your head? A cardboard box is underappreciated. No accessible healthcare? Hopefully you're a winner in the genetic lottery. What the fuck is a mammogram anyway? Finding any of this hard? Well, try harder. And wrap your head around the fact that there's probably something wrong with you. Maybe you're lazy. Maybe you lack the desire and drive to be an American. Maybe you're a sinner who deserves your hunger pangs. There's some justice for you, Freedumb style.

Today ... On National Do Something Nice Day, do something not nice. Find someone worse off than yourself, and lecture them why you're better than they are. Feel free to joke around with them, just make sure you're laughing at them, not with them.

OCTOBER 6

Ties that bind?

"They came here – the exile and the stranger, brave but frightened – to find a place where a man could be his own man. They made a covenant with this land. Conceived in justice, written in liberty, bound in union, it was meant one day to inspire the hopes of all mankind; and it binds us still. If we keep its terms, we shall flourish."
(Lyndon B. Johnson)

"Again, isn't a covenant a gathering of witches?"
(Freedumb Fighter)

Then ... I believed that America was indeed a covenant. What a compelling notion. I believed, as Americans, we were bound together by purpose. That purpose is rooted in the idea of liberty and justice for all. Those roots had nothing to do with the color of your skin, where you worshipped or if you worshipped, who you loved, whether you lived in a small town or a big city – they were roots that put us all on equal footing. They were roots from which our aspiration and achievement grew. They were roots that demanded our care and attention. Our diligence and vigilance. If you wanted to be a part of the greatest country in the world, that's what you were looking at. That's what we were all looking at.

Now ... But what about the witches? We Freedumbers want nothing to do with witchcraft.

First off, any gathering of women should be considered dangerous. And witches are the worst. Who knows what kind of magic they might be up to. Bewitching agricultural produce? Producing sickness? Creating storms? Putting spells of seduction on unsuspecting men? Witches are bad news. And have you ever noticed that feminists have a witch-like quality to them? How do you think women got the vote? That's right, they cast a spell to make it happen. How do you think women first got the chance to work outside the home? You are correct. sir, they cast a spell. That's some badass black magic. Sorry, lost my train of thought, now what was President Johnson blathering on about?

Today ... Protect yourself against any and all witches out there. Maybe hang a little garlic off your AR-15. Or is that for vampires?

OCTOBER 7

What does it mean?

"Patriotism is when love of your own people comes first; nationalism, when hate for people other than your own comes first."
(Charles de Gaulle)

"Don't dare tell me what it means to be a patriot."
(Freedumb Fighter)

Then ... The former French President made an important distinction here. And for the record, we Americans are patriots, not nationalists. And, it seemed obvious, our patriotism must never have anything to do with hating our fellow Americans. Loving our country doesn't demand hatred of someone else. American patriotism doesn't force or encourage us to hate. It's about being proud not prideful. And it is strong enough to weather debate and disagreement. If we truly embrace being the land of the free, we must have the courage to respect, if not love, others. Love of country should bring us together to solve problems, take advantage of opportunity, and build on American potential. If it didn't do that, it was something other than patriotism.

Now ... We Freedumbers aren't ones to quibble over subtle distinctions.

Nationalist or patriot, what's the difference? And who the fuck cares? They're just words, and words don't matter. The important thing, from a Freedumber's point of view, is that if you love America, there's a lot you have to hate. A lot of people you have to hate. Of course, your hate comes from a place of superiority. So, the only people you really have to hate are the lesser Americans. Which is easy enough, because you know them when you see them. You gotta respect that.

Today ... Name your five favorite patriots. Helpful hint: Don't think too hard. Thought starter: Jesus of Orange. Jesus of Orange. Jesus of Orange. Jesus of Orange. And Jesus of Orange.

OCTOBER 8

Where are you?

"We shall overcome because the arc of the moral universe is long but it bends toward justice."
(Martin Luther King Jr.)

"I don't bend. Ever."
(Freedumb Fighter)

Then ... You could argue that determination and patience are an essential combination for those pushing for progress. The reality is that the change we desire always comes too slowly, with smaller steps than we'd like – but come, it will. I believed the goal of justice for all was the holy grail for America, and for all humanity. Americans must push to balance the scales of justice today, and for the long haul. Generation upon generation. Progress will not always appear as a straight line, questions will emerge about how far we've truly come, and the pendulum can swing in unexpected ways. Still, our commitment cannot waver. For if we waver, if our commitment disappears, America as we know it will disappear. And the promise of what America could have been, would become no more than a footnote in history.

Now ... A footnote would be fine with us Freedumbers.

We don't see a "moral universe" as any kind of preferred destination. The Marvel universe is entertaining. The Metaverse is useful. And the Xverse is where the action is. But the moral universe sounds suspicious. A little woke. It sounds a little too open, too understanding and decent. Potentially open to good things for other people. It sounds like a place without privilege or built-in advantage. A place where white men might have to give up something. A place where Christendumb might not reign supreme. So, let's pull back on this whole moral universe thing. A footnote is a future worth fighting for. Just stay strong.

Today ... Build a Freedumb ark with your kids. Use popsicle sticks. Helpful hint: Once built, focus on who, and what, you keep off the ark. Thought starter: White rhinos are preferable to black rhinos.

OCTOBER 9

Today, a Freedumber's version of a beloved poem by Robert Frost:

The Road Not Shunned

Two roads diverged in my neighborhood
And glad I could not stomach both
And be one Freedumber, long I stood
And looked down one as far as I could
To where it promised honor and growth;
Then took the other, less just, less fair,
And clearly having the stronger claim
Because it was jackassy, fit to ensnare;
And as my sneers and my chilly glare
Had told the weak to shoulder blame,
Both roads that morning unequally lay,
Just one besmirched by the do-gooder pack.
Oh, I kept it blocked for another day!
Knowing how easily men fall astray,
I rejoiced at everything they lack.
I shall proclaim this alibi
Somewhere ages and ages hence:
Two roads diverged in my town, and I –
I took the one more corrupted by,
And America reaped all the difference.

OCTOBER 10

Are you nuts?

"The people who are crazy enough to think they can change the world are the ones who do."
(Steve Jobs)

"My world isn't going to change on my watch."
(Freedumb Fighter)

Then ... I think we can all agree that Steve Jobs changed the world as we knew it. From where I sat, we needed a lot more of his kind of crazy. It's so easy to be a naysayer. It's so easy to say "It'll never happen", "It can't be fixed" or "It can't ever be solved." And I'm not just talking about technology. We can't all be Steve Jobs, but we can all be difference-makers. That's because I believe we Americans all share a bit of the 'crazy' gene. We're crazy enough to believe in a brighter future. It's the kind of crazy, I thought, that serves as an antidote to fear by fueling our courage, strengthening our resolve and defying 'realistic' expectations.

Now ... Excuse me, but nobody is crazier than us Freedumbers.

One thing we're really crazy about is the word "no." It's key to the power of not solving, not building, not overcoming. Or wanting to. Having no as your North Star is an amazing thing to behold. For example, by saying no to action on climate change, you get to see more droughts, floods, hurricanes, wildfires and heat domes. By saying no to a woman's right to choose, you get to create more poverty, more mental health issues, riskier pregnancies, and more women in vulnerable situations. And by saying no to stricter gun control laws, you get to live with more mass shootings. More and more mass shootings. More and more and more mass shootings. That's the kind of crazy that can make America great again.

Today ... Start saying no in Russian. "Nyet" has a real authoritarian vibe that you'll find both comforting and effective. Practice in front of a mirror by saying "Nyet to Democracy!"

OCTOBER 11

Are your passions under control?

"The life of a good man is a continual warfare with his passions."
(Samuel Richardson)

"I don't fight my passions, there are too many bigger enemies out there."
(Freedumb Fighter)

Then ... Samuel Richardson was an 18th century English writer. To me, his thought about "continual warfare" signaled the importance of reason in the life of a good person. All of us should have our passions. We need men and women of passion to help push us forward. But reason – the power of the mind, the power to think and to be thoughtful – must be in the driver's seat. Passion without reason doesn't make room for common sense or objectivity. Unbridled passion allows the end to justify any means necessary. I believed passion should be guided by a sense of responsibility – a reasoned responsibility to your best self, to your fellow citizens and your country.

Now ... We Freedumbers are passionate about our lack of restraint.

For Freedumbers, a great again man is a privileged man. An advantaged man. An entitled man. And every great again man has the right to protect what's his – with great again reason. And bad behavior. We would passionately argue you can't hold us responsible for that.

Today ... Unbridle your passion. We passionately agree all women should be homemakers – whether they want to be or not, and that it's well past time to do something about it. Helpful hint: Get'em young and train'em right. Thought starter: Push your local school board to ban teaching STEM classes to girls. Let's make being a dependent woman great again!

OCTOBER 12

Are you game?

"Champions keep playing until they get it right."
(Billie Jean King)

"I'm taking my ball and going home."
(Freedumb Fighter)

Then … I saw Billie Jean King as a champion in tennis and life, a powerful advocate for both gender equality and social justice. In 1973 she beat Bobby Riggs in the "Battle of the Sexes" tennis match – which was a moment for the ages, and just fun to watch. She showed the determination and resilience needed to be a champion. If you wanted to win anything of value, playing until you got it right was part of the gig.

I thought the same was true for America. If we truly aspired to greatness, there were things we needed to champion, things we needed to get right – gender equality and social justice among them. Progress is not a sure thing or an easy thing, but it's an American thing. We just needed to keep grinding. We needed to hang in there together and keep playing until we could declare "Game over."

Now … We Freedumbers have taken our ball and gone home.

Back in the day, when Riggs was up against the Feminazi, our money was on the old white guy wearing the short shorts. It was a chance to show women who was boss, head-to-head, on national TV. And yet, somehow, we lost. It was a bad look for us men. Regardless, fact is fact. Men are superior. Always have been. Always will be. But we don't ever want to play Billie Jean King in tennis ever again. Not our game to play.

Today … Hold your own "Battle of the Sexes." Helpful hint: Challenge some random woman to a game of pickleball. When you lose, tell her your rotator cuff is not quite right or say you're getting over a groin pull. Then tell her she got lucky, go home and declare yourself the winner.

OCTOBER 13

Do you think you're favored?

"Anyone who does wrong will be repaid for their wrongs, and there is no favoritism."
(Colossians 3:25)

"With God on my side I can do no wrong.'
(Freedumb Fighter)

Then ... I saw doing wrong as a choice. It takes something away from the person making that choice. And it does damage not only to ourselves but those around us. Good people can make a mistake, do something wrong, and fall short of their own expectations. Bad people, on the other hand, make a habit of it and expect nothing more. Often without shame or conscience. But if you believe in a day of judgment, doing wrong, will eventually have consequences. It's always good to remember that all races, colors, creeds and sexual orientations have both good and bad in them. No group has the market on goodness. Or badness. At least that was the perspective of my God. And in the end, she didn't play favorites.

Now ... For us Freedumbers doing wrong isn't a choice it's an obligation.

Wrongdoing isn't wrong if it serves the cause. Take, for example, casting a vote. Perhaps the most important vote cast by an American citizen is the vote for President. The super cool thing about being a Freedumber is that a candidate's character isn't a factor when casting a vote. That simplifies an awful lot, and opens up some super interesting choices. Dishonesty? Doesn't matter. Pussy grabbing? No problem. Making fun of the disabled? Classic! Disparage a war hero for getting caught? What a loser. Undermining and disrespecting American democracy? That's what great againess demands. Mercifully, Freedumb's God looks favorably upon those who serve the cause.

Today ... Win God's favor. Helpful hint: Deface something. Thought starter: Vandalize one of those woke "In This House, We Believe ..." lawn signs.

OCTOBER 14

Ever wonder what if?

"If you talk to the animals they will talk to you and you will know each other. If you do not talk to them, you will not know them and what you do not know, you will fear. What one fears, one destroys."
(Chief Dan George)

"I'm not talking to animals or anybody else I don't know."
(Freedumb Fighter)

Then … The words of Chief Dan George carried a timeless wisdom. Fear is destructive. I believed his nod to the importance of connection should inform every aspect of our lives. Fear of the unknown, of what is different and foreign, can define who we are. And it can define the relationships we have, not only with people, but with all aspects of the world around us. If we're uninterested in truly knowing, or if we do not seek some depth of understanding, we are left with a void too easily filled by fear. And living in fear doesn't encourage clear thinking or constructive action. Still, at the moment of truth, I believed we in America would overcome our fear and find the will and the way to reach out and connect.

Now … Talking to animals? Who am I, fucking Dr. Doolittle.

Why should we connect when we can divide and conquer? Why be forced to rethink any of our relationships? With anything or anybody. What if Mother Nature really wasn't our bitch? What if we got serious about climate change? What if 'tree-hugger' became something to aspire to? What if Native Americans were seen as more than an easily forgotten people? That's simply too much 'what if' for a Freedumber. For the love of God, disconnect.

Today … On National Indigenous Peoples' Day, take out a full-page ad in your local newspaper. Remind all the Native Americans out there that they lost. We conquered. And we don't have to listen to any of their spirit-talking, nature-loving wisdom.

OCTOBER 15

What is your duty?

"I believe in the equality of man; and I believe that religious duties consist in doing justice, loving mercy, and endeavoring to make our fellow creatures happy."
(Thomas Paine)

"I believe that my religious duties consist of ... judgment."
(Freedumb Fighter)

Then ... For a man who has always struggled to see the upside in organized religion, I found the "religious duties" identified by Thomas Paine came as a pleasant surprise. A belief in equality and justice. Mercy that comes from a place of love. And working toward the happiness of our fellow men and women. I could buy into that. It was thinking very much in line with the way I believed God would have us behave. Whether religious or not, this spirit encapsulated a kind of big-heartedness that I felt was very American in nature. Believe in whatever faith you want or in nothing at all. Just aspire to be a decent human being. Kind. Thoughtful. Respectful. Do that duty, and you will have done your job as an American citizen.

Now ... We Freedumbers see our religious duty a little differently.

For us, our duty anchors itself in judgment. Of others. It is judgment that requires no empathy, no thoughtfulness or respect. We know someone who's begging to be judged when we see them. And we are here to make life hell for those other people. We do so proudly in the name of the God of Christendumb - knowing that those we judge are lesser people. One can only hope the passion for our duty is contagious. Let us pray.

Today ... Read your bible. Cross out any passages related to kindness, compassion or caring. Use an orange marker to highlight any passages in the holy book referring to vengefulness. Helpful hint: You may want to also highlight any passages calling for stoning and burning.

OCTOBER 16

Can you live a simple life?

"My religion is very simple. My religion is kindness."
(Dalai Lama)

"My religion is simple too. No kindness needed."
(Freedumb Fighter)

Then ... I thought, wow, "religion is kindness". That's a beautiful thought. Kind is generous. Kind is considerate and supportive. Kind is helpful. Kind is even friendly. If you're going to anchor religion in one thing, you could do a lot worse than kindness. Just imagine if we anchored ourselves – our hearts, minds and souls – in kindness. That doesn't mean we can't be ambitious, competitive and independent. Kindness isn't an obstacle. I always found Americans to have a great capacity for kindness. A kindness is rooted in our strength, courage and sense of responsibility. From where I sat, kindness was as American as the Fourth of July.

Now ... A religion of kindness? You gotta be kidding.

The 'Dolly Lama', whatever that is, is speaking blasphemy. Christendumb, the religion of Freedumbers, is the one and only true religion. It's short on compassion, but long on subjugation and domination. If you want to knock on heaven's door, you have to see the sacredness of power and control. Hard to understand? No worries, just let go and believe.

Today ... Get on your knees and pray – pray that you can be the hardship that breaks the spirit of some kind soul trying in some small way to make the world a better place.

OCTOBER 17

Are you burdened?

"Prejudice is a burden that confuses the past, threatens the future and renders the present inaccessible."
(Maya Angelou)

"When others say prejudice, I hear justice."
(Freedumb Fighter)

Then ... Maya Angelou gave a sobering encapsulation of the damage done when judgment is based on ignorance and fear. It impacts everything. Yesterday. Today. And tomorrow. Prejudice weighs down opportunity, freedom, justice, and our collective goodness as a people and country. When we choose to understand history from a 'white first' perspective, that prejudice prevents us from fully learning from the past. And that lack of learning will cast a shadow over not only us, but our children and grandchildren. I didn't believe that was the legacy America was looking to leave.

Now ... OK, we've heard enough from Maya Angelou.

History *is* white. That's learning number one. When all is said and done, we believe the others got what they deserved. That's justice. Pure and simple. That's learning number two. If their life was, or is, in some way burdened, confused, threatened or limited, that's on them. That's learning number three. History lesson over.

Today ... Don't remember their names. Daunte Wright, Andre Hill, George Floyd, Breonna Taylor, Atatiana Jefferson, Freddie Gray ...

OCTOBER 18

How do you respond?

"Between stimulus and response there is a space. In that space is our power to choose our response. In our response lies our growth and our freedom."
(Viktor Frankl)

"I get lost in space."
(Freedumb Fighter)

Then … When a Holocaust survivor says something, you listen. Frankl's "space" was the opportunity to choose. About who you are and what you believe. The space is where ambition and attitude come in. The space is where we can decide to show up, where we can decide to step up. I believed Americans would always step up. We just do. We step up to solve, to encourage, to help, to build. That's who we are. We don't stand by and watch – we're not spectators. We don't shut our eyes or turn away. And we don't waste the space we're given.

Now … There are few things us Freedumbers appreciate as much as a wasted space.

Space to think? That's sounds way too thoughtful. And kind of 'science-y' too. Both of which are red flags. Name a stimulus and we have a ready-made response. No space needed.

Today … Ignore Victor Frankl. And Anne Frank. And Elie Wiesel. If you don't read any of them, you can blame the Jews for the Holocaust (if that was even a real thing). Bam! Why search for space when all you need is the Freedumb to respond.

OCTOBER 19

What kind are you?

"We need optimism to make progress – yet that alone isn't enough. To contend with environmental crises and make life better for everyone, we need the right kind of optimists: those who recognize that the world will only improve if we fight for it."
(Hannah Richie)

"What environmental crises?"
(Freedumb Fighter)

We need to rethink our relationship with the environment.

Then: Let's treat Mother Nature as we would our own mother, but …

Now: Let's treat Mother Nature like we're Motherfuckers.

OCTOBER 20

Are you up for a challenge?

"The challenge of leadership is to be strong, but not rude; be kind but not weak; be bold but not a bully; be thoughtful but not lazy; be humble but not timid, be proud but not arrogant; have humor, but without folly."
(Jim Rohn)

"The challenge of leadership is to give your followers what they want."
(Freedumb Fighter)

Then … Leadership isn't easy. And truly great leaders are rare. That said, I believed America has, and has had, more than our fair share of them. As Jim Rohn observed, leaders walk a line. It's often a fine line, but the bottom line is that we expect leaders to do what's right. That requires a particular kind of strength and boldness: to make hard decisions that aren't always popular; to care for the marginalized and vulnerable when others may be less than concerned; to strive for better when you could get away with leaving things as they are. Like I say, leading is a tough gig. We needed our best to answer the call.

Now … It is the Freedumbest among us who should lead.

What we need are leaders who draw no lines. Think a rude, unkind, arrogant bully who has no sense of humor unless they are laughing at other people (especially the disabled) or shooting their dogs. Talk about great again! We need leaders who make decisions consistent with the best of what Freedumb has to offer. That won't involve striving for better. That won't involve protecting the vulnerable or marginalized. But it will involve chaos and fear. And it will require us all to be less than our best. Commit now!

Today … Create a leadership moment. Helpful hint: People can't follow behavior they don't see. Thought-starter: Knock over the recycling bins in your neighborhood on collection day or snicker at someone with Down's Syndrome and get your kids to film it and post you in action.

OCTOBER 21

What do you look forward to?

"The quality I look for most is optimism: especially optimism in the face of reverses and apparent defeat. Optimism is true moral courage."
(Ernest Shackleton)

"We are on the verge of the apocalypse."
(Freedumb Fighter)

Then ... Defining optimism as moral courage was a powerful thought and one that, I believed, tapped into something inherent in the American character. Optimism isn't about closing your eyes and hoping. It's not about wishful thinking. Optimism is about a belief in our capacity for progress, and having the will and wherewithal to act on its behalf. It's the energy to overcome and get good, constructive things done. An energy that believes the future must be better than the past – and works to make that belief a reality. And, I thought, it's an energy that puts one foot in front of the other until the ultimate destination is reached.

Now ... Freedumb's energy is anchored in a sense of doom.

Everywhere we turn, we see the apocalypse. Love is love – the pink apocalypse. Equal pay for women – the financial apocalypse. Trans people – the bathroom apocalypse. Books with the word "gay" in them – the library apocalypse. Civility – the fucking political correctness apocalypse. History including black people – the learning apocalypse. Consequences for sexual assault against women – the consensual apocalypse. Science is real – the vaccine apocalypse. Voter rights – the electoral apocalypse. Democracy – the globalist apocalypse. Police reform – the lawless apocalypse. And on and on and on it goes.

Today ... Be vigilant. Be on the lookout for more warning signs that the end is near. Helpful hint: Be wary of the obvious. Thought starter: Obviously, a second black President would break us. But so would a woman President or a gay President or a Hispanic President or any President who still believes democracy is a thing.

OCTOBER 22

What do you have to lose?

"I have nothing to lose by standing up for my beliefs. So I'll go to jail. We've been in jail for 400 years."
(Muhammad Ali)

"Why do black people always have to come across as so hard done by."
(Freedumb Fighter)

Then … Muhammad Ali was an American icon, and hero. He was a man of conviction, who stood up for what he believed in. He lost his heavyweight title and went to jail for refusing to fight in the Vietnam War. He also had a way with words. The above quote might not be quite as poetic as "Float like a butterfly, sting like a bee," but the idea of 400 years of jail time should get our attention. We can't truly know or feel what other people experience. I can't fathom what it must feel like to have "been in jail for 400 years." No white person can. The truth is, you can't really walk in other people's shoes. Not for a mile. Not for a step. That said, I held on to the belief that seeking to understand carried an upside of its own.

Now … We Freedumbers aren't really seekers by nature.

We don't get bogged down in trying to understand the circumstances of others. Life is tough. There are winners. And there are losers. And we Freedumbers figure we know all we need to know about the losers. We certainly know that losers would benefit from emulating us winners. So, for example, black people should stop bitching and moaning about how tough they've had it in America – and just try harder, like us white people. Let's not make things more complicated than they have to be.

Today … Play a practical joke on some loser. Help hint: You know a loser when you see one. Thought starters: Make a 'Get out of jail free' card and give it to the first black person you see.

OCTOBER 23

What do you depend on?

"The fate of America cannot depend on any one man. The greatness of America is grounded in principles and not on any single personality."
(Franklin D. Roosevelt)

"The fate of America does depend on one man."
(Freedumb Fighter)

Then ... I always understood that America was bigger than any one man. Even a great man such as President Roosevelt. America begins and ends with "we the people": inclusive of principles such as freedom, equality of opportunity, and justice for all. As Americans, we push toward fulfilling our potential, achieving a better America together. Leadership plays an important role, but we never have been, nor ever will be, a dictatorship. Or a country vulnerable to the appeal of a demagogue. Our democratic foundation grounds, defines and protects us. No one man could be bigger than we the people. Ever.

Now ... We Freedumbers know the one man is out there.

His name: Jesus of Orange. A man so great again he should be President for life.

Today ... Play 'Lead me on'. It's a game where you rank order the characteristics most important for a leader in the Freedumb movement. For example, what matters more, contempt for the environment or contempt for fair elections? Hostility toward independent women or hostility toward voting rights? No integrity or no compassion? It's tough stuff, but it's a game the whole family can enjoy.

OCTOBER 24

What's your truth?

"We hold these truths to be self-evident: that all men are created equal; that they are endowed by their creator with certain inalienable rights; that among these are life, liberty and the pursuit of happiness."
(Thomas Jefferson)

"I'll tell you what's self-evident or not."
(Freedumb Fighter)

Then ... There may be a more powerfully inspiring sentence in the English language, but I had yet to come across it. To me, the words written by Thomas Jefferson *are* America. Powerful. Ambitious. Straightforward. Energetic. Aspirational. This is America's truth. This is why people come to America. This is why people want to be American. This is why people are proud to call themselves American. Our country demands the best from its citizenry. It speaks to opportunity and possibility. It invites ideas and dreams. Whenever I read these words, I came away thinking better was always on the horizon. I believed that truth should be self-evident to us all.

Now ... For us Freedumbers, self-evident isn't evident at all.

We Freedumbers will give you the real truth. The idea that all men are created equal is a misstep right out of the gate. Men aren't created equal. They are created white, and then stained by other colors. That's the real truth. Or, if you want to be a little more poetic, try "White men lead, all others plead." Plead to white men for hope. Plead to white men for liberty and justice. Plead to white men for opportunity. Now that's aspirational. Any other perspective would be alien. That should be self-evident to all.

Today ... Do something self-evident. Helpful hint: Correct a 'real' truth with a declared truth. Thought starter: Just spell it out – forget we the people, democracy is only as good as the dictator who runs it.

OCTOBER 25

Today, five Top Trending Movies (Freedumber favorites):

Cancun
A modern-day thriller that tells the inspiring story of a heroic politician who leaves his constituents freezing in the dark during a midwinter power outage while fleeing with his family to a sun-drenched beach locale in a foreign country. What will it take to bring him back home? Did 'home' want him back? Is there something to see here?

The Brain
A thought-provoking comedy charting the rise of an Alabama politician who doesn't know the three branches of American government, argues he can't be a racist because he was a football coach, and believes World War II was fought against the forces of European socialism. Now he's an intellectual leader in the world's greatest deliberative body.

Mr. S. Goes to Washington
A wild romp of a farce about a habitual liar who makes his way into the US House of Representatives by fibbing about everything from the schools he attended to being a college volleyball star to writing Broadway plays to helping sick dogs to even saying his mother died as a result of 9/11 – only to be embraced by his party as one of their own.

The Fist Pump
The riveting story of a real American hero. The man from Missouri, a man elected by the people, who incited insurrectionists on January 6th 2021. He shook his fist in solidarity, then ran away to save himself so he could write a book on what it takes to be the kind of manly man America needs today. Prepare yourself for bravado on every page.

Girls' Night Out (R-rated)
A dramedy that follows the trials and tribulations of a couple of AR-15 toting frenemies who bring a fresh kind of leadership to Congress by cursing, name-calling, and finger-pointing their way to social media fame while accomplishing absolutely sweet fuck all. Contains shocking scenes involving a vaping, groping moviegoers and a tantric sex guru who teaches sword fighting.

OCTOBER 26

Do you see what I see?

"A pessimist sees the difficulty in every opportunity; an optimist sees the opportunity in every difficulty."
(Winston Churchill)

"I like to make it difficult for anybody seeking opportunity."
(Freedumb Fighter)

Then ... As Winston Churchill realized, how you choose to see the world makes a difference. For me, optimism sat at the heart of the American character. Whether immigrant or native-born makes no difference. Americans are all about possibility. Optimism and possibility fueled our dreams and guided our actions. Americans believe tomorrow will be better than today. We believe racism can be overcome; we believe ignorance and intolerance can be overcome; we believe injustice and inequality can be overcome. Maybe not tomorrow, or the next day, but someday. We don't quit after a setback, or become apathetic when the journey gets hard. That's not who we were. The harder the struggle, the stronger we got.

Now ... We Freedumbers know woke when we see it.

Hope is a threat. Possibility is a weapon. And the libtard mob won't hesitate to use them. Racism helps give society its structure. Intolerance provides lines that help keep order. Entitlement allows for disinterest in the struggle of others. That shouldn't be so difficult to get your head around.

Today ... Fine tune your woke detector. Helpful hint: If it walks like a duck, swims like a duck and quacks like a duck, then you may have a woke duck on your hands. Thought starter: Invite them to go hunting with you. Accidents happen.

OCTOBER 27

Are you a game-changer?

"The ignorance of one voter in a democracy impairs the security of all."
(John F. Kennedy)

"The ignorance of one voter is something to cherish."
Freedumb Fighter)

Then ... I believed we Americans took citizenship seriously. Being an informed voter is fundamental to that responsibility. Simply voting isn't enough – we need to learn about the issues and candidates. An informed and thoughtful vote should sit at the top of every American's 'to do' list. Who you vote for, and what they bring to the table, can have lasting consequences.

Would you vote for someone who is both passionate and prudent? Would you vote for someone interested in working together with others to govern, legislate and solve? Would you vote for someone who will listen and debate in good faith? Would you vote for someone who agrees that compromise isn't capitulation and that give-and-take is part of the democratic process? I thought informed voting was key to constructive, common-sense governing. Informed voting would contribute to all of us sleeping a little better at night. President Kennedy's words were a warning I figured we would do well to heed.

Now ... We Freedumbers see that warning as an invitation.

An ignorant voter is key to America getting back to greatness. We believe voting is so important, you shouldn't overburden it with critical thinking or common sense. Why? An ignorant voter can be led anywhere. An ignorant voter can elect ignorant representatives. Ignorant representation can lead to a lot of really dumb stuff, Freedumb stuff. And those will always be moments to cherish.

Today ... Show off your ignorance. Helpful hint: Do it for America. Thought starter: Tell your local representative the most effective way to serve his constituency is to stop considering the needs of the people.

OCTOBER 28

What are you hearing?

"Education is the ability to listen to almost anything without losing your temper or your self-confidence."
(Robert Frost)

"Now that really pisses me off."
(Freedumb Fighter)

Then ... I thought Robert Frost offered a unique perspective on what education can teach us. Certainly, the ability to listen is critical to deeper understanding and greater appreciation, but to be able to listen to unpleasant or critical words without getting angry or feeling threatened can be a challenge. To listen to something you disagree with, or take exception to, takes a level of discipline and composure that requires some real effort. Anger is the lazy man's emotion and it's seldom helpful. Freedom demands both responsibility and restraint. As we struggle toward a more perfect union, being 'educated' would hold us in good stead.

Now ... I realize reflection is an unnecessary speed bump on the way to getting pissed off.

Remember, your anger needs a daily outlet. Have you been doing your stretching, and punching your pillow every morning?

Today ... Find a fresh target to attack. Helpful hint: What are songbirds really singing about anyway? Thought starter: Direct a little well-aimed vitriol at sparrows, robins, and the ever-irritating warbler. Just in case. Nobody should have to put up with a woke warbler.

OCTOBER 29

Is it too late?

"It's never too late to give up your prejudices."
(Henry David Thoreau)

"There are some things just too valuable to ever give up."
(Freedumb Fighter)

Then ... I looked on Henry David Thoreau's assertion as another call to action. Hard but hopeful. It's never too late. It's never too late to get better. Prejudice of any kind is a pox. It has always been with us, and perhaps always will be. Still, as Americans, each of us has the opportunity to let go of the judgments we make based on things other than reason or actual experience. Our prejudices grow from fear and ignorance. In order to give them up, or at least confront them, we had to overcome both.

Now ... Prejudice is the last thing we Freedumbers would give up.

OK, the second last thing. Guns, of course, would be the last thing. But with that as inspiration, let me leave you with this thought: I'll give you my prejudice when you pry it from my cold, dead hands.

Today ... Work your prejudice. Helpful hint: Keep connecting the dots. Thought starter: Have you heard that gay men are poisoning our water supply, that "Happy Holidays!" really means "Have a lousy Christmas!" and that Barack Obama was actually born in Wuhan, China.

OCTOBER 30

What's love got to do with it?

"A new command I give you: Love one another. As I have loved you, so you must love one another."
(John 13:34)

"That can't be in the bible!"
(Freedumb Fighter)

Then ... The "new command" is not an easy one, but I believed love is what gave us a chance. A chance to connect with one another, to understand one another, to respect one another. Love opens up possibility. The possibility to overcome our fear of things that are foreign and different. The possibility to overcome judgments based on that fear. The possibility to reconsider our behavior based on that fear and those judgments. And for a people who express love of country like no other people on the planet, it would seem love is something we Americans do indeed carry in our heart. We love the flag, we love the Statue of Liberty, we love the Fourth of July, we love hot dogs and beer at a baseball game. We love a lot of things. Maybe putting a little more love in our hearts for our fellow Americans wasn't the impossible task it sometimes seemed.

Now ... We Freedumbers only have so much love to give.

We love our country so much, we don't have a whole lot left in our heart for the people who actually live in it. Loving is hard and can leave you vulnerable. Loving takes effort and can make you uncomfortable. Loving takes sacrifice and can encourage compassion and understanding. In other words, to love one another has no place in making America great again.

Today ... Rewrite some bible passages to make them even more Christendumb. For example: "Love turning your back on your fellow man." Or "Save all my love for you and yours."

OCTOBER 31

What do you respect?

"Respect for the God-given dignity of every human being, no matter their race, ethnicity or other circumstances of their birth, is the essence of American patriotism. To believe otherwise is to oppose the very idea of America."
(John McCain)

"Disrespecting the dignity of others is my right as an American."
(Freedumb Fighter)

Then ... I believed John McCain gave us words to live by. I felt that respect for the dignity of every human being was sacrosanct. What is America, if not the place where respect and dignity for all is the goal? How can you be a patriot without striving for that goal? How can you call yourself an American without working to make that goal a reality? Race should not dictate dignity. Not in America. Ethnicity should not dictate dignity. Not in America. Religion should not dictate dignity. Not in America. Gender and sexual orientation should not dictate dignity. Not here in America. That's what I believed.

Now ... Not John McCain again. Fuck me.

First, we consider the source of the thought. In this case, John McCain. A war hero, a statesman, an independent thinker. A man of integrity and conviction. Why on earth would you listen to, let alone embrace, anything he would say? Remember, he got captured by the enemy. What a loser! And we Freedumbers are winners. Besides, for us, patriotism isn't that big an ask, but it does demand some thoughtlessness in who and what you respect. Respect people who look like you, think and believe like you, and live like you. To believe otherwise is to disrespect the very idea of what will make America great again.

Today ... It's Halloween, so let's put a little scare into an unsuspecting target by undermining their dignity. Helpful hint: Think north of the border. Canada's always shoving their decency and niceness in our face. Thought starter: Let's hit them below the belt. Calling them the 51st state might hurt (and frighten) them now more than ever.

NOVEMBER 1

What measure of man?

"The ultimate measure of a man is not where he stands in moments of comfort and convenience, but where he stands at times of challenge and controversy."
(Martin Luther King Jr.)

"The ultimate measure of a man is me."
(Freedumb Fighter)

Then ... When I stood up to recite the Pledge of Allegiance, I was very proud to think of myself as an American. I believed that by any measure, the American people measured up. To me, Americans were defined by their courage. Sometimes in big ways such as stepping up for their country, but more often in small, everyday ways that mattered to their neighbors. In ways that mattered to their community. Sure, we appreciate comfort, but we Americans wouldn't seek it out to the detriment of doing our part, or doing what is right and just. We don't have an 'S' on our chest and wear a cape, but I believed an American would always bring the courage of their convictions wherever and whenever it was needed.

Now ... We Freedumbers take the measure of an American with a different yardstick.

Simply put, we are the measure. And what does the measure demand? Well, there's whiteness. That's critical. There's manliness. That's essential. And there's the belief in Christendumb. That's a righteous prerequisite. With those as your metrics, you can't go wrong or do wrong.

Today ... Imagine the ultimate measure of a man: the perfect man. Helpful hint: He actually does exist. Thought starter: Visualize a white, foul-mouthed, morally corrupt, egomaniacal sociopath with an intoxicatingly beautiful orange tan. And comb over.

NOVEMBER 2

What are you looking for?

"People only see what they are prepared to see."
(Ralph Waldo Emerson)

"People don't see what I'm prepared to see."
(Freedumb Fighter)

Then ... There's a fundamental truth in Emerson's thought above. People don't see things they are not ready for. One thing America has always been prepared to see is the future. Maybe it's our inherent optimism that drives our courage to step forward. Maybe it's our formidable energy that compels our ambition to get after what's next. Maybe it's our eternal confidence that unleashes our creativity in defining 'what if'. Whatever the reason, nothing could stop America from moving forward. Nothing could stop us from building, from creating, from improving. Nothing could stop us from envisioning a better future. We have always pushed to see an America that shines brighter.

Now ... We Freedumbers get no joy from the thought of a brighter future.

'Brighter future' is woke-speak. Freedumbers prefer to put on our 'greatness goggles,' and stare into the idyllic past. A past that is familiar. A past that is comfortable. A past that doesn't challenge our beliefs or attitudes. Loving the past doesn't require building anything. It doesn't require learning or growth, confidence or courage. Going back requires so little. The only thing it requires is fear. Imagine an America scared enough to embrace white Christendumb nationalism. Scared enough to abandon democracy. Scared enough to run from liberty and justice for all. An America scared of science and objective fact. Forget the 1950s, we want to take America back to the dumb ages!

Today ... Go dumb. Helpful hint: Be bold. Thought starter: Look directly into the sun and dare it to bring a brighter day.

NOVEMBER 3

What defines your destiny?

"It is your character, and your character alone, that will make your life happy or unhappy. That is all that really passes for destiny. And you choose it."
(John McCain)

"Character has nothing to do with destiny."
(Freedumb Fighter)

Then ... I thought John McCain was a real-life American hero. A patriot. A man of character. A man to be inspired by. So I put a lot of stock in his thoughts on character. I believed there to be a direct line from traits like discipline, integrity, courage and compassion to goals such as attaining happiness, maximizing potential and fulfilling one's destiny. Not to put too fine a point on it, but lack of character isn't a blueprint much good for anything. Destiny included. And coming up short on the character front will always be a choice. An un-American choice at that.

Now ... Character is a luxury we Freedumbers can't afford.

To Freedumbers, lack of character is very helpful in getting America back to greatness. Lack of character shrugs off lying and hypocrisy. It embraces intolerance and gives prejudice a pass. It values ignorance over understanding, cruelty over compassion, and coarseness over civility. That said, character isn't destiny. Ultimately, the color of your skin: that's destiny. Your gender: that's destiny. Your heterosexuality: that's destiny. Christendumb: that's destiny. Lack of character is just there to help things along.

Today ... Show'em what you're lacking. Helpful hint: Look for low hanging fruit. Thought starter: Berate any black or brown service person you happen to come across. Announce your displeasure at the treatment you received – however good it might have been. Feel free to make a scene.

NOVEMBER 4

Do you see a fire hazard?

"The mind is not a vessel to be filled, but a fire to be kindled."
(Plutarch)

"Education should extinguish the fire. Any fire. All fire."
(Freedumb Fighter)

Then ... I liked the distinction made above by the ancient Roman philosopher Plutarch. Education can't simply be an information 'dump.' We want our children to develop the capacity to think. To think critically, and for themselves. To question, and be fuelled by their curiosity. To think through issues and solve problems. We want education to open our children's minds, their eyes and their hearts. We want them to think and do in ways that make us a better country. We want them to learn what it means to be a good and responsible citizen. Admittedly, that's a lot of freight for our educational system to carry. That's why education is so important. And I thought that's why we, as parents, needed to support it in every way so that it would light a fire to a brighter future.

Now ... We Freedumbers would prefer to piss on any fire leading to a so-called better future.

But it's easy to run dry, so we need more fire extinguishers. Thank the God of Christendumb for Moms for Liberty. They are an increasingly powerful organization committed to two things. First, developing a school curriculum that ensures our kids learn absolutely nothing – except the ten commandments. And second, providing their founders with a lot of adventurous sex. Think of them as a pail of water, fighting educational fire wherever they find it – and as a group for any woman looking for a little sexual *ménage à trois*. Who says Freedumbers can't embrace diversity?

Today ... Start a local chapter of FFFD (Freedumb Fighting Fire Department). Helpful hint: Fires need to be put out at the source. Thought starter: Barge into your kid's school Principal's office and demand less science, white history only, no civics, math for Boys, marksmanship, and lots more Christendumb ethics (using the 'God Bless the USA' Bible of course).

NOVEMBER 5

Today, two more Freedumber Public Service Announcements:

PSA #7:

Will you never be expected to change your name when you marry. Or never be questioned if you keep your name? Will your ability to make important decisions, or your capability in general, never be questioned depending on what time of the month it is? Can you be determined and ambitious without being called a bitch? Will your careless driving or poor financial decisions never be attributed to your gender? Welcome to the club! Call 1-800-FREEDUM to learn more on all the best things about being man.

PSA #8:

Can you go about your day-to-day life without seeing ads for products to make your crotch smell 'meadow fresh'? Can you attend public events without concern about whether you should do something different with your hair? Can you say 'motherfucker' in public without being a disgrace to your gender? Will you never be expected to spend your life ten pounds underweight if you want to look your best? You lucky guy! Call 1-800-FREEDUM and talk to our representatives about how to help your woman make you proud.

NOVEMBER 6

What choice do you have?

"All your life, you will be faced with a choice. You can choose love or hate … I choose love."
(Johnny Cash)

"All your life, you will be faced with a choice. You can choose love or hate… I choose hate."
(Freedumb Fighter)

Then … I believed that love is the most powerful force on the planet. I thought love came as close to a superpower as we humans could have. True, as the 'man in black' suggested, it's a choice. To choose love defines what you say and do, how you think and what you feel, and ultimately the kind of person you are. To choose love took courage, humility. and generosity. Love opened you up. That's why when we chose love, amazing things could happen. Did happen. And I thought Americans were always open to doing the amazing.

Now … We Freedumbers have a different superpower.

We hate.

Today … Hate harder. Forget Johnny Cash. God's watching.

NOVEMBER 7

Are you having fun?

"It's kind of fun to do the impossible."
(Walt Disney)

"It's kind of fun to do the incomprehensible."
(Freedumb Fighter)

Then ... I believed Walt Disney captured the mindset of what it was to be American. Americans loved to take a rip at doing the impossible. Doing the impossible can take many shapes and forms, but it always takes courage. It always takes going beyond the boundaries of expectation. In big moments, like the moon landing that inspired the world in 1969. As well as more earthly moments such as the courageous rescue missions of the Cajun Navy in the wake of Hurricane Katrina in 2005. To more everyday moments like a community rallying around a bullied boy who was knocking on doors and desperately looking for friends in 2023. The best of America is impossibly brave and giving. Impossibly kind. Impossibly determined. And that can be awe-inspiring to see. It's also impossibly life-affirming.

Now ... We Freedumbers don't see any benefit in attempting the impossible.

So, our focus is the incomprehensible and the inexplicable. Freedumbers find life-affirming fun in leaving people speechless, at a literal loss for words. From groundless claims of stolen elections to antisemitic COVID conspiracy theories, from defending a dicktator want-to-be ex-President to celebrating America because "You have a right to decide who you hate", Freedumbers seek to make the unbelievable a reality. Doing and saying the incomprehensible must be an everyday occurrence if we are to push America toward its deserved destiny. Can you say "great again"?

Today ... Bring back the R-word. Talk about inexplicably offensive and cruel – why did 'retarded' ever fall out of favor? Helpful hint: Target Special Olympians. Thought starter: Follow the lead of a great again politician from Ohio who went out of his way to remind us all that no matter how well a participant might perform, they were still "a fucking retard."

NOVEMBER 8

Do you know your limits?

"Never be limited by other people's limited imaginations."
(Mae Jemison)

"I like limiting other people's imaginations."
(Freedumb Fighter)

Then ... Dr. Mae Jemison is an engineer and former NASA astronaut, and the first African-American woman to travel into space. It's safe to say she knows something about defying expectations. Americans never let limited imaginations win. We dream big. Americans never let the fears, concerns and doubts put a ceiling on what we can accomplish. The American imagination has given us everything from the electricity that powers our homes to the airplanes that fuel our travel to the smartphones that seem to run our lives. The American imagination gave birth to a country that believes in life, liberty and the pursuit of happiness. And in that pursuit, Americans have forever imagined better lives for themselves and their children. Americans even imagined a more perfect union, and a country that would be a force for good. In America, as the saying went, "If you can dream it, you can do it."

Now ... We Freedumbers wonder why other people have to imagine better for themselves.

After all, that doesn't do anything to help us. Better lives, for others? True liberty, genuine justice, real opportunity? What if dreams really do come true? None of that will do much for Freedumb's cause. It's not that we Freedumbers are asking for the moon. We just want to maintain and strengthen our built-in advantage. And our sense of privilege. And our feeling of entitlement. And our feeling of superiority. Is that so much to ask? Our imperfect union would be perfect if we could all come together and make that belief a reality. And that kind of perfection doesn't take much imagination at all.

Today ... Perfect yourself. Helpful hint: You're almost there. Thought starter: Actually, you are there, you entitled son of a gun. Imagine that. Have a great again day!

NOVEMBER 9

What's it all about?

"I care about decency and humanity and kindness. Kindness today is an act of rebellion."
(Pink)

"Kindness today is a waste of time."
(Freedumb Fighter)

Then ... I admired Pink. Her thought above was one of the reasons why. Calling out kindness as an act of rebellion reframes the act itself. Rebelling through kindness and decency can re-energize our humanity. At a time when fear and anger seem to dominate what many of us say and do, and how we interact with one another, acting with kindness and decency takes courage. Allowing fear and anger to define who we are not only feels wrong, it feels un-American. Courage doesn't always mean confrontation. Courage doesn't always require aggression. And courage should never be uncaring. Doing something nice for someone else might be the most courageous thing anyone can do. I believed there was no better time to be a rebel for the cause of kindness.

Now ... Fuck that.

We Freedumbers like to keep it real by keeping it cruel, coarse and uncaring. That's being an authentic American. The upside is obvious. Besides, it's fun to be mean to other people. Being kind can actually be dangerous. It could give the false impression that we are all created equal, all of us deserving of decency and respect. That type of acknowledgement is a slippery slope that no Freedumber wants to ride down. Ultimately, it could even threaten our sense of superiority. Time to quash the rebellion.

Today ... Call out any acts of kindness. If you see something, say something. Helpful hint: Pay special attention to any kindness directed toward immigrants. After all, as the Freedumbest of the Freedumbers himself said, "They are poisoning the blood of our country."

NOVEMBER 10

What race are you running?

"Human history becomes more and more a race between education and catastrophe."
(H.G. Wells)

"I won't tolerate education."
(Freedumb Fighter)

Then ... I found a sense of urgency and timeliness in the words of H.G. Wells. With the world getting seemingly more complicated by the day, with our issues dividing us more than ever, learning seemed to be imperative. If we don't learn, we are stuck. Without learning, we're stuck with mediocrity. Stuck with ignorance. And a lack of curiosity and critical thinking. We're stuck on the edge of darkness. That darkness won't look anything like the land of the free. And that's as accurate a definition of catastrophe as I could think of.

Now ... I'm stuck. Proudly and patriotically so.

It's simple. We've tolerated learning for too long. If we can effectively confront the catastrophic impact of education, learning and understanding on our kids and culture, we've got a better than fair shot at becoming great again. It's well past time we see darkness as destiny.

Today ... Be the intolerance you want to see in the world. And look good being intolerant by wearing a golden pair of high-top sneakers for only $399 – brought to you by the Jesus of Orange himself!

NOVEMBER 11

What is your intention?

"What is the quality of your intent? Certain people have a way of saying things that shake us at the core. Even when the words do not seem harsh or offensive, the impact is shattering. What we could be experiencing is the intent behind the words. When we intend to do good, we do. When we intend to do harm, it happens. What each of us must come to realize is that our intent always comes through."
(Thurgood Marshall)

"I have only the highest quality intent."
(Freedumb Fighter)

Then ... I never believed that the road to hell was paved with good intentions – that's a perspective grounded in cynicism. Intention matters. It may not guarantee a desired result, but good intentions are always better than the alternative. I thought Americans were people of good intention. I thought Americans were people with a good heart. We were people who wanted to do the right thing, to make things better. To help. To contribute. To improve on what was, and aim for what could be. I believed our intent would always come through loud and clear.

Now ... We Freedumbers never hide our intention.

We intend to take back America. To take it back from all the others. Take America back to when things made sense. When we all felt great about everything. You remember. A time when we could help blacks by keeping them as slaves. A time when gays were seen as mentally ill, and treated as such. A time when women knew they didn't know anything. A time when everyone from Native Americans to Hispanics to Orientals were not seen as fellow citizens but served as the butt of our jokes. What could be the harm in that intention?

Today ... Go old school. Buy some sheets, a few crosses and lots of matches. Poke a couple eyeholes in the sheets, and step up to be a great again pillar of your community. Helpful hint: Don't overthink where to stake your ground, any patch of green grass will help get the message out.

NOVEMBER 12

Are you ready to lift your gaze?

"We are striving to forge our union with purpose. To compose a country committed to all cultures, colors, characters and conditions of man. And so we lift our gaze, not to what stands between us, but what stands before us."
(Amanda Gorman)

"I strive to forge differences."
(Freedumb Fighter)

Then ... I thought Amanda Gorman was proof that wisdom didn't have to wait for old age. This quote, taken from her inaugural poem "The Hill We Climb," was a point of inspiration. This particular passage struck me as a poignant articulation of the challenge we face in America today. For me, it comes down to commitment. We are a "union with purpose." As a country and people, would we rise to our purpose? Or not. Would we represent the best humankind has to offer? Or not. Would we be the force for good the world desperately needs? Or not. Would we provide a safe haven, and offer the possibility of something better to those yearning to breathe free? Or not. I believed we could lift our gaze and answer the question of commitment with a definitive yes.

Now ... We Freedumbers prefer lewd limericks to lofty ideals.

We dream of a smaller America. Smaller in ambition, smaller in mind and heart. Smaller in responsibility, in purpose and potential. A union based on exclusion rather than inclusion. A union based on privilege and fuelled by entitlement. A union based on a single color and creed. To be great again demands that we lower our gaze.

Today ... Write a poem. Helpful hint: If it doesn't rhyme it ain't gonna shine. Thought starter: "There once was a man in Tallahassee, who didn't know his head from his assy ..." (OK, OK, great again effort. Right idea, but there are better targets out there. Keep practicing.)

NOVEMBER 13

How are you developing?

"If you can develop this ability to see what you look at, to understand its meaning, to readjust your knowledge to this new information, you can continue to learn and grow as long as you live."
(Eleanor Roosevelt)

"I'm not going to change my mind."
(Freedumb Fighter)

Then ... I realized "learning" was easy to say, tough to do. In fact, as Eleanor Roosevelt suggests, it's a skill we need to develop. It's easy not to seek to understand. It's easy not to grow. It's easy to think what you have always thought, do what you have always done, and know what you've always known. That kind of approach is certainly one way to live, but it seems fundamentally lacking. It lacks curiosity and courage, energy and ambition. In other words, you might say it lacks 'Americanness'. I thought we might start by understanding that.

Now ... We Freedumbers are blessed with amputated development.

We have severed ourselves from learning and thinking. We don't need to see anything. We've seen enough. We don't need to understand anything. We know what we need to. And what we don't know, we make up. And we do this without any sense of conscience or shame. Did you know COVID was designed to spare Jews and the Chinese? That's a Freedumber fact. Mass shootings happen because of Prozac. Also, a Freedumber fact. Gun ownership in the US is just the same as in Switzerland. Another Freedumber fact. The US government was responsible for 9/11 – they used controlled demolitions. A great big Freedumber fact. Let's call it like it is: When you stop learning, you gain a lot of insight into reality that others fail to see.

Today ... Make up your very own Freedumber fact. Helpful hint: Link pizza, vaccines, cannibalism and democracy together as a threat. America needs your insight.

NOVEMBER 14

What is your dream?

"I have a dream that my four little children will one day live in a nation where they will not be judged by the color of their skin, but by the content of their character."
(Martin Luther King Jr.)

"I have a dream that my little children will never grow up to live in a nation where they are judged by the content of their character."
(Freedumb Fighter)

Then ... I believed that if we are to be judged here on earth, it should be based on how we behave and what we contribute. Judge us on our integrity. Judge us on our work ethic. Judge us on our compassion and decency toward our fellow human beings. Judge us on our honesty, our generosity. Judge us on our willingness to learn and be better. Judge us on our courage to do the right thing, the hard thing. And let us agree that the color of one's skin is indicative of only one thing - the color of one's skin. There are good and bad in white and black. There are good and bad in every race, color or creed. The question we all need to ask ourselves, I thought, was "Are we good enough to be called American?"

Now ... We Freedumbers are tired of hearing from Martin Luther King Jr.

Freedumbers are above judgment. And insulted by any hint of it being aimed at us. It's an unfair weight for us to carry especially when our lack of character is focused on the most noble of goals - taking America back to greatness.

Today ... Stay strong and promote the cause. Helpful hint: Work dumber not harder. Thought starter: 'Freedumb Buttons' can help spread the word with messages like "Character Doesn't Count" or "Unmake Someone's Day" or 'Just lie baby'.

NOVEMBER 15

What is it that fills you?

"May the God of hope fill you with all joy and peace as you trust in him, so that you may overflow with hope by the power of the Holy Spirit."
(Romans 15:13)

"I don't see God as having anything to do with hope."
(Freedumb Fighter)

Then ... Hope was a powerful thing. The God I believed in was the God of hope. And if God really did bless America, we had to embrace the hope she offered, because hope was energy-giving. It fostered possibility. It led to solutions. It supplied the energy needed to confront inequality and injustice. Hope gave oxygen to the possibility of a more perfect union. Hope gave oxygen to the idea that our country could lead, by example, to a better place. A place of less suffering, injustice and inequality. A place of greater peace and joy. That's when we make miracles happen. The key was to keep the faith.

Now ... We Freedumbers have lost faith in hope a long time ago.

No disrespect to the Bible, but hate is a safer bet than hope. Hate puts a ceiling on possibility. So, immigrants can hope all they want. It ain't happening for them. Hate limits equality. So, women can hope all they want. It ain't happening for them. Hate puts strict parameters around liberty and justice for all. So, the blacks and browns can hope all they want. It ain't happening for them. Hate sets conditions on life, liberty and the pursuit of happiness. So, the gays can hope all they want. Sure as shit, it ain't happening for them. The white, straight men of Christendumb know God's will. And we alone do God's work. No miracles, or hope, needed. There's something to put your faith in.

Today ... Make some mischief. Helpful hint: create some false hope. Thought starter: Tell a newly arrived immigrant family you're going to give them some help settling in, and then do absolutely nothing to help them. Too funny, right. Bonus points if you call yourself an "Indian giver."

NOVEMBER 16

What are the fundamentals?

"In short, there are certain fundamental requisites for wise and resolute democratic leadership. It must build on hope, not fear; on honesty, not on falsehood; on justice, not on injustice; on public tranquility, not on violence; on freedom, not on enslavement."
(Edmund Ezra Day)

"Wise leadership is overrated."
(Freedumb Fighter)

Then ... I believed Edmund Ezra Day captured the 'must have' traits of any great democratic leader. It seemed straightforward enough to reject leaders who look to build on fear and lies, injustice and violence. It's hard to imagine how such leadership could have a place in America. It's even harder to imagine the American people encouraging and supporting such leadership. Nothing sustainable, nothing worth sustaining, could be built on fear and falsehood. On injustice and threats of violence. That's why I always believed wise leaders were a prerequisite for our great country.

Now ... What we Freedumbers want to see in our leaders is wisdumb.

Wisdumb isn't wisdom. Wisdom brings with it a sense of integrity, thoughtfulness and responsibility. And those are non-starters as far as we're concerned. Wisdom doesn't undermine the tenets of democracy. Wisdom doesn't use fear to stoke discord and division. Wisdom doesn't turn a blind eye to injustice. Wisdom doesn't just make shit up as you go along. So, we Freedumbers want leaders with the strength of character to reject wisdom, deny responsibility, dismiss hope, discard honesty, spurn justice, renounce tranquility, embrace thoughtlessness, and repudiate any sense of togetherness. And that takes real wisdumb.

Today ... Take the lead. Helpful hint: Come up with some words of wisdumb. Thought starter: "You must be unkind to achieve a greater again kindness" or "You must lie to achieve greater again integrity" or "You must be uncaring to achieve a greater again compassion."

NOVEMBER 17

How hard do you work?

"We are all born ignorant, but one must work hard to remain stupid."
(attributed to Benjamin Franklin)

"I don't work hard at being stupid. It comes naturally."
(Freedumb Fighter)

Then ... There's an important distinction between ignorance and stupidity. Ignorance is not knowing. Stupidity is not thinking. We may not know what it feels like to be the descendants of slaves, but it takes some real stupid to assert slavery was beneficial to black people. We may not know what it's like to be a woman considering an abortion, but it takes some real stupid to support that someone else should be making the decision for her. We may not know what it's like to be a healthcare worker in a pandemic, but it takes some real stupid to see them as the enemy. We may not know what it's like to struggle with our gender identity, but it takes some real stupid to see those people as a threat to our way of life. Ignorance can, at least at times, be forgiven, stupidity is a much tougher proposition. Still, I never thought either had much of a place in the American experiment.

Now ... We Freedumbers see ignorance and stupidity as the kissing cousins of greatness.

And fortunately, we Freedumbers have been blessed with an unlimited capacity for both.

Today ... Just be yourself. Helpful hint: Make a statement. Thought starter: Put a bumper sticker on your car that reads "Your in America. Speak English."

NOVEMBER 18

So where are we?

"And so I close by quoting the words of an old Negro slave preacher who didn't quite have his grammar right but uttered words of great symbolic profundity, and they were uttered in the form of a prayer: 'We ain't what we ought to be. We ain't what we want to be. We ain't what we gonna be. But, thank God, we ain't what we was'."
(Martin Luther King Jr.)

"Why can't we put all this progress in reverse and go back to the way things was."
(Freedumb Fighter)

The path to greatness always has a fork in the road.

Then: What could be, but …

Now: What used to be.

NOVEMBER 19

Today, the Gettysburg Address, as given by a Freedumber:

Four score and a lot of years ago our white fathers brought forth on this continent, a new nation, conceived in anger and agenda, and dedicated to the proposition that all men aren't created equal.

Now we are engaged in a great culture war, testing whether that nation or any nation so conceived and so dedicated, and so pure, and so perfect, can long endure. We are met on a great battlefield of war. The world can never forget what we are doing here: Battling women, who want equal pay. Battling people of color, who want a fair chance at buying a house in the suburbs. Battling radicals who care about the environment and are committed to giving our children and grandchildren a sustainable future. Battling teachers who believe education involves questioning, learning and critical thinking. Battling doctors and nurses who think vaccines and healthcare are aimed at keeping us well. Battling those who believe that guns kill people.

It is for us to be here dedicated to the great task remaining before us – to get angry and to resolve that government of the Christendumb people, by the Christendumb people, for the Christendumb people, shall not perish from the earth.

NOVEMBER 20

What's on your mind?

"Our progress as a nation can be no swifter than our progress in education. The human mind is our fundamental resource."
(John F. Kennedy)

"You don't want to put too much pressure on the American mind."
(Freedumb Fighter)

Then ... I had a lot of faith in the American mind. I believed that with focus and commitment, we could think our way through pretty much anything. As President Kennedy suggests, it's our go-to tool in the toolkit. The American mind must be nurtured, cultivated and exercised. It must be taught to think critically. It must be familiar with history so as to inform the future. It must learn to appreciate what science can offer. It must be schooled to respect the responsibilities of citizenship, the importance of democracy, and every individual's contribution to it. Progress comes from knowing better, from being better, and from seeing what better might look like. That's why critical thinking never seemed like a wasted endeavor.

Now ... I understand we have to protect the American mind from critical thinking.

We Freedumbers believe America thinks way too hard. We think too much about racism. Haven't we thought about it long enough? We think too much about intolerance. Is it really that big a deal? We think too much about inequality and injustice. Doesn't everybody have enough rights as it is? Freedumbers believe we must liberate our minds from the tyranny of thinking. Which, by definition, makes education a problem rather than a solution. Critical thinking will never get us to the greatness Freedumb offers. Critical thinking will never get us to the mind-numbing decisions and actions necessary to fulfill America's destiny.

Today ... Redefine critical thinking. Be critical of anything you start thinking about too much. Or opt for a second lobotomy. It's always better to be dumb than sorry.

NOVEMBER 21

Who will lead?

"Clearly no one knows what leadership has gone undiscovered in women of all races, and in black and other men of color."
(Gloria Steinem)

"Clearly, white men must lead."
(Freedumb Fighter)

Then … The greatest resource America had was the American people. Our diversity of talent, capability and leadership was limitless. To fulfill our promise, I believed we needed to tap that resource in its entirety. To do so, we had to untether ourselves from using color, gender, sexual orientation or religious belief as a filter for our leadership possibilities. Gloria Steinem laid it out pretty clearly. The land of opportunity was no place for opportunities missed. 'What if' cannot be an American regret. If greatness is to be part of America's future, our leadership must be accessed from the most talented and capable among us. To me that seemed pretty clear.

Now … Please, just stop.

White men just know better. White men just do better. White men just *are* better. It's due to that 'special sauce' produced when you mix the superior race with the superior gender. If the leadership of white man has fallen short, or does fall short, understand it's not white man's fault. No matter the situation or circumstance, fault or blame for any failure must fall elsewhere. Clear enough?

Today … Lead on. Helpful hint: Look for a victim who's really asking for it. Thought starter: Steal a barbie, break a Barbie, and post the video of you in the act. Separately, consider buying a couple of Ken and Alan dolls and convince them to become full-fledged Freedumbers. Just don't let yourself have too much fun playing with dolls. You know what that can lead to.

NOVEMBER 22

How do you exercise your strength?

"We in this country, in this generation, are – by destiny rather than choice – the watchmen on the walls of world freedom. We ask therefore that we might be worthy of our power and responsibility, that we may exercise our strength with wisdom and restraint, that we may achieve in our time and for all time that ancient vision of peace on earth, good will toward men."
(John F. Kennedy)

"I'm watching out that this 'goodwill toward men' thing doesn't get out of control."
(Freedumb Fighter)

Then ... These remarks were to be delivered in Dallas, Texas, on November 22, 1963. JFK was a beacon of hope and optimism. He believed America had an obligation to lead. Leading through strength, responsibility and wisdom feels like what the world needed from America. The American intention is anchored in building a better world. A world and country, more just, and free. I believed that Americans took their part of that responsibility seriously. As an obligation. An obligation that asks for the best we've got – heart, mind, and soul. It's an ask not all can rise to, but one I believed America could deliver on, for we were indeed worthy watchmen.

Now ... We see goodwill as another in the tsunami of threats coming at us.

The world doesn't need it, and more importantly, America is better off without it. Goodwill, that is. Imagine if we genuinely protected the freedom of minorities and the vulnerable. Imagine if we truly respected the rights of women, people of color, and all those in the queer community. Imagine if we took religious freedom seriously. Imagine if we took a hard look at the privilege and the advantage baked into our system. Stop the madness!

Today ... Embrace being a watchman. Helpful hint: Look the part. Thought starter: Design a custom-made ball cap for you and your pals. The front could read "Watchman of Freedumb" and on the back "The BIPOC stops here."

NOVEMBER 23

What is owed?

"I believe in the dignity of labor, whether with head or hand; that the world owes no man a living but that it owes every man an opportunity to make a living."
(John D. Rockefeller)

"I believe in indignity."
(Freedumb Fighter)

Then ... I believed in the dignity in and of all things. Labor perhaps first and foremost. I don't know if the world actually owes us anything, but I did believe America would be better off if each and every one of its citizens had a legitimate opportunity to make a fair wage. A living wage. A fair opportunity to find dignity in a day's work – in everything from fair working conditions to fair weekly hours, and from fair maternity leave to paternity leave. I felt that with dignity of labor as a foundation, we Americans would have the legitimate springboard needed to chase our dreams.

Now ... We Freedumbers get indignant at the thought of fairness.

Somebody's gotta do the shit work. And we ain't doing it. That's only fair. Shitty working conditions. Shitty hours, shitty pay. How else are lesser Americans going to help America? Shitty maternity leave, no paternity leave – well, tough shit. Lack of affordable childcare. Lousy inner-city transportation. Tough shit. It's important that other people experience and understand: unrelenting hardship is their destiny. And with that comes a certain reality. Dignity has no place in the lives of other people.

Today ... Shame someone. Helpful hint: Shouldn't new immigrants work for free, just for the honor of living in America? Thought starter: Suggest that your town council institute a 'Begging for Pennies' hour in front of City Hall every Sunday.

NOVEMBER 24

What do you hope for?

"I had always hoped that this land might become a safe and agreeable asylum to the virtuous and persecuted part of mankind, to whatever nation they might belong."
(George Washington)

"Do us all a favor and find asylum elsewhere."
(Freedumb Fighter)

Then ... I believed if America was a magnet for dreamers, it was also a haven for the persecuted and oppressed. I don't mean a so-called 'open border' policy, but rather an America with an open door and a welcome mat. So many in those "huddled masses yearning to breathe free" have come to our land of opportunity and done amazing things. They come with the hope of a better life. They come with the hope of giving their family something more. They come with the hope that hard work and some grit can make their dreams come true. I thought America was the place where ordinary people, from all over the world, hope to come and do extraordinarily American things.

Now ... We don't need even one more of those kind of people.

We want people to fear the thought of coming to America. We want people to understand that America doesn't care about who's tired or poor or huddled in a mass. Go breathe somewhere else. And just know America doesn't have the virtue to open our doors to the persecuted of mankind.

Today ... Plan a trip to the Statue of Liberty. Take a picture with the family, and then give that bitch a piece of your mind. It's time to turn off the torch, the party's over.

NOVEMBER 25

What's the answer?

"Some problems are so complex that you have to be highly intelligent and well informed just to be undecided about them."
(Laurence J. Peter)

"There's a simple answer to every problem. Just ask me."
(Freedumb Fighter)

Then ... Laurence J. Peter's quip spoke to the difficulty of solving difficult issues – and the need to keep an open mind as we face them. Being engaged and undecided leaves open the possibility for robust debate and a genuine exchange of alternative ideas. That's what I thought solutions to our most intractable problems demanded. Problems such as racism, inequality and injustice. I always believed that America housed more than enough of the necessary intelligence, curiosity and awareness to provide some traction against those kinds of complex issues.

Now ... We Freedumbers could save us all a lot of time.

We don't see complex problems. We see easy solutions. Freedumbers don't get hung up on the need for intelligence or understanding in solving problems. And we are undecided about nothing. The solution to racism? Get the black and browns to stop whining and moaning and send all the shithole immigrants back where they came from. Problem solved. The solution to inequality? Tell those who feel unequal to just shut up, show some gratitude and then get on their knees and pray to the God of Christendumb. Too easy! And injustice? Well, that's not really a problem in the first place. Bam. Just stay dumb simple, and watch America pole vault to unimaginable great againess.

Today ... Conduct a problem-solving session. Get some friends together, head down to the basement with a few beers, and puzzle out some solutions for what ails us. Helpful hint: Start with the '3 Ds' – democracy, diversity and decency. Thought starter: A dicktator.

NOVEMBER 26

What do you wonder about?

"I would rather have a mind open by wonder than one closed by belief."
(Gerry Spence)

"I wonder why people aren't more closed-minded."
(Freedumb Fighter)

Then ... Wonder, by one dictionary definition, is "a feeling of surprise mingled with admiration, caused by something beautiful, unexpected, unfamiliar, or inexplicable." That sounds enriching. It sounds inspiring and full of possibility. In order to see things differently, it stands to reason you must be open to the unexpected, the unfamiliar. I always believed that the American mind was an open mind. Americans want to feel wonder. We want to feel the surprise of experiencing something new or different. We are open to admiring something unfamiliar or unexpected. Wonder helps fuel the dynamism of America. It helps to fuel our evolution as a culture and society. That sounded like a beautiful thing to me.

Now ... We Freedumbers are looking to the day when wondering will stop.

We wonder about nothing, except why you'd wonder about anything. We see nothing to admire, let alone anything of beauty, in the unexpected or unfamiliar. A Freedumber's mind is immune to wonder. What's unfamiliar, foreign, alternative, atypical is bad. What's unusual, uncommon, out of the ordinary is bad. Freedumbers admire sameness. That is, people similar to us in how they look, think and believe. Wondering is a waste of time.

Today ... Wonder less. Helpful hint: Create the 'Seven Un-Wonders of World' and wonder no more. Thought Starter: Why wonder about over-watering grass, it's meant to be green. Or why wonder about a teacher walking down the hallway with a gun, when it's clearly going to get students to toe-the-line on hall passes. Or why wonder about the difficulty of women having to go out of state for an abortion, when those women are baby killers. Un-wondering is wonderful.

NOVEMBER 27

Where do you stand?

"Books and ideas are the most effective weapons against intolerance and ignorance."
(Lyndon B. Johnson)

"Intolerance and ignorance aren't the enemy."
(Freedumb Fighter)

Then ... I thought that books and ideas fostered thought and provoked curiosity. I believed they could inform. Could cultivate understanding and empathy. Could challenge beliefs and assumptions. Books could force us to think critically. They could combat complacency and passivity. They could instigate change – of opinion and mindset, and of behavior too. Exposure to other cultures, countries and peoples through books and ideas could open us up to the world. Books and ideas could bring us closer together. They could connect us to others in ways that foster trust and respect. Books and ideas may not be a panacea, but in the battle against intolerance and ignorance, they couldn't hurt.

Now ... That's why we Freedumbers have to take book banning and burning more seriously.

Freedumbers are waging a war against books and ideas. And we're not getting the support we need or the credit we deserve. Without intolerance and ignorance, where would we be? It's time to take a stand before it's too late.

Today ... Commit to being bookdumb. Helpful hint: The more books gone, the better. Thought starter: Get the matches, collect some firewood, and have the little lady go out for some marshmallows. The kids will love to see *Fahrenheit 451* and *The Great Gatsby* go up in flames.

NOVEMBER 28

What works for you?

"The strongest streak in the American character is a fierce pragmatism that mistrusts blind ideology of every stripe and insists on finding what really works."
(Eric Liu)

"I'm fiercely blind."
(Freedumb Fighter)

Then ... I believed that at the end of the day, Americans want to get things done and move forward. We are not blind followers. Of ideology, or anything else. We don't get caught up in false promises or in hollow, let alone hateful words. We can see through that stuff. The extremes don't trap us. We look for things that help. We are all about problem-solving, about addressing issues. We love to debate, argue and exchange ideas, but what we really like is working things through to get to the other side. We are, and always have been, a can-do kind of people and country. We aren't a people seduced by simplistic ideologies or narrow-minded panaceas. I always thought we had too much common sense for that.

Now ... We Freedumbers have an uncommon sense of the way the world ought to be.

A funny thing happens to a Freedumber when we shut our eyes: we begin to see a lot of problems. For example, democracy is a problem – it allows too many people to vote. That's bad for American greatness. Teachers are a problem – they want kids to learn, expand their minds, and feel comfortable with who they are. That's bad for American greatness. Then there's Barbie. That's right, the doll. Have you seen the movie? It actually makes fun of men. Big problem! Thank God it was a box office flop.

Today ... Lay down the law. Helpful hint: Do the unthinkable and withhold sex from your wife until she agrees that college should be a 'For Boys Only' thing. Higher education just gets in the way of girls having babies.

NOVEMBER 29

What's your way?

"Cheating is not the American way. It is small, while we are large. It is cheap, while we are richly endowed. It is destructive, while we are creative. It is doomed to fail, while our gifts and responsibilities call us to achieve. It sabotages trust and weakens the bonds of spirit and humanity, without which we perish."
(Terrence McNally)

"My way is the American way."
(Freedumb Fighter)

The American way sets a high bar.

Then: Heed the call of your gifts and responsibilities, but …

Now: Reset the bar to sabotage humanity with all you've got.

NOVEMBER 30

Can you face the truth?

"In contrast to totalitarianism, a democracy can face and live with the truth about itself."
(Sidney Hook)

"I always tell the truth."
(Freedumb Fighter)

Then ... I believed America was the greatest democracy in the world. And one of the things I loved most about America, about Americans, was that as proud and patriotic as we are, we are also courageous enough to acknowledge our faults. America will always be a work in progress. Our Founding Fathers recognized both the greatness of our union and the imperfections in it. As the saying goes, the truth can hurt – but facing the truth is necessary if we are to get better. Facing the truth is necessary if we are to fulfill our destiny. Facing the truth is necessary if we are to honor our potential. It was as straightforward and difficult as that. For the land of the free and the home of the striving – our struggle was a noble one.

Now... Well, rest assured, Freedumb's truth is going to hurt.

If you believe you're a victim of intolerance, injustice, and prejudice, here's some truth for you. Tough shit.

Today ... Give people some truth. Helpful hint: Dress it up as a fun fact. Thought starter: Freedumbers are going to put an end to fact-checking once and for all. Really, really soon. Fun fact!

DECEMBER 1

Are you a man of principle?

"A man's country is not a certain area of land, of mountains, rivers and woods, but it is a principle; and patriotism is loyalty to that principle."
(George William Curtis)

"This is a man's country. Period."
(Freedumb Fighter)

Then ... I always believed America to be a principled country. And I believed that Americans are a principled people. Our country was anchored in the principle of freedom for all, and the best of what that principle could unlock. More specifically, both as a country and a people, we recognize and reach for the ideals of justice, democracy and equality of opportunity because those ideals are core to the American experiment. Commitment to them forms the basis of American patriotism. And serves as the foundation of America's exceptionalism, its greatness and its place as the world's wellspring of hope. That was something worth pledging allegiance to.

Now ... We Freedumbers are unprincipled on principle.

We won't be weighed down by the chains of principle. You can talk about land, mountains, rivers, woods, or high-minded ideals all you want. But the most important thing to know about America is that it's a man's country. A country for men like us. White men. Straight men. Men who follow the God of Christendumb. Men unafraid to let ignorance be their guide. Men, who through the power of narcissistic self-belief consider themselves superior to any and all. Men righteous enough to believe they can say and do without consequence. Men so brilliant, they need not understand history, respect science or concern themselves with fact, in order to have all the answers. Why look to ideals or high-minded principles to guide us, when the men of Freedumb stand ready to lead us backwards to the America of our dreams.

Today ... Show some manly insight. Helpful hint: Listen to the commencement rant from the 'Field Goal Philosopher.' Thought starters: Women's lives really begin when "she starts living her vocation as a wife." Great again! The most important title any woman can hold is that of "homemaker." Great again! The ladies are so lucky to have the benefit of our wisdumb.

DECEMBER 2

What do you do unto others?

"Do not mistreat or oppress a foreigner, for you were foreigners in Egypt."
(Exodus 22:21)

"Sometimes you have to send a message."
(Freedumb Fighter)

Then ... My God was welcoming. She had her arms wide open, ready to embrace each and every one of her children. She didn't care where you come from, what you look like or who you love. She believed that being a good person was the most important thing. And my God put a premium on courage. The courage not to be threatened by difference. The courage to listen, learn, and try to understand people who don't look or believe as we do. The courage to advocate for people who are vulnerable and need our help – be it someone from another country or someone down the street from where you live. I always believed that one of the reasons God blesses America is that we are indeed the home of the brave. And we have the kind of courage needed to do her work. Hearts, minds and arms wide open.

Now ... Freedumb showed me the power of a God that prefers clenched fists to open arms.

Freedumb's God isn't so much welcoming and open as he is adversarial and aggressive. Which, aside from being kind of fun, sends a message that needs to be heard. The specific missives that need to be sent are many and varied. For example, skin color matters. Whiteness is next to godliness. Gender identity matters. Manliness is next to godliness. Poverty is a character flaw. And everything from AIDS to hurricane Katrina to maternal mortality rates for black women are punishments for unforgivable sins. Thank the Lord.

Today ... Get out there and have some thank the Lord kind of fun.

DECEMBER 3

Today, the Beatitudes of Christendumb:

Blessed are the mean in spirit: for theirs is the kingdumb of heaven.

Blessed are they who attack: for they shall be comforted.

Blessed are the bleak: for they shall inherit the earth.

Blessed are they who hunger and thirst for chaos: for they shall be filled.

Blessed are the vengeful: for they shall obtain mercy.

Blessed are the deniers: for they shall see many other election results to deny.

Blessed are the nihilists: for they shall be called the children of Jesus of Orange.

Blessed are they who persecute the vulnerable: for theirs is the kingdumb of heaven.

DECEMBER 4

What are you willing to lose?

"When we lose the right to be different, we lose the privilege to be free."
(Charles Evan Hughes)

"I wish 'different' would just go away."
(Freedumb Fighter)

Then ... This quote from Justice Hughes struck me as bang on the money. We can't be truly free without embracing our diversity. Different peoples, religions, cultures. Different traditions and perspectives. All connected by foundational American values: Freedom. Justice and opportunity for all. Democracy. The right to life, liberty and the pursuit of happiness. I believed diversity, underpinned by these values, helped us learn, grow and evolve. Evolve into a stronger and smarter nation. A stronger and smarter people. Diversity inspired us to search and learn. About others, and also about ourselves. It's the kind of inspiration that fueled American greatness, and something to be celebrated.

Now ... We Freedumbers are keeping the fireworks in their box on this one.

Diversity lets the devil in our house. Freedumbers prefer to celebrate sameness. If we want to celebrate something, let's throw a party for uniformity, homogeneity (not to be mistaken for homosexuality) and, dare to dream, purity. 'Different' is the arch-enemy of all things American.

Today ... Fantasize. Maybe one day soon DEI will stand for the mass Deportation and Expulsion of Immigrants.

DECEMBER 5

Can you see the light?

"Religious controversies are always productive of more acrimony and irreconcilable hatreds than those which spring from any other cause … And I was not without hopes that the enlightened and liberal policy of the present age would have put an effectual stop to contentions of this kind."
(George Washington)

"The fight is against enlightenment. In any form."
(Freedumb Fighter)

Then … I believed George Washington's thought possessed a timeless wisdom. If believing in God helps make you a better person, cool. What isn't helpful is when 'the organization' interjects itself into connection between us and God. Christianity is no better or worse than any other religion in that context. Basically, it's rooted in organized religion's eternal desire to win. To be the last one standing. And that, unfortunately, can bring with it a lot of acrimony, fear and tribal bad behavior. But enlightenment? Not so much. That's why I was grateful America has a long-standing commitment to the separation of church and state. One that prevents the American government from favoring one religion over another or imposing religious beliefs on its citizenry. I counted that as a blessing.

Now … We Freedumbers believe that church should be the state.

We see America as a Christendumb nation. A white Christendumb nation. A nation that stands in judgment of others, using religion as a weapon. For example, if you truly believe we are all God's children, we Freedumbers are going to give you a little religion - our religion, the only real religion. In the end, every day is judgment day. That doesn't make America a compassionate, civil or sensible nation. Let alone a thoughtful one. But it does bring us closer to being great again.

Today … Imagine Christendumb flourishing in its full glory. Helpful hint: There is no need for a state when you have the right church. Thought starters: Could all statehouses become churchhouses? Should we replace the State Department by the Church Department? And would the President deliver a Church of the Union address?

DECEMBER 6

What makes you happy?

"Happiness is not achieved by the conscious pursuit of happiness; it is generally the by-product of other activities."
(Aldous Huxley)

"I'm happiest when 'schooling' other people."
(Freedumb Fighter)

Then ... I believed most Americans intuitively got what Aldous Huxley was poking at: happiness isn't a destination. It's a product of the things you do every day. The basic stuff. From what I've seen, happiness comes from a sense of contribution. It comes from small acts of kindness and generosity. And yes, it comes with success. That said, it's clear that material success doesn't always measure up to the happiness you get from being a good person. For a country and a people who dream big, sometimes the best thing in the world is simply smiling at someone, and receiving a smile in return. Or so I used to think.

Now ... We Freedumbers are generous with our all-knowingness.

Take tipping for example. We've taken it next level. For us, tipping isn't so much about giving money as it is about giving instruction. We want the people who serve us to be the best servants they can be. So, we're happy to carry the burden of instructing the waitress who's being run off her feet as to how to better get us our check in a timely manner. Nice tip. Or instruct the cashier at the grocery store to smile more as customers come down her aisle. Nice tip. Or instruct a stewardess how she could make our flight more enjoyable with a free drink perhaps. Nice tip. These people may not be happier for our instruction, but we Freedumbers have no doubt they'll be the better for it.

Today ... Chase your happiness. Helpful hint: Is there anybody out there in more desperate need of tips than women drivers. Thought starter: A little road rage could teach some little lady a lifelong lesson. Get your finest glare ready and declare school is in session.

DECEMBER 7

Is that fair?

"It is not fair to ask of others what you are not willing to do yourself."
(Eleanor Roosevelt)

"Some people were born to ask, others born to answer."
(Freedumb Fighter)

Then ... I thought Eleanor Roosevelt's statement put a little meat on the bone of responsibility and obligation. What's fair is always the subject of animated and energetic discussion here in America, but the 'fair ask' is a powerful thing. If we ask people for respect, we must be respectful ourselves. If we ask people to be honest, we must be honest too. If we ask people to be brave, we must also be brave. The fair ask holds us accountable. Accountable to our fellow Americans. The fair ask raises the bar on our behavior. It encourages us to think and to understand, to learn and to empathize. The fair ask can never be too much to ask.

Now ... We Freedumbers know life is unfair. And we mean to keep it that way.

That doesn't mean we can't ask questions. First off, why can't we make our country even more unfair in our favor? Why can't we ban black history and learn only about great white men? Just asking. Why can't queer people just straighten up? Just asking. Why can't non-believers in Christendumb be subject to forced conversion? Just asking. Why can't we do away with elections and appoint a dictator for life? Just asking. Why can't we ban those woke electric vehicles and make all our cars coal-fired? Just asking. Why can't kids take guns to pre-school? Just asking. Why can't women be satisfied with satisfying their man? And having babies? And making dinner? And bringing us another drink? Just asking.

Today ... Just keep asking. Helpful hint: If someone dares to ask you a question, flip them the middle finger as an "asked and answered." Thought starter: You can always follow-up with a question of your own like "Where are you from?"

DECEMBER 8

Do you dream of great things?

"Every great dream begins with a dreamer."
(Harriet Tubman)

"Some great dreams deserve to die."
(Freedumb Fighter)

Then ... I felt the American dream was the stuff of legend. It captures the imagination of people within America and around the world. These were people who believed in what could be, and who acted on their belief. Harriet Tubman was among America's greatest dreamers. She dreamt of what might come to be – if. If she helped slaves escape to freedom by way of the Underground Railroad. If she risked her life so that others might have one of their own. Her entire life was an act of courage. We can't all be Harriet Tubman, but I saw Americans as dreamers, unafraid to dream big. And bravely. Americans dared to dream that genuine greatness, and the goodness that comes with it, were within our grasp.

Now ... We Freedumbers have all the ammo we need to be dream killers.

Where Americans dream of 'what if' and see possibility, Freedumbers dream of 'what if' and see problems. So we dream of ending other people's dreams. Kiss goodbye to liberty for all.

Today ... Say what everybody is thinking. Helpful hint: Blame Lincoln. He gave away our country to the blacks. Thought starter: "Honest Abe" doesn't do him justice. What about 'Ugly Abe' or 'Incompetent Abe' or 'Race Traitor Abe'?

DECEMBER 9

Why do you do it?

"Do nothing out of selfish ambition or vain conceit. Rather, in humility, value others above yourselves."
(Philippians 2:3)

"If you're not above others, you're below them."
(Freedumb Fighter)

Then … Humility is a rare trait. I thought perhaps it was even a sacred one. Humility allows you to be proud, but not too proud. To know, but not be a know-it-all. Confident, but not overly so. Humility allows you to see others as equals, as equally deserving – of respect, of freedom, of justice. Humility allows for introspection. Humility can open our eyes to others' truth. And the realization that how things are for us, might not be how things are for others. Others may not have the same opportunities, the same freedoms, the same shot at the pursuit of happiness. I believed humility carried the power to connect, solve and heal. It was energizing to imagine where this underappreciated virtue might take us.

Now … We Freedumbers don't believe in humility, but are open to vain conceit.

We understand that every once-in-a-while, the good book says stuff that just needs to be set aside. This particular verse was a big swing and a miss. Freedumbers know God's will. We know what to attend to, and what to ignore. What to do and not do. We know the difference between right and wrong: we are right and others are wrong. We know what stands next to godliness, for we have been specially chosen. What's good for us is great for America. No question. And no need to be humble about it. With the white, straight men of Christendumb in the driver's seat, the journey back to greatness is destined to have us winning so much that, as Jesus of Orange suggested, we might actually get tired of winning.

Today … Brag. Helpful hint: Do a little showing off. Thought starter: You could post a pic of your Jesus of Orange Signature Edition God Bless the USA Bible on Facebook and watch your friends turn green with envy.

DECEMBER 10

What's happening?

"The American Dream is that dream of a land in which life should be better and richer and fuller for everyone, with opportunity for each according to ability or achievement."
(James Truslow Adams)

"You can't have my American Dream."
(Freedumb Fighter)

Then ... What James Truslow Adams described was foundational to the America I knew. And I believed the American Dream may be the most powerful invitation the world has ever known. It speaks for us and to us, as a country and people. As a country, we invite dreamers from around the world to the possibility of a better life. As a people, it challenges us to take our shot. And then to keep on taking it. It is the opportunity to create, achieve, and grow. To unlock our individual and shared potential. And reach for better. That's the opportunity. That's the goal. I believed America was steadfast in its resolve to make this the country where the dreams of all could come true.

Now ... For us Freedumbers, the American Dream isn't a promise, it's a piece of property.

And we are the sole owners. The American Dream was never intended as something meant for everybody. Others are welcome to embrace the fantasy or the illusion – just so long as nothing ever comes of it. No better life. No richer life. No fuller life. We Freedumbers could never stomach that. Could you imagine some dark-skinned immigrant besting the best efforts of a native-born white man? Could you imagine some uppity other becoming more successful than a devoutly believing white man? Could you imagine taking orders from a woman? Talk about the American nightmare.

Today ... Protect the white dream. Start a local chapter of the NAAWP (National Association for the Advancement of White People). Helpful hint: It never hurts to have a mission statement. Thought starter: "No fried chicken or water melon for me."

DECEMBER 11

What will you defend?

"We defend the foundations laid down by our fathers. We build a life for generations yet unborn. We defend and we build a way of life, not but for America alone, but for all mankind."
(Franklin D. Roosevelt)

"I don't really believe in mankind."
(Freedumb Fighter)

Then ... President Roosevelt's words crystallized the role of America in the world. And I believed his remark carried a timeless relevance. The land of the free and the home of the brave has a global obligation. We must embody the best that freedom and bravery can offer. For ourselves and for the future – a sustainable future. We must uphold the ideals of liberty and justice for all. We must care a little more and work a little harder. We must be open to new ideas and ways of doing things. We must invite and welcome. We must ensure that access to the pursuit of happiness is a genuine promise and not merely puffery. Clearly, that's no small obligation. Still, I believed our collective fate somehow depended on America's commitment to delivering on this outsized expectation.

Now ... I realize believing in mankind doesn't put America first.

We Freedumbers don't really acknowledge a world outside America. It's only full of other people. And that is, of course, a problem. Other people mattering takes our eye off the ball. This is our time. This is our country. Our way of life is ours. Nobody else's. This is our chance to taste the sweet fruits of Freedumb. And that's what we'll defend. The best defense being a good offense, we aim to take, take and keep taking until there is no more. Besides, it's hard to take 'the globe' seriously when maps are always flat. Explain that!

Today ... Go where few men have gone before. Helpful hint: Dabble in meteorology. Thought starter: Climate change doesn't exist, but are UFOs to blame for America's extreme weather?

DECEMBER 12

What are you worried about?

"I'm more worried about being a good person than being the best football player in the world."
(Lionel Messi)

"I don't worry about being a good person as long as I'm a great American."
(Freedumb Fighter)

Then ... I thought Lionel Messi's quote deserved more than just passing consideration. What if each and every American worried a little bit more about being a good person? A good influence. A good contributor. A good father, son, parent and spouse. A good neighbor. A good friend. What if we began our day with a commitment to do at least one 'act of goodness' before our head hit the pillow that night? What if that act of goodness was aimed at a perfect stranger? What if that act of goodness offered you absolutely no material benefit? There's no doubt we worry about a lot of things these days, but shifting some of that worry toward being a better person might give us a lot less to worry about.

Now ... One last time: for us Freedumbers, goodness has nothing to with greatness.

Being a fucking better person isn't worth the effort. Worrying about being a good person isn't going to move the needle on what actually makes a difference. Being a good man isn't going to protect white entitlement or advantage, let alone supremacy. It isn't going to protect white men from being infringed upon by justice for blacks, equal rights for women, or opportunities for immigrants. Being a good man isn't going to protect our manliness from being undermined by everything from the toxicity of responsibility to the corrosiveness of compassion to lack of appreciation for mediocrity. So, forget about being a good person - and get serious about acting like a great again American.

Today ... Throw a holiday party. Helpful hint: Invite the "Field Goal Philosopher" to make a speech. Thought starters: Topics could include 'Gays and a deadly sin sort of pride' or 'IVF, surrogacy and other degenerate cultural values' or 'Women and the shame of working for a living.' Long live the great again American!

DECEMBER 13

What's your view?

"A man who views the world at fifty the same as he did at twenty has wasted thirty years of his life."
(Muhammed Ali)

"I've got a lot more important things to do with my life than to spend time learning."
(Freedumb Fighter)

Then … I believed a good life demanded a commitment to learning. And that learning wasn't something that ended in kindergarten, elementary school, high school or college. Nor did learning happen only when school was in session. How we experienced life should bring insight. It should help us see things more clearly, more deeply. Experience should open our hearts and minds. If we're not learning and growing from our experience, then what are we doing? Confirming our biases? Protecting our comfort zone? Hardening our prejudices? No doubt life gives us a lot to learn. About ourselves, about our communities, our country and the world. Perhaps the first lesson is that we don't know quite as much as we think we do.

Now … Why learn when you can act out.

Our view of the world is anchored in the energy and genius of the 'terrible twos'. You remember: "Gimme, gimme, gimme, it's mine!" Cry and throw a tantrum when you don't get what you want. Hit and kick those who tell you to do things you don't want to. Believe that you're the center of the universe and that everything revolves around your wants and whims. Why try moving on from that?

Today … Class is in session. Helpful hint: Throw a temper tantrum. Thought starter: Think of a local pharmacy administering vaccines as your playpen. After berating any and all shot givers and takers, don't forget to pick up a pack of diapers on your way out.

DECEMBER 14

What can you do?

"Don't let what you can't do interfere with what you can do."
(John Wooden)

"I'll do my best to get in the way of what you can do."
(Freedumb Fighter)

Then … I believed the "Wizard of Westwood" captured the potential power of can-do America. And can-do Americans. It's easy to get derailed by obstacles and problems. Seeing the issues that ail us as a brick wall, and focusing on what you can't do, is in the end an energy taker. To achieve the seemingly impossible, we need to take one small step at a time. The truth is there is no miracle cure for racism, nor is there a vaccine to protect us from being infected by intolerance. There is no over-the-counter drug to make us more aware of inequalities in society, nor a booster shot to lessen ignorance. Still, doing what we can might just help create a constructive ripple that might work to change the game.

Now … We Freedumbers don't like to use the C-word. Constructive, that is.

Why worry about obstacles when you can be one? We Freedumbers love to get in the way, and we take pride in being the biggest roadblock we can be. So, to all the women out there, don't ever forget that it's a man's world, and sorry, the future will never be female. No doubt the gays and queers have dreams for the future of their communities. Well, whatever they might be, they won't be getting any 'double groom' wedding cakes from Freedumb's bakery. So too for the migrants crossing our southern border yearning to breathe free. Inhale a little Freedumb and realize our oxygen is hazardous to your health. I could go on, but…

Today … Run an errand. Helpful hint: Be the message you want to send. Thought starter: Head to your local big box store and demand to speak to a white English-speaking, preferably male, sales rep. Or better yet, get in the face of the manager and tell him to hire some real Americans – then make sure not to buy anything. Message sent.

DECEMBER 15

Do you feel lucky?

"Parents and schools should place great emphasis on the fact that it is all right to be different. Racism and all the other 'isms' grow from primitive tribalism, the instinctive hostility against those of another tribe, race, religion, nationality, class, or whatever. You are a lucky child if your parents taught you to accept diversity."
(Roger Ebert)

"Instinctive hostility is the best hostility."
(Freedumb Fighter)

Then ... I believed that in the land of the free, it should be OK to be different. Our country was founded on the idea that you being you is your right. Your right as an American citizen. That's a great thing. And we should celebrate the diversity our freedom has cultivated. So vibrant and dynamic. Different is fun, interesting, and life-affirming. As we challenged ourselves to move beyond "primitive tribalism," I thought we must, as Roger Ebert suggested, teach our children that 'you doing you' – whoever you might be – was a core component of American greatness.

Now ... Diversity puts us Freedumbers into panic mode.

Freedumbers love all things tribal. The tribe makes us feel safe. Different people aren't fun. Different races and nationalities are confusing. Different religions, lifestyles and cultures aren't life-affirming. They are life-destroying. We don't look for people or experiences to learn and grow from. We are looking for comfort and confirmation. Life is easier when your worldview is Freedumber simple.

Today ... Consider home schooling your kids. Imagine the curriculum!
8:30 – 9:30: Hostility toward the gays.
9:30 – 11:30: Hostility toward blacks, browns and every other color.
11:30 – 12:30: Lunch and some Newsmax TV.
12:30 – 1:30: Hostility toward science.
1:30 – 2:30: Hostility toward black history.
2:30 – 3:00 Hostility with prayer.

It's your chance to make your kids feel like the luckiest kids in the world.

DECEMBER 16

Are you distracted?

"Skip the religion and politics, head straight to the compassion. Everything else is a distraction."
(Talib Kweli)

"Politics with religion is the answer."
(Freedumb Fighter)

Then ... Rapper Talib Kweli's words came as something of a lightning bolt. It's tough to beat compassion as a building block to something better – our better angels, if you will. Belief can help, but too often doesn't. Power can help, but too often doesn't. Religion and politics both aim to win believers and achieve control. Too often they work to distract us from who we really are. I believed that people are, by nature, good. I believed that if we could think and feel without falling prey to the distractions that often surround us, we'd have a chance. A chance to truly put our hearts into how we live with one another. Imagine our country if we were just a little more concerned about the suffering of others. What if we decided to suffer 'together'? To interact and connect, in order to relieve the suffering around us. Just imagine.

Now ... We Freedumbers see compassion as a distraction.

Compassion distracts us from the intolerance we need to fulfill our destiny. Compassion, and its criminal cousins, kindness and empathy, distract from the prejudice required for pushing us to the promised land. And the entitlement needed to enjoy the push. Bottom line, compassion is an existential threat that must be eradicated. Focus, Freedumbers, focus!

Today ... Don't get distracted. Helpful hint: Start your day with a creative visualization exercise. Thought starter: Imagine meeting some of those migrants struggling in various states of hardship and need. Then visualize telling each one of them to be grateful or fuck off out of our country. You'll love the smell of great again in the morning!

DECEMBER 17

What's your choice?

"Despair was a choice. Hatred was a choice. Anger was a choice. I could choose to give up or to hang on. Hope was a choice. Faith was a choice. And more than anything else, love was a choice. Compassion was a choice."
(Anthony Ray Hinton)

"Anger and hate aren't choices, they are necessary ingredients to greatness."
(Freedumb Fighter)

Then ... Anthony Ray Hinton had a pretty amazing story. Wrongly convicted for murder, he spent 28 years on death row before being released on appeal in 2015. Now an author and activist, he fights for justice reform and serves as an inspiration to many, given his struggle and perseverance. If he can speak of choosing love and compassion, then why can't we all? The choice confronts us all. Every day. Choice in how we interact with one another. How we respond to the issues, obstacles and opportunities we face on a daily basis. It seems all too easy now to exist in a dark hole of hatred and anger, but choice also invites the possibility of good. What if we put our faith in goodness? Being good. Doing good. All it took was the right choice.

Now ... Goodness, in all its forms, is really the beginning of the end.

We Freedumbers understand the pernicious nature of goodness and are on the front lines of stopping it from doing its dirty work. Hate and anger are our weapons of choice, a choice we make on behalf of American greatness. Being hateful and angry isn't as easy as it looks. It takes sacrifice. You have to begin by sacrificing your conscience. Put that little voice inside you on mute and get on with the task at hand. Goodness must be stopped. That's the real American way. When you think about it, "life, liberty and the pursuit of hatred" has a nice ring to it.

Today ... Play a game. Helpful hint: A couple rounds of "sleep with, marry, or off a cliff" can always be great again fun for the whole family. Thought starter: Sleep with cruelty, marry hate, and throw the unholy trinity of wokeness – compassion, hope, and love – off the highest cliff you can imagine.

DECEMBER 18

Today, two final Freedumber Public Service Announcements:

PSA #9: Are you unlikely to get your ass grabbed by strange men? Are you never going to be called a whore or slut because of your gender? Are you never going to have to wear makeup to make yourself 'look better'? Are you never going to shave your armpits or legs for a social occasion? Could you care less? Call 1-800-FREEDUM and talk to a kindred spirit about how women have it so good. He will share your conviction that women should always be grateful to men for the opportunity to look their best while doing what they're told.

PSA#10: Can you advocate for your gender without being called anti-family? Can you bring emotion into a debate, without being called hysterical? Can you speak with some authority, whether or not you know much about the topic being discussed? Can you divide up household chores, do 20 per cent of them, and declare you're doing your fair share? Call us at 1-800-FREEDUM and connect with someone who appreciates the many burdens you bear – man that you are.

DECEMBER 19

What are your three words?

"Explore. Dream. Discover."
(attributed to Mark Twain)

"Fuck. Your. Feelings."
(Freedumb Fighter)

Then … I thought the three words attributed to Mark Twain perfectly encapsulated the opportunity that is America. Explore your potential. Dream of what could be. And discover what you're made of. At its best, America is a limitless possibility. We need to continue to push against any limitations to that possibility based on race, creed, gender or socio-economic status. That said, America is a country where the improbable and the miraculous happen every day, because if you give the American people a chance – even a snowball's chance in hell – you best watch out. Amazing is commonplace in America. We share the belief there's something better on the other side of our dreams. And that shared belief drives us forward. I believed that as an American, you feel that in your bones.

Now … This is our country and we don't care what you feel in your bones, or anywhere else.

We are happy to let others explore, dream and discover. Others should feel free to discover whose country this really is. Explore to quickly discover their limitations. Dream so as to see the dead end that is their destiny. If you feel that's somehow not right, just or fair, well then, we have just three words for you. (see Freedumb Fighter quote above)

Today … Take ownership. Create a list of tenant rights for all non-Freedumbers. Helpful hint: Start with a blank piece of paper. Thought starter: End with a blank piece of paper.

DECEMBER 20

Who are you?

"I discovered one must keep a freshness and a source of joy intact within, loving the daylight that injustice leaves unscathed … In the depths of winter, I finally learned that within me there lay an invincible summer."
(Albert Camus)

"Talking about fucking climate change doesn't bring me any joy."
(Freedumb Fighter)

Who you are is revealed, and your joy can be defined, in times of difficulty.

Then: I believed character must be anchored in courage, but …

Now: Expand your carbon footprint.

DECEMBER 21

What's your tolerance level?

"Tolerance is the best religion."
(Victor Hugo)

"Tolerance has no place in religion."
(Freedumb Fighter)

Then … I loved when smart people simplified religion to one word. I often found the distillation to be both inspirational and instructive. Victor Hugo's choice of tolerance is a good example. If people jumped on board the idea of tolerance, it could become the foundation for how we live our lives. For how we constructively engage with our fellow Americans – regardless of color, creed, gender or sexual orientation. Our communities and country would feel different. Safer. More peaceful. Even more dynamic. I could tolerate that.

Now … We Freedumbers embrace intolerance as a guiding light.

Intolerance is the rocket fuel for becoming great again. We Freedumbers aren't interested in understanding. Different races, religions, cultures, or sexual orientations? Not interested. We already know they are inferior. We already know they are deviants. We already know they are threats. And none of that is to be tolerated. We've already made the mistake of giving them an inch. Don't even think about giving them a mile. It's time to take back our inch.

Today … Take one step closer to heaven. Helpful hint: Lower your tolerance level. Thought starter: Have a zero-tolerance policy for any of the D-words: diversity, different, divergent, disparate, dissimilar, distinctive. (Discrimination, being the exception to the rule, is all good.)

DECEMBER 22

Could there be a mistake?

"There are seasons in every country, when noise and impudence pass current for worth; and in popular commotions especially, the clamors of interested and factious men are often mistaken for patriotism."
(Alexander Hamilton)

"Any real patriot knows that noise, impudence and commotion are the key to America's destiny."
(Freedumb Fighter)

Then ... Patriotism wasn't a moving target. It was a commitment etched in stone. Impervious to passing circumstance, let alone the impudence of self-interested men. It's anchored in a genuine love of and appreciation for our country. It's about commitment to liberty for all. Justice for all. It was about acknowledging the 'united' bit in the United States of America, including the seeking of common ground with our fellow citizens. It was about challenging the status quo if it fell short of what could be. It was about aiming for and building an even better America. Patriotism wasn't rooted in self-interest, or making noise to get attention or causing commotion for the sake of chaos. In America, we know a true patriot when we see one.

Now ... 'Divided we stand, united we fall' does have a kind of undeniable appeal.

Make no mistake, we Freedumbers know division is fundamentally a good thing. A patriotic thing. Division stirs up distrust, disrespect, and opens the door to Freedumbness. And that's not only worthy but an essential element of our patriotism. How else are we to become the white, paternalistic, Christendumb nationalist country of our destiny? And noise isn't without benefit if it allows you to drown out common sense. Commotion isn't a waste of time if it can overwhelm clear-headedness. Makes sense, right? A clearer blueprint of what it is to be a real patriot would be tough to come by.

Today ... Polish your patriotic bona fides. Helpful hint: Be a warrior in the war on Christmas. Thought starter: Frame any book with the word 'holiday' in it as an attack on Christmas and conspiracy against Christendumb.

DECEMBER 23

Which way are you headed?

"The good man is the man who, no matter how morally unworthy he has been, is moving to become better."
(John Dewey)

"Getting better is for other people."
(Freedumb Fighters)

Then ... The American philosopher John Dewey didn't dabble in the shallow end of thought. I believed the idea that, being good is as much about where you're headed as where you are, gave us all a shot at redemption. The possibility to improve, contribute, and make amends. To me, Americans were made of strong stuff: getting better was all about having the strength to learn from our mistakes, be better for ourselves and everybody around us.

Now ... Enough about good men – what about us Freedumbers?

For example, we're pretty amazing at playing the vicdumb. Have you ever been bullied by a Barbie doll? We have! Have you ever been disrespected by having to earn the same money as a woman for doing the same job? We have! Have you ever felt threatened by someone wearing a mask to protect themselves from COVID? We have! Have you been disobeyed by people refusing to be categorized as either man or woman? We have! Have you been made to feel uncomfortable by a black man walking on your side of the street? We have! Have you felt inconvenienced because your landscaper is still learning English? We have! Have you ever been upset by the thought that love is love? We have! Woe is the man of Freedumb!

Today ... Now that Christmas is coming, do more than just play the vicdumb. Helpful hint: Think season's greetings. Thought starters: Mock survivors of school shootings as 'media prosti-tots.' Or verbally attack actresses for wearing 'whore dresses' to protest sexual harassment. Or advocate the arrest of trans people for their choice of bathroom. Merry Christmas!

DECEMBER 24

What's your limit?

"Our thoughts and imaginations are the only real limits to our possibilities."
(Orison Swett Marden)

"I won't imagine that. You can't make me."
(Freedumb Fighter)

Then … Orison Swett Marden was a 19th century writer who focused on how to live a successful life. He believed there is nothing that couldn't be overcome by brainpower and creativity. No problem too big, no issue too complex, no set of circumstances too dire. Imagine that. Some might say that the above quote is naive and overly romantic. I would say, "What's the alternative?"

Now … Here's an alternative – the end of imagination.

For us Freedumbers, a lack of imagination is critical – except, of course, when talking conspiracy theories. In the push to take America backwards, brainpower and creativity have no place. Why be better when we can be great again. Freedumbers don't want an America that thinks or imagines. So put your brain out to pasture, kick your imagination out of the house, and start pushing America back to greatness.

Today … Stifle your kid's imagination. Helpful hint: Go hard and you won't have to go often. Thought starter: Tell them Santa's dead. And say the blacks and gays killed him because they didn't get what they wanted for Christmas.

DECEMBER 25

Today, the (abridged) Freedumber version of a popular Christmas carol:

On the first day of Christmas,
my true love gave to me
A cartridge for my AR-15.

On the second day of Christmas,
my true love gave to me
Two M4 speed magazine loaders,
And a cartridge for my AR-15.

On the third day of Christmas,
my true love gave to me
Three backup night sights,
Two M4 speed magazine loaders,
And a cartridge for my AR-15.

On the fourth day of Christmas,
my true love gave to me
Four quick deploy bipods,
Three backup night sights,
Two M4 speed magazine loaders,
And a cartridge for my AR-15.

On the fifth day of Christmas,
my true love gave to me
Five time-delay hand grenades,
Four quick deploy bipods,
Three backup night sights,
Two M4 speed magazine loaders,
And a cartridge for my AR-15.

DECEMBER 26

What does heroism look like?

*"A hero is no braver than an ordinary man, but he is braver
five minutes longer."*
(Ralph Waldo Emerson)

"I have more bravery in one finger than most men do in their whole body."
(Freedumb Fighter)

Then ... I thought Emerson spoke to the potential hero in all of us. The upside of courage can happen in a moment. Being brave didn't always have to be a matter of life and death, but I believed it always involved transcending your comfort zone to do something good, something of value. And a lot can happen in five minutes. A heart can open. A hand can reach out. A mind can change. A soul can lighten. This may not sound monumental, but it signals the everyday acts of courage we need. Such acts require us to overcome our fear and prejudices, and step outside of who we were to become who we could be. Just give yourself five minutes, step up, and do something to make the home of the brave proud. I had no doubt we all had it in us.

Now ... We Freedumbers don't need five minutes to prove we're heroes.

We can do something heroic with the flash of a finger. Our middle finger. And we love using it. But we're no 'one trick pony' type hero. We can also point our finger to assign blame. And we're heroic enough to blame poverty on the poor, homelessness on the homeless, and intolerance on those who shouldn't be tolerated. But rest easy, we'll never point a finger at ourselves. Clearly, we're no ordinary heroes.

Today ... Award yourself a trophy. Acknowledge the hero that is you. Helpful hint: No little figurine cup is good enough for you baby. Your type of heroism is too rare for that. There's a big, beautiful gold middle finger in your future!

DECEMBER 27

Have you applied yourself?

"The price of success is hard work, dedication to the job at hand, and the determination that whether we win or lose, we have applied the best of ourselves to the task at hand."
(Vince Lombardi)

"That's a price I won't pay."
(Freedumb Fighter)

Then ... I was all for listening to somebody who has a trophy named after him. Vince Lombardi is an American icon and he knew a lot about what it takes to be successful. I thought his statement captured a fundamental trait of the American character. You could count on us to take our best shot – and our best shot was as good as it gets. We will work hard. We will be determined. We will apply our very best to whatever lies in front of us. And never quit. In a way, I believed that to be the price of admission for being an American.

Now ... We Freedumbers believe there's a lot of quit in the American character.

We believe, America's success, its ability to be great again, requires us to pay a different price. Quitting is that price. We can't afford to be tolerant. That won't contribute to getting our greatness back. So we've got to quit trying. We can't afford to have a conscience or feel shame. That won't contribute to being great again. We can't afford to build bridges, open our hearts, or lend someone in need a helping hand. That won't contribute to getting us back to greatness. So, we've got to just quit trying.

Today ... Succeed at something. Helpful hint: Quitters always win. Thought starter: Be a winner, quit stalling, call Jesus of Orange your President for Life, and bask the sweet glow of Freedumb.

DECEMBER 28

What do you do in the dark?

"It is during our darkest moments that we must focus to see the light."
(Aristotle Onassis)

"During our darkest moments, others can't see what you're doing."
(Freedumb Fighter)

Then ... I thought focusing on the light had a practical application. It meant looking for common ground to build solutions and unlock opportunities. It meant not closing your eyes to compromise and trade-offs. It meant giving up a little for the potential of moving forward. It meant remembering you're an American, not a warrior of some tribe. Our darkest moments demanded our best selves. It's when our responsibilities became something more than simply words on some piece of paper. It's when we have to live up to what it is to be American. That was a light worth focusing on.

Now ... We Freedumbers love dark moments.

In fact, we aim to create them. You can get away with stuff in the dark. You can conspire, you can enable and avoid in the dark. You don't have to hold yourself accountable in the dark. You don't have to listen to your conscience in the dark. Darkness blinds you to injustice and inequality. It blinds you to the cruelty of intolerance and prejudice. It blinds you to pain caused by ignorance. And we wouldn't have it any other way. Three cheers for dark ages!

Today ... Take a moment. Creating darkness is exhausting. Just remember the old Freedumber saying "It's always darkest before the dawn of more darkness." Hopefully, that'll feed your spirit and give you the strength to carry on.

DECEMBER 29

What are you?

"I am not a product of my circumstances, I am a product of my decisions."
(Stephen R. Covey)

"I consider myself a finished product."
(Freedumb Fighter)

Then … There was a reality check for all of us in Stephen Covey's words. Clearly, we all come from different situations and circumstances. That said, it is ultimately our decisions that determine who we are and what we're about. That's an essential part of being American. We didn't look to blame. We didn't look for an excuse. We didn't rationalize. We took accountability for what we said. We took responsibility for what we did. While the notion of a self-made man has always felt a bit exaggerated, it is in some way what every American man aspires to be. That aspiration comes to life with our decisions. The decisions between right and wrong, good and bad. The decisions to help or harm, contribute or obstruct. The decisions to respect or disparage. It all came down to what kind of 'product' you wanted to be.

Now … With us Freedumbers, what you see is what you get.

We always call it like it is. So, we've decided the world doesn't matter. We've decided democracy doesn't matter. We've decided governing doesn't matter. We've decided truth and justice don't matter. We've decided education doesn't matter. We've decided minorities and immigrants don't matter. We've decided common sense and civility don't matter. We decided future generations don't matter. We've decided the only thing that matters is us. And that makes for one helluva product.

Today … Call one more as you see it. Helpful hint: The fucking #MeToo movement should have been dead on arrival. Thought starter: Harvey Weinstein got a bad rap.

DECEMBER 30

Are you in a good place?

"I still believe in a place called Hope, a place called America."
(Bill Clinton)

"Hope is one four-letter word we refuse to use."
(Freedumb Fighter)

Then … I was a believer. In hope. In the promise of America. In the land of the free and the home of the brave. This was not false hope, delusion or illusion because I also believed, not only in America, but in Americans. You know, we the people. I believed Americans wanted America to be better. Better for all. I believed that America remained a force for good. I believed in the goodness of the American people.

Now … We Freedumbers can't figure out why hope is such a big deal.

It's just more woke bullshit. Did you know "woke" was originally a term that emerged among the blacks, as early as the 1930s, to signal the need to be awake to the racism they believed confronted them in American society. Can you imagine that? Better we shut our eyes and go to sleep. And hope? Fuel for the woke. It's got to be stopped! Bottom line, you can "believe in a place called Hope" all you want, but that isn't a place called America.

Today … Teach your kids the 'w-word' is the baddest of bad things. And 'hope' isn't much better (unless it's attached to something like a great white hope, obviously).

DECEMBER 31

Are you having fun yet?

"Be strong, believe in freedom and in God, love yourself, understand your sexuality, have a sense of humor, masturbate, don't judge people by their religion, color or sexual habits, love life and your family."
(Madonna)

"Wait, did someone just say masturbate out loud?"
(Freedumb Fighter)

Then ... Girls just wanted to have fun. Me too. And as I thought about it, maybe more masturbating would actually be the answer to everything. Maybe if some of us straight white men masturbated more, we wouldn't be so hard on other people. Maybe we wouldn't be so hard on the queer community or on women wanting equal rights. Maybe we wouldn't be so hard on Muslims or other people who believe differently from us. We wouldn't be so hard on gun control advocates or movies starring Barbie. We wouldn't be so hard on the climate or on people who think the environment is kind of important. We wouldn't be so hard on people who believe in science and want to learn history, read books and keep an open mind. Maybe, just maybe, masturbating is the solution hiding in plain sight. Whether it is or not, what was the downside to giving it a shot?

Now ... We Freedumbers know where to draw the line.

We're OK with mass shootings, but don't make light of masturbation. It's a sin, you know. Besides, you could go blind. End of story.

Today ... Time for a New Year's resolution. So, one last thought: Whatever you do, don't say the M-word, don't think the M-word, and heaven forbid, don't do the M-word if you really want to make America great again!

ACKNOWLEDGEMENTS

The author would like to step outside his Freedumbness, and take a moment to thank a few good men for the example they set, and the inspiration they provided: Clive, Ken, Kevin, John, Brad, Mark, Fritz, Randy, George, Tomer, Tom, Bill, Abe, Pat, Alan, Mark, Richard, Rick, Ed, Dave, Tim, Will, Ray, Billy, Michael, John. And the women I have to thank are way too numerous to name. Just know that you are all men and women who make me proud to be an American. Also special thanks to my man Sam, without whom this book would never have been written.